# A STORM FORETOLD:
# COLUMBIA UNIVERSITY
# AND MORNINGSIDE HEIGHTS, 1968

CHRISTIANE CRASEMANN COLLINS

# Publisher's Information

EBookBakery Books

Author contact: crasemann@aol.com

ISBN 978-1-938517-48-8

© 2015 by Christiane Crasemann Collins

*Cover design by Amy Bernstein*

For Sue Carlson
good friend
and helpmate!

Christiane C.C.

# DEDICATION

*In memory of Robert (Bob) McKay:*
*His vision and determination inspired*
*the grassroots movement to succeed*
*against all odds.*

In a photo taken in 1995, Bob McKay, center, stands with 1960s gymnasium protest colleagues, left to right, Tom Mencher, Helen Mencher, author Christiane Crasemann Collins, and Suki Ports.

# CONTENTS

Preface..................................................................................VII

Chapter 1: Morningside Park ...........................................1

Chapter 2: Park and Gown............................................11

Chapter 3: The School on the Rock (1961–1964) ..............43

Chapter 4: Morningsiders United (1962–1965) ...............55

Chapter 5: A Funeral under the Trees (1965–1967) ...........77

Chapter 6: Never Look a Gift Horse in the Mouth (1966–1967)..93

Chapter 7: Gym Crow (1967) .......................................133

Chapter 8: Up Against the Fence! (February 1968)...........155

Chapter 9: Winds of Change (March 1968) .....................167

Chapter 10: Grassroots Triumph (April 20–26, 1968).......185

Chapter 11: The Icon is Demolished (March 3, 1969) .......209

Epilogue................................................................227

Chronology.............................................................235

Cast of Characters ....................................................245

Organizations...........................................................251

About the Author ......................................................253

*Figures may be found on pages 108 to 131.*

# PREFACE

From today's perspective, events that took place on the Upper West Wide of Manhattan in 1968 and that are narrated here could be titled "Morningside Park: A Civil Rights Battleground." Though they represent a small segment of the Civil Rights Movement of the 1960s and the country's continuing struggle for civil rights, they provide an important example of an emerging grassroots movement that united multiethnic communities that, convinced of their rights, bravely opposed a major educational institution.

Most publications on the 1960s focus on the student uprising at Columbia University and barely mention the community context. The student uprising was, indeed, a historic episode, and its complexity begs for further examination. But this narrative takes a long view of the urban circumstances and Columbia University's geopolitical strategy (or lack of it) dating from the late nineteenth century decision to settle on the Upper West Side of Manhattan, later called Morningside Heights.

Even before Columbia's move uptown in 1896, developments on the Heights were conditioned by geographic and natural features, primarily the majestic Hudson River to the west and a dramatic declivity to the east. Of these parameters, the river was immutable, while the embankment facing east allowed a few options. Parks on both sides were designed by premiere landscape architects Frederick Law Olmsted and Calvert Vaux.

The university's plan to transform its site into a campus responded to the physical geography without taking advantage of its unique natural features. McKim, Mead & White's 1894 master plan for the central campus would remain the only real *plan* ever considered by the university. Columbia leadership was guided by the idealistic ambition of creating an "acropolis of knowledge" on the Hudson that would occupy and control the entirety of Morningside Heights. Isolated from the excitement of an evolving metropolis, this utopia became an enclave that permitted only select people within its walls. Racial minorities, African American or Hispanic, and lower class people were not welcome. Undesirables were removed by evicting them from purchased real estate. These actions, justified by a need for "expansion," did not demonstrate any sensible planning consideration. Emptied buildings were frequently left vacant, demolished, or offered to other institutions willing to conform to the "acropolis" ideal.

Within this context, the focus of this narrative is Columbia's intention to build a gymnasium in Morningside Park, first discussed with city officials in 1958. More than a decade later, the decision by the university's Board of Trustees in March 1969 to terminate the construction placed it into a category historians designate as "unbuilt" projects. The reasons for buildings remaining unbuilt or unfinished are varied and often unknown. Some are utopian dreams, not even intended to be realized. In other cases, it is lack of funds, a change in politics and cultural circumstances, or even natural disasters.[1]

Numerous complex and conflicting issues that evolved over many decades caused Columbia's gymnasium in Morningside Park to remain unbuilt. Some of the issues pre-existed the initial decision to embark on this project. Over its history, the "Gymnasium in the Park" had ramifications not only in Morningside Heights and surrounding neighborhoods but also more broadly in New York City and beyond. Rather than its architectural design (which did have its critics), the discord regarding the gymnasium involved primarily what the project represented in relation to Columbia's urban and cultural attitudes and pursuits, and its significant encroachment upon a public park.

After World War II, the townscape on Morningside Heights gradually changed from one of visual transparency in which small shops and street activity provided amenities and a sense of neighborliness for academic affiliates, students, and other residents to a sterile environment where vacant, or new, opaque buildings presented long stretches of blank walls along the sidewalks. Security became an issue for those who were supposed to benefit from these changes, and private guards became the norm.

---

[1] Alison Sky and Michelle Stone, *Unbuilt America: Forgotten Architecture in the United States from Thomas Jefferson to the Space Age* (New York, McGraw-Hill, 1976). Introduction by George R. Collins, 1–13..

Safety concerns were cited to justify the fortification of Morningside Heights against a presumed threat from the surrounding neighborhoods: West Harlem, Manhattan Valley, and Manhattanville. The strategy of building a defensive enclosure, truly a "cordon sanitaire," to protect the "white" institutions was perceived as racially motivated by the communities and some elected officials, with suspicion that it would lead to a gated academic community comparable to an exclusive ghetto. A sequence of institutional actions and urban events over several years culminated inexorably in "a storm foretold" crisis in 1968.

Columbia's Bicentennial year, 1954, marked the beginning of escalating threats affecting the ethnic diversity of Morningside Heights, as well as the adjacent areas. Within the context of Columbia's "urban strategy" and racially motivated decisions, the Morningside Park gymnasium project emerged as a focal point. It became the issue that united the surrounding communities, alerted devotees of Olmsted parks along with advocates of the environmental movement, and eventually drew the attention of Columbia's faculty and students. The historic climax united the diverse grassroots movement that had emerged on the Heights and in its surrounding neighborhoods. The gymnasium in Morningside Park became the icon of Columbia University's racism, envisioned as a bulwark against the imagined threat of Harlem.

Morningside Park was truly a civil rights battleground, and this narrative describes the decades of events that led to the triumph of a grassroots community. As it is used here, the term "community" describes a loosely coordinated, ethnically mixed groundswell of black, Hispanic, and white citizens bound together by their strong convictions about their civil rights as they opposed institutional strategies and fought for control of their urban environment. The author uses "black" for community members in Harlem who proudly used this term to describe their ethnicity in the 1950s and 1960s; the more current "African American" is also used in this narrative where it is more appropriate. The grassroots West Harlem Morningside Park Committee succeeded in exposing the racism and arrogance of a leading educational institution that was symbolized by its project to construct its own gymnasium on public land in Morningside Park—considered Harlem's turf by the neighborhood—with only a small share designated for community use.

As the wife of George R. Collins, a member of the faculty of Columbia's Department of Art History and the School of Architecture, the author, Christiane Crasemann Collins, was embedded in this grassroots movement. From 1950 to 1968, the Collins family, including three young sons, lived in an apartment overlooking Morningside Park. George Collins' specialty was history of architecture and city planning, and the author concentrated on those subjects as well. After obtaining her master's degree in art history from Columbia, the author collaborated with her husband on several publications and also published on her own. Her interest in urban planning and parks merged with her involvement in the Morningside neighborhood. Providing open space for the children, preferably parks, was a challenge. To the east, Morningside Park was visually enticing, though not very accessible or inviting. Reaching Riverside Park, to the west, required crossing the university campus along 116th Street (where the Columbia security force prevented running or rolling balls on the steps of Low Library).

In addition to these family related experiences, Christiane Crasemann Collins considered Morningside Heights, the surrounding neighborhoods, and the parks to be her urban laboratory. She became active in the neighborhood groups and with local families—African-American, Hispanic, and white—and owing to her Chilean background, her fluency in Spanish inspired a special trust and welcome. Thus, the author was in a real sense "community," thoroughly involved in the grassroots movement that opposed insensitive institutional attitudes and actions. As a participant and keen observer in the 1960s, she carefully hoarded the ephemera pertaining to long years of protest, guided by the conviction that these were historic events that ought to be recorded in order to give human faces and voices to the voiceless. In 1984, she donated the resulting archive, including photographs, notes on interviews and meetings, posters, and correspondence, to the Schomburg Center for Research in Black Culture of the New York Public Library. It forms the "Christiane C. Collins [CCC] Collection of the West Harlem Coalition for Morningside Park and Urban Problems of the Contiguous Communities: West Harlem, Manhattan Valley, Morningside Heights and Manhattanville." Drawing on the CCC Collection and some other sources, this chronicle-cum-memoir is composed as a "history from below" or from the ground up, an approach to writing cultural history that differs from the "high" perspective tradition of historiography.[2] A recent tendency in the discipline laments the scarcity of sources for research. This difficulty is overcome for the areas covered by the CCC Collection, which was admirably organized and indexed by Janice Quinter and the staff at the Schomburg Center. Another source used in this narrative is *Crisis at Columbia: The Cox Commission Report of the Fact-Finding Commission Appointed to Investigate the Disturbances at Columbia University in April and May 1968.* Immediately following the events referenced in this title, the Executive Committee of the Faculties of Columbia University requested appointment of a fact-finding commission to investigate and report on the uprising. Harvard Law Professor Archibald Cox chaired the commission; hence, its name. The published report is a condensation of the formal testimonies at public hearings, which are documented in the holdings of Columbia University's library.

The 2008 program of the "Columbia 1968" retrospective included lectures, informal talks, and responses by/in the media, resulting in a surge of commentary in print and film.[3] An aspect that came into focus at that time was the role that racism at Columbia University played in linking African American students, white students, and faculty to the grassroots opposition. However, the role of Columbia University's urban antecedents that culminated in and were symbolized by the gymnasium project in Morningside Park have never been fully scrutinized. This

---

[2.] Peter Burke, ed., *New Perspectives on Historical Writing*, 2nd. ed. (Pennsylvania State University Press, 2001).

[3.] About 350 participants in and observers of the 1968 uprising at Columbia gathered on the campus for a twentieth reunion in 1988 to discuss the causes and results of their revolt, which helped spawn similar events on other campuses across the country. A discussion of the events of 1968 and 1988 and a look at Columbia in the intervening years may be found in: Morris Dickstein, "Columbia Recovered," *New York Times Magazine*, May 15, 1988, 32–35, 64–68.

chronicle is intended to help fill that gap, relating and documenting the decisions made by Columbia University's Board of Trustees and administration, and New York City's elected officials, that commenced when the Columbia campus was located on Morningside Heights. Decades in the making, the grassroots opposition of the communities surrounding Morningside Heights (West Harlem, Manhattanville, and Manhattan Valley) is documented here—a history as well as a tool of empowerment.

The term "expansion" as applied to Columbia's urban strategy was a misnomer; numerous incidents show that "expansion" activities were driven by racism. Urbanism as an expression of racism vis-a-vis ethnic and economic minorities fostered bonds between diverse people, and, in the late sixties, with the black students at Columbia and with black organizations. Within a long festering context, the gymnasium in Morningside Park became an icon of Columbia University's racism, planned as an institutional bulwark against the imagined threat of Harlem.

Termination of the Columbia University gymnasium project in response to persistent grassroots opposition deserves to be recognized as a triumph for civil rights and participatory planning.

**Author's note:** An early version of this manuscript was written in the 1970s. Footnotes referring to the earlier version do not cite locations of source materials that were later assigned at the Schomburg Center. The author continues to hold a collection of material not directly related to the topic of this narrative; it is named Christiane Crasemann Collins Collection (CCC Collection).

**Acknowledgments:** Because of this book's long history, it would be impossible to list all those who contributed to its making, but the author is grateful to all of them.

That said, special thanks is surely due to Vicky Cullen for her professionalism and continued dedication as my editor and dear friend.

# 1

## MORNINGSIDE PARK

The 1807 Commissioners' Plan for New York laid out a rigid grid of streets for Manhattan Island extending from 23$^{rd}$ Street all the way to 155th Street. It was a plan oblivious to topography, property lines, or existing roads. Shortcomings were soon apparent. In 1866, the Central Park Commissioners were empowered to revise the grid layout for the west side of Manhattan, and Morningside Park was one result of this revision.[4] Its unique natural features would not surrender to rigid geometry. On the other hand, there were questions about its suitability for development as a park at all.

In his report of March 14, 1867, Andrew H. Green, founder of the American Scenic and Historical Preservation Society, as well as Commissioner and Comptroller of Central Park, expressed his doubts about the grid plan: "On the easterly side of the district in question . . . from 110 Street north to Manhattan Valley, the ridge of rocks almost verdureless, mainly between 9$^{th}$ and 10$^{th}$ avenues, breaks so abruptly towards the east as to render the streets that have been laid over it in rigid conformity with the plan of the city, very expensive to work, and when worked so steep as to be inconvenient for use."[5]

---

[4.] Edward Hagaman Hall, "A Brief History of Morningside Park and Vicinity and an Account of the Aqueduct Pump Controversy in 1916," *Twenty-first Annual Report of the American Scenic and Historic Preservation Society: 1916* (New York, 1917), 537–598 (Appendix C).

[5.] Ibid., 557.

Commissioner Green proposed abandoning the side streets between what became Morningside Avenue and Morningside Drive from 110th to 123rd Streets. In November of that same year, he proposed that a park occupy this lacuna within the regular grid of neighboring streets. The following spring, on March 3, 1868, the Commissioners of Central Park accepted his suggestion and authorized him, as Comptroller, to acquire title to the necessary lands.

The steep ridge rising from the Harlem Plain had been a factor in the area's land use and history since colonial days. For three-quarters of a mile, this formidable outcropping of gneiss rock separated the flat farmland in the plain below on the east from the area on top of the bluff to the west, then called "Harlem Heights." (Originally a Dutch village organized around 1658, this section of Manhattan was named after the city of Haarlem in the Netherlands.)

Only one road is known to have connected the "Plain" and the "Heights" across this declivity.[6] This road branched off in an easterly direction from the old Bloomingdale Road, crossing what became the grounds of the Cathedral Church of St. John the Divine on the southern portion of the ridge. The road descended into the Plain between the present 112th and 113th Streets, taking advantage of the gentler contours of the slope at that point. The lane then turned northeasterly, emerging at the eastern border of the future Morningside Park between 117th and 118th Streets. The 1873 design by Frederick Law Olmsted and Calvert Vaux for Morningside Park incorporated vestiges of this historic road, which provided the only grade-level access to the park from the Heights. The disappearance over the years of this trajectory contributed to Morningside Park's reputation as a barrier between diverse communities. In retrospect, plans for the Columbia campus favored the ridge as a bulwark, while reviving the historic road might have ameliorated eventual problems.

During the Revolutionary War, particularly on the occasion of the Battle of Harlem Heights, the road connecting Bloomingdale Road with roads in Harlem Plain and another road running southerly to

---

[6.] Ibid., 549.

what became Central Park were of considerable military significance. The declivity formed a natural line of defense, reinforced in the War of 1812 by fortifications erected on the bluff to fend off British attacks from the north. The remains of a stone blockhouse perched on a steep rock outcropping 45 feet above 123rd Street were evident until the site was occupied by a public school in 1964 (see Chapter 3). Two other blockhouses, built of wood within the later Morningside Park, also disappeared. Their locations, however, are known: one was situated below 121st Street, and the other where the historic road turned down the hill between the future 113th and 114th Streets at Morningside Drive. Until the spring of 1968, the remains of the stone blockhouse were recognizable in the form of an earthen mound notably unrelated to the natural contours of the site. The historic significance of this small, eroded hill escaped the attention of the planners who proposed placement of Columbia University's gymnasium in Morningside Park.

In addition to topographical challenges, there were administrative obstacles to the creation of Morningside Park. Before the Commissioners of Central Park were able to make much progress in shaping a park out of the rugged stretch of land between the Heights and the Plain, a city government reorganization took the matter out of their hands. In the spring of 1870, their office was dissolved and succeeded by the Department of Public Parks. Surveys, cost estimates, and a layout for the proposed park were prepared under the auspices of this new city department and presented by its Engineer in Chief, M. A. Kellogg. (See Figures 1a and 1b for maps of Morningside Heights showing the location of Morningside Park east of the Columbia University campus.) Subsequently, the Parks Department took planning of Morningside Park to the landscape team of Frederick Law Olmsted and Calvert Vaux, who had worked previously with the Commissioners of Central Park and the Department of Public Parks in various capacities, notably from 1858 to 1873 on their *Greensward Plan* for Central Park.

Frederick Law Olmsted is considered to be the father of landscape architecture in America. More recently, he has become recognized as a pioneer environmental and urban planner, committed to the concept of physical form as an instrument of social planning. His understanding of the cultural impact of civic design was far ahead of his time and often in conflict with the public officials with whom he worked. He was deeply committed to the realization that future democratic societies would be achieved in an urban rather than the traditional agrarian context. In the park systems that consumed much of his life and gained him international renown, Olmsted explored ways in which the benefits of close contact with nature and landscape could become available to the inhabitants of urban centers. His "landscape parks" offered recreational possibilities to all social classes and a variety of tastes. These islands of green respite could be reached without requiring expensive travel to the periphery of the cities. Olmsted considered his parks to be integral elements in the lives of urban dwellers, used by people going to work and spending leisure time with their families and friends. Calvert Vaux was trained as an architect in his native England. His partnership with Olmsted was strained at times, because his contributions to their collaborations—as, for instance, in Central Park—were not fully acknowledged compared to Olmsted's rising notability. Their friendship, however, endured, and Vaux achieved acclaim for his architecture. Even after dissolving their partnership, they worked together on Riverside and Morningside Parks,[7] submitting their "Preliminary Study by the Landscape Architect[s] of a Design for the Laying Out of Morningside Park" on October 11, 1873.[8] Unfortunately, the plan drawings that accompanied the study have been lost.

The land set aside for Morningside Park had not been selected in accordance with Olmsted's ideas for parks and recreation, but rather for economic and practical considerations. While recognizing the challenge of the unusual site, the "Preliminary Study" of 1873 bluntly expresses the planners' unhappiness with the narrow dimension and roughness of the park's terrain.

---

[7.] Francis R. Kowsky, *Country, Park & City: The Architecture and Life of Calvert Vaux* (New York: Oxford University Press, 1998), 3–9.

[8.] Albert Fein, ed., and Frederick Law Olmsted, *Landscape into Cityscape: Frederick Law Olmsted's Plans for a Greater New York City* (Ithaca, NY: Cornell University Press, 1967), 333–341.

The study document indicates that, from the beginning, Morning-side Park was the subject of opposing ideas on how to make it available for public use. Discords and conflicts have continued to be its fate.

On the one hand, the Parks Department was anxious to convert the land into a recreational area by developing a variety of facilities; on the other hand, Olmsted saw the impossibility of building attractions without destroying the uniqueness of the site as well as incurring great expense. The text of the 1873 report gives a range of suggestions for the narrow, steeply inclined stretch, which rarely reached more than 100 yards in width. The plan offers a "design with nature" that would enhance vistas within the future park, and into it from the periphery. The edge of the street bordering the park on the west, later called Morning-side Drive, would be shored up to allow creation of a promenade with balconies overlooking the bluff. The view of the dramatic rock outcrop-pings from the avenue below along the eastern side would be softened and enhanced by plantings. The original slopes were apparently quite bare, and Olmsted anticipated problems in selecting vegetation and trees that would flourish without much attention. He envisioned the level area at the northeastern end as a meadow surrounded by a path leading to a walkway below the ledge extending from 122nd to 114th Street, and exiting at the southern end of the Park. The level area just north of 110th street and below the most picturesque rock formations would be converted into an artificial lake surrounded by "tropical" vegetation. Overlooking it, on a slight rise to the west, was to be an esplanade on the so-called "plateau" or "upper meadow." This scenic stretch offered the only level access into the Park from the Heights.

Olmsted's Old Plan of 1873 included an exhibition pavilion with access from below by stairs and inclined walks. Emphasizing an entrance to the Park from the south was intended to establish a link with Central Park, located only one block away across 110th Street. However, though it did offer sweeping views of Morningside Park, a soon-to-be-constructed elevated railroad along 110th Street obstructed this possible connection between the two parks. Figure 2 shows the revised General Plan for Morningside Park of 1887, by Frederick Law Olmsted and Calvert Vaux.

This second plan contains several changes, some of them prompted by the arrival of the elevated railroad.[9] (Figure 3, a view from "the EL," the elevated train station at 110th Street, shows the southern portion of Morningside Park with the Cathedral of St. John the Divine in an early stage of construction and St. Luke's Hospital to the right of the cathedral. Figure 4, "Cathedral Heights," an oil on canvas done in summer or early fall of 1905 by Earnest Lawson, was painted from the same location.) The original emphasis on a southern entrance facing Central Park was shifted to highlight both sides of Morningside Park at 116th Street, and its southern portion was shielded from the increased noise and traffic along 110th Street by a densely planted embankment. The artificial lake was abandoned because of cost and an inadequate water supply.

Overall, the 1887 version is less ambitious and simpler than the earlier one, thus conforming more closely to Olmsted's ideals of park design. He welcomed the decision by the Parks Department to give up on the exhibition pavilion with its brightly illuminated approaches enticing evening use.[10] The new plan did include a modest shelter and comfort station on the upper meadow.

An interesting exchange of letters between Olmsted, then in Brookline, MA, and Vaux, in New York, discusses the revision of the Old Plan.[11] The letters date from the first two weeks of September 1887, shortly before the report and revised plan were presented to the Parks Department on October 1 of that year. In his two letters to Vaux, Olmsted expresses more candidly than in the official report his thoughts as to what Morningside Park should and should not be. On September 3, he writes: "This main motive, the ag[g]randizing of the view downward and eastward from the west side, and the freshening, gracing and enriching of the view upward and westward from the east side, is a totally different motive from any commonly had . . . in a city square or small park or local pleasure ground." All Olmsted's efforts were to be devoted to "the simple pursuit of the leading purpose," to persuade the Parks

---

[9.] Ibid., 441–457.

[10.] Ibid., 451.

[11.] The Library of Congress, Manuscript Division, Olmsted Papers, Box 30. The author is grateful to William Alex for having brought these letters to her attention.

Department and his partner Vaux to stop insisting on features that he considered impossible, unnecessary, and in conflict with his concept of what Morningside Park should be.

One of the points of contention, and one that was to cling to the Park throughout its history, was whether it could be made safe at night. The 1873 plan observes, "Argument is hardly necessary to prove that by no appropriate treatment could a ground having the natural features of Morningside Park, be made a safe and reputable place of resort at night."[12] The report accompanying the revised plan of 1887 insists, "The topography of the Morningside property is all against an intention to adapt it to night use; to do this would add greatly to its original cost and compel a much more expensive system of maintenance."[13]

As an alternative, Olmsted proposed a well-illuminated promenade along the periphery, and keeping the walks inside the Park to a minimum. In his September 3 letter to Vaux, Olmsted suggests that they should "omit all walks south of 120th Street, inside the Park, except one, (which could be secluded), from north to south, and one for crossing at 116th Street . . . [and] keeping the 'plateau' in a natural forest character . . . with nothing artificial except the one upper walk south from the foot of the 116th Street stairs." It is not entirely clear whether Olmsted's purpose was to keep people out of the Park for their own safety or to protect the Park's uniqueness from the intrusion of what he considered extraneous elements. Olmsted even suggests a footbridge as an alternative to the paths. He writes to Vaux, "Considering the declivity as offering the same obstacle to communication as the river, . . . I should say that . . . it would not be theoretically unreasonable to have it foot-bridged at three points, 113th, 116th, and 119th Streets."

Vaux, on the other hand, thought that well-illuminated walks running east-west were essential because the Park was located between two areas that would soon be densely built up. His premise was that "the park was intended to be occupied as well as looked at." The final plan presented on October 1, 1887, shortly after this exchange of letters, represents a compromise of the two positions. Considering the events

---

[12.] Fein and Olmsted, *Landscape into Cityscape,* 338.
[13.] Ibid., 451.

that impacted Morningside Park in the twentieth century, the problem of safety lingered and generated a range of alterations to the Olmsted/Vaux design.

An elaborate retaining wall of granite blocks supporting Morningside Drive and balconies on the crest of the bluff were partially completed by the architect Jacob Wrey Mould on the basis of the Old Plan before work on the rest of the Park began. Existing sparse vegetation was supplemented with extensive planting. Greenery was used to mollify the "fortified" eastern aspect of the retaining wall. To enhance the dramatic character of the site, additional rocks were brought in to create special effects. Paths were alternated with steps following the contours of the escarpment and the descent into the Plain. As a result, unexpected vistas would open to a later stroller skirting rock formations and approaching the level area below, which featured a tree-studded meadow and grassy playing fields.

The original design of Morningside Park reflected what Olmsted envisioned in his September 3, 1887, letter to Vaux: "The great merit of all the works you and I have done is that in them the larger opportunities of the topography have not been wasted in aiming at ordinary suburban gardening, cottage gardening, effects. We 'have let it alone' more than most gardeners can. But never too much. Hardly enough." As a result of this aesthetic, a segment of Manhattan's original scenery—most of it long vanished—was intended to be preserved as a rare still point within an ever changing urban context.

William H. Whyte pointed out that "for most of the people most of the time, the edge of the open space *is* the open space," and in this respect Morningside Park, facing some 30 city blocks along both sides, fulfills its function as a city park admirably.[14] Its elongated shape offers the greatest periphery possible per square foot, short of becoming a mere strip or boulevard.

---

14. William H. Whyte, *The Last Landscape* (Garden City, NY: Doubleday and Company, 1968), 171–173.

The value of a landscape park in a modern metropolis has been questioned, and is considered by some to be a romantic, elitist anachronism.[15] Increasing demands for recreational use have placed burdens on existing nature parks. Under the threat of encroachments, they may even disappear altogether. However, barring human interference or unusual disasters, nature is more enduring and requires less maintenance than manmade creations. The survival of Morningside Park over more than a hundred years and several brutal intrusions testifies to the resiliency of a natural landscape within a densely built-up urban environment.

An air of neglect hung over Morningside Park from the beginning, undoubtedly enhanced by the controversies over its purpose. It was constructed with limited funds. The poor soil and the steepness of the ground hampered planting. Samuel Parsons, Landscape Architect of the Department of Public Parks while the work on Morningside Park was taking place, comments in his memoir that the construction of the walks and steps was of inferior quality and would cause difficulties in upkeep. "Unfortunately," he wrote, "Morningside Park was built economically."[16] In spite of the rocky ground, the ravages of erosion on the steeper slopes, and a minimum of maintenance, bushes and trees grew well. Sheltered from the westerly winds and benefiting from the morning sun, the trees developed to an impressive size with some of their crowns reaching above the level of Morningside Drive. Thriving Park species include maples, elms, sycamores, oaks, black locusts, and osage oranges, among other varieties.

Morningside Heights west of the Park remained rural for some time after Park layout began, but major changes were in store just before the turn of the century. In 1897, Columbia University moved from downtown to its present location west of the park. Low Library was built during 1895–1897, between Broadway and Amsterdam Avenue facing 116th Street, and became the center of the university's growing campus.

---

[15.] George F. Chadwick, *The Park and the Town; Public Landscape in the 19th and 20th Centuries* (New York: Praeger, 1966), 314.

[16.] Samuel Parsons (edited by Mabel Parsons), *Memories of Samuel Parsons, Landscape Architect of the Department of Public Parks, New York* (New York: G. P. Putnam's Sons, 1926), 58–66.

Construction of the Episcopal Cathedral Church of St. John the Divine commenced in 1892 and St. Luke's Hospital in 1896, both adjacent to Morningside Park between 111th and 113th Streets.

The development of Columbia University on Morningside Heights is the subject of numerous publications. It need not be repeated here except in discussion of university decisions and actions that affected evolving urban tensions. The architects McKim, Mead & White provided a master plan for the university in 1894 that shaped Columbia's physical and cultural vision. The plan's genesis and legacy is aptly presented by architectural historian Barry Bergdoll[17], whose account details Columbia's relationship to New York City's grid plan and McKim's Beaux Arts Plan, as well as the university's ambition to achieve Ivy League status. The latter required an expansion and a building program at times in conflict with McKim, Mead & White's master plan and its architectural style. Throughout the ensuing years of impressive academic achievements and physical growth, trustees, administration, and star faculty of "Columbia University in the City of New York," as it soon proudly called itself, disregarded their adjacent neighborhoods and any reasonable concept of urban planning in their determination to build an ivory enclave. The following chapters chronicle the interwoven circumstances and events that led inevitably to a "crisis foretold" with Morningside Park as contested turf.

---

[17.] Barry Bergdoll, Hollee Haswell, and Janet Parks, *Mastering McKim's Plan: Columbia's First Century on Morningside Heights* (New York:Wallach Art Gallery, distributed by Columbia University Press, 1997).

# 2

## PARK AND GOWN

Columbia University is forever shaped by its perch atop Morningside Heights. Early in its history, the university opted to create its own inflexible campus framework within the Manhattan grid in the form of McKim, Mead & White's master plan, and to develop into a self-contained "ivory tower" rather than a dynamic urban complex. (The Figure 5 aerial photograph of Morningside Heights includes Columbia University's campus, and the Cathedral of St. John the Divine at lower center. The university's Morningside Park athletic field is located to the right and downhill from the cathedral.)

With its perimeter buildings emphasizing its geographic enclosure, it became known as "the acropolis on the Hudson." McKim, Mead, & White's campus layout specified several major buildings and adjusted to Manhattan's street grid, but disregarded the prominent natural features of the site. Notable in the McKim plan is the absence of open vistas toward the Hudson River, its scenic shores, and Riverside Park and Drive, which were designed by Frederick Law Olmsted in 1873. Eastward views over the bluff and Morningside Park toward the Harlem Plain and distant East River were not considered in the design. Classical buildings imposed their uniform base and cornice lines on natural rises in the site's terrain. An exception in the early decades was the northern part of the campus, which descended to an open "grove," reflecting the design of the Chicago Columbian Exposition on which the campus was partly based, and, perhaps unintentionally, the aesthetics of nearby Morningside Park.

Conforming to the street grid, the building-enclosed court in front of Low Library was bisected by 116$^{th}$ Street, a major cross street. The street functioned as a typical city block, with parked vehicles and vendors, until Columbia closed it off in 1954. Attracted by the renown and location of Columbia University, other institutions moved to Morningside Heights. Within the confines of this chosen territory, in consort with the other institutions, and enjoying the tacit consent of the city government, Columbia University embarked on the creation of a utopia conducive to intellectual pursuits—an urban enclave from which all social deterioration, crime, decay, and undesirable tenants were to be excluded. This mindset considered Morningside Park a significant, natural barrier rather than a bridge, and, within the context of this narrative, it evolved into a catalyst for controversy.

When Olmsted described the Park's escarpment as an obstacle to communication comparable to a river, he was referring to its physicality. It had not yet become a feature dividing two social worlds within sight of each other. Irwin Edman, in his autobiography *Philosopher's Holiday*, describes living with his family on Morningside Avenue, east and just below the Park, during the first decade of the twentieth century: "It was a quiet, bourgeois neighborhood, although neither I nor anybody else knew the word then. Harlem meant not the world of Negroes or of 'swing' but of middle-class domesticity."[18] The neighborhood began to change a few years after Edman wrote this. (Figure 6, the cover of *The Unfolding of Artistic Activity* by Henry Schaefer-Simmern [University of California Press, 1948], shows a black child sitting on a rock, possibly in Morningside Park. The book's foreword was written by John Dewey.) In the 1930s, Harlem became a tourist-attracting mecca of "swing" and increasingly evolved into an African-American neighborhood with problems of poverty and crime.[19]

---

[18.] Irwin Edman, *Philosopher's Holiday* (New York: Viking, 1938), 162.

[19.] These and the following developments are described in detail in *The Community and the Expansion of Columbia University: Report of The Faculty Civil Rights Group at Columbia University* (December 1967) and also in *Columbia and the*

Before the 1940s, the university's neighborhood was predominantly white and middle class. Between 1950 and 1957, its African-American and Hispanic populations increased from approximately 8,000 to 15,000, according to a study conducted by Skidmore, Owings & Merrill, not including Morningside Gardens and General Grant Houses. (Figure 7, a map published in 1963 in "A Guide to Morningside Heights, New York City," shows the General Grant public housing, Morningside Gardens rental housing, and Morningside and Riverside Parks.)

Inexpensive housing could be found in older Morningside Heights buildings where landlords converted spacious apartments into "single room occupancy" (SRO) units. The landlords collected substantially more rent by crowding several families into an apartment formerly occupied by only one. The tenants in these SROs were mostly poor and elderly, many were on welfare, and some were students in the academic institutions. An increase in crime was routinely ascribed to local tenants from ethnic minorities, although much of it could be traced to intruders from other parts of the city.

Alarmed by the deterioration of the neighborhood and in order to coordinate efforts to combat this trend, the institutions on Morningside Heights banded together in 1947 to form "Morningside Heights Inc."[20] The list of the incorporating institutions is notable, particularly as several were *invited* to locate on this New York acropolis. The association's purpose was "to promote the improvement of Morningside Heights as an attractive residential, educational, and cultural area." This aspiration resembled an American suburb draped in an academic gown: economically and culturally homogeneous and free of "undesirables,"

---

*Community: Past Policy and new Directions: Report by Columbia College Citizenship Council Committee for Research*, written by Marc Rauch, Bob Feldman, and Art Leaderman c. 1968.

[20.] Morningside Heights Inc. originally had 14 institutional members: Barnard College, the Cathedral of St. John the Divine, Columbia University, Corpus Christi Roman Catholic Church, the Home for Old Men and Aged Couples, International House, Jewish Theological Seminary, The Julliard School of Music, Riverside Church, St. Luke's Home, St. Luke's Hospital, Teachers College, Union Theological Seminary, and Women's Hospital. By 1968, the number had increased substantially.

thus implying discrimination along economic and racial lines. The area in which Morningside Heights Inc. wished to achieve this insular campus encompassed all of the Heights, and its boundaries required watchfulness. On the west, Riverside Park and the Hudson River promised a permanent, secure enclosure. The other three sides, however, posed latent threats.

Over the years, the success and/or failure of schemes to "hold the ghetto" affected urban development and the cultural environment on the Heights and in adjacent neighborhoods. It is unclear how decisions were made: were there discussions at meetings of Morningside Heights Inc., or did Columbia University, its most eminent member, present the others with these schemes? Apparently, urban planning professionals were not consulted. The absence of such advice—which might have guided Morningside Heights Inc., and particularly Columbia University, toward a sensible, comprehensive, long-range urban plan—had dire consequences lasting into the present. It was lamented by architects and urbanists, even by members of Columbia's administration and faculty, as well as by generations of alumni, particularly when the university used "expansion" as an umbrella term for "holding the ghetto." In 1966, the *Columbia Daily Spectator* cited an unnamed "high level" university administrator as referring to negligent and "haphazard" planning. The same article mentions a 1963 speech by Vice President Lawrence Chamberlain in which he lamented the lack of coordination between Columbia's educational program and its planning strategy.[21] These were only a few of several criticisms coming from Columbia affiliates.

It is particularly tragic that the university administration and trustees were oblivious to their own School of Architecture, recognized to be in the forefront of urban planning expertise. By the time Morningside Heights Inc. was considering improvement options for the area, Columbia's School of Architecture had modernized its curriculum under the influence of Dean Joseph Hudnut. Already in the 1930s, its faculty included several pioneers in urban planning; the "Town Planning Studio," headed by Henry Wright and the German exile Werner

---

21. *Columbia Daily Spectator*, March 4, 1966.

Hegemann, was established in 1935. Both men were well known among the coterie of urbanists associated with the Regional Plan of New York. In the 1960s, the Columbia architecture faculty was involved in a number of conferences whose subjects could have benefited what the university considered its "expansion" activities. These included five forums on "The Shape of Cities of Our Time" convened by the Architectural League and the Museum of Modern Art in New York. At the first of these, well-known scholar Vincent Scully presented a keynote address entitled "The Death of the Streets," and architect Paul Rudolph discussed the need for "civic" space and comprehensive planning. The tendency of urbanism to move beyond the functional city planning of the modern movement to embrace a more humanistic, cultural, and multi-use approach was widely discussed.

Despite a wealth of knowledge, for most of these decades the School of Architecture at Columbia was not consulted or permitted to make suggestions regarding the university's "expansion" and building projects. (This ban would not be lifted until 1969 in response to demands from the faculty and students of the School of Architecture, and the recommendation of I. M. Pei, who had been invited to design a comprehensive master campus plan. (See chapters 9 and 10.)

Columbia University missed opportunities to embark on a course of noteworthy urban development, choosing instead to ignore experience derived from American and international urban plans. A recent study of the manner in which the administration, dominated by a myopic president, and the trustees conducted the affairs and finances of the university reveals an astonishing lack of coordination and foresight, and lack of communication between the various entities.[22] Without a clear vision or awareness of needed synergy between academic and urban planning, years of haphazard decisions wasted economic resources and opportunities.

From the 1940s on, in the name of "expansion" but without any apparent plan, the university acquired as much real estate on Morningside Heights as possible. However, "expansion" as an explanation lacked

---

[22.] Robert A, McCaughey, *Stand, Columbia: A History of Columbia University in the City of New York, 1754 –2004* (New York: Columbia University Press, 2003).

validity in view of the fact that Columbia invited other institutions to occupy vacant buildings or lots that could have formed the basis for a comprehensive university expansion initiative. Some of the acquired buildings remained vacant for extended periods or were demolished, which failed to make the neighborhood safer or attractive for those affiliated with the institutions. It also effectively convinced the "community" that the university intended to fortify its enclave with a barrier against the intrusion of ethnic minorities from the surrounding areas—African-Americans from West Harlem, Hispanics and an ethnic mixture from Manhattanville and Manhattan Valley to the north and south.

To prevent encroachment from the north, Morningside Heights Inc. persuaded the New York Housing Authority to sponsor a large, lower-income housing project, General Grant Houses, while a middle-income cooperative housing complex, Morningside Gardens, was sponsored by the institutions. In the early 1950s, in the name of urban renewal, a vast clearance razed 25 densely populated acres of mixed-use cityscape, primarily low-rent housing. New construction began in 1953. Both projects stressed racial integration, and claimed to give first priority to the displaced families. This was heatedly questioned, as many dwellers of the so-called "slum" were forced into worse neighborhoods. Sterile in design, and obviously intended as a rampart sealing off Morningside Heights from the north at 123rd Street, the housing on both sides of Amsterdam Avenue was nevertheless proclaimed a major achievement by the institutions.

In another effort, Morningside Heights Inc. commissioned the architectural firm Skidmore, Owings & Merrill to undertake a $75,000 study of the neighborhood. The report was presented to the City in 1959 in the hope of enlisting financial support for the rehabilitation of Morningside Heights. By 1961, the New York City Planning Commission and the Board of Estimate[23] approved the project. Federal support was also

---

[23.] The New York City Board of Estimate was a governmental body. Under the 1897 charter of the City of Greater New York, the Board of Estimate and Apportionment was given responsibility for budget and land-use decisions. It was composed of eight ex officio members: the Mayor of New York City, the New York City Comptroller, and the President of the New York City Council, each of whom

requested. David Rockefeller, then chairman of Morningside Heights Inc., went personally to Washington, DC, to obtain advance funding from the Federal Renewal Administration for preliminary planning. Awareness of the confrontation between neighborhoods and the radical slum clearance plans advocated by urban planner Robert Moses had led to making citizen participation a legal requirement. Moses was not actively involved with the proposals for Morningside Heights, although his ideas presumably inspired the drastic urban renewal action to the north of it.

The Morningside Renewal Council (MRC) was set up 1962, under the law requiring citizen participation in the formulation of urban renewal plans. The MRC was made up of representatives of tenant and other community organizations, political associations, schools, churches, and many institutions. From the beginning, the meetings were characterized by town-gown tensions. These increased when the General Neighborhood Renewal Plan (GNRP) was released in 1964.

During intense discussions at MRC meetings, the interpretations and connotations of the terms urban "renewal" or "rehabilitation," as well as "slum" and "blight" were indicative of speakers' stands. Morningside Heights Inc., representing Columbia's position, referred to urban renewal as "redevelopment," if not outright as "expansion." Neighborhoods in decline were rarely called "slums," which they really were not. On the other hand, preference for the term "blight" had the meaning of a disease that ought to be prevented from infecting surrounding areas. This justified eradication of neighborhoods demonstrating "blight," and the people living in them moved away.

It became customary to designate as "community" those groups and individuals not affiliated with the institutions, or, if affiliated, standing in opposition to institutional policies. This "community" embraced an ideal-based, ethnically and economically diverse group of people from Morningside Heights as well as the surrounding neighborhoods. In the years leading to the events of 1968, the "community" evolved into a

---

was elected citywide and had two votes, and the five borough presidents, each having one vote. In the 1960s, it was simply referred to as the Board of Estimate.

"grassroots" movement bonded by civil rights ideals and opposition to racism.

MRC meetings became forums for a diversified community to voice sharp criticism of institutional expansion policies and the secretive, ruthless way in which they were carried out. It was clear that the preliminary GNRP, released by the MRC in the fall of 1964, would primarily benefit the institutions. Its purview even expanded beyond Morningside Heights, comprising approximately 600 acres extending from 104th Street to 125th Street, and from Riverside Drive east to 8th Avenue, thus separating West Harlem from Central Harlem. It was divided into five project areas, with 14 blocks in the immediate environs of Columbia University "excluded from project activity." Thus, the GNRP virtually handed the heart of Morningside Heights to the institutions for disposal as they pleased. Setting aside this enclave destroyed any hope for comprehensive multi-use neighborhood planning, and the privilege extended to the institutions angered the community groups. Strong reactions were provoked by the inadequacy of relocation provisions for lower income families and tenants in the SROs. The GNRP actually prided itself on supporting the city's official policy of abolishing all SROs. There was no program to take care of the occupants of these buildings; they were simply urged to leave the neighborhood and disappear.

West Harlem was hardest hit regarding relocation because of the extensive clearance envisioned for Project Area II, east of Morningside Park. It was the proposed widening of 8th Avenue that was suspected of being an attempt to separate West Harlem from Central Harlem, which would change its cultural character—truly a divide-and-conquer approach.

The inequities of this preliminary 1964 GNRP drew criticism from a wide range of parties, including the City Commissioner on Human Rights, Manhattan Borough President Constance Baker Motley, Congressman William F. Ryan (D., 20th District, which included the area in question), the Morningside Renewal Council, ARCH (Architects' Renewal Committee in Harlem, founded in 1964), The Faculty Civil Rights Group at Columbia University, and others.

After stormy public hearings, a revised GNRP was approved by the Board of Estimate in April 1965. (See also Chapter 4.) The changes in the plan affected primarily the area designated for Columbia's building program. A moratorium of a decade was declared on any further expansion beyond projects already proposed. Columbia quickly made eleven additions to this list, but had to accept the inclusion of the fourteen blocks immediately surrounding the campus into the comprehensive plan for the whole neighborhood.[24]

These changes, as well as revisions concerning relocation of facilities and cancellation of the widening of 8th Avenue, had been worked out prior to the Board of Estimate hearing at the urging of Borough President Motley. The compromises were considered to be highly unsatisfactory by members of the community, as well as by Columbia University officials. The university had apparently entered into a "gentleman's agreement" regarding the expansion moratorium—or so it seemed at first. In fact, an official letter from Columbia's Board of Trustees to the Board of Estimate, dated December 13, 1965, denies that "Columbia University has consented to the restrictions . . . to be imposed on its future development."[25]

Within weeks after the Board of Estimate meeting, Columbia bought two more SROs and proceeded to clear them of tenants, and so it went. Over the following years, Morningside Heights Inc., or its real estate arm Remedco, continued to buy up property on the Heights, ignoring the plans formulated by the GNRP, endeavoring rather to be steps ahead of it, or acting in spite of it. Designating these moves "expansion" had little to do with an actual physical need to enlarge facilities. It was rather an effort to gain total control over use of the land. The acquisition of real estate took on the character of a territorial war, waged primarily by Columbia University against the community and the City of New York as well.

---

[24.] *The New York Times*, April 23, 1965.
[25.] A copy of this letter was presented to the Cox Fact-Finding Commission, May 1968.

This urban policy was destroying the diverse character of the neighborhood, without bringing about the improvements originally envisioned by Morningside Heights Inc. More than 150 buildings were acquired and some 7,500 persons displaced.[26] Structurally sound buildings, which could have been renovated, were left vacant or were demolished, leaving empty lots. This tactic hardly qualified as sound economic policy, but it was nevertheless condoned by the Columbia Board of Trustees. Neither the trustees nor the university administration seemed to be aware of its repercussions. Vacated buildings and empty lots reduced safety, and street life decreased. Urban amenities diminished for those living and working in the neighborhood, the faculty and students, and others affiliated with the various institutions gathered on this "acropolis." Neighborhood stores and restaurants were forced to vacate their premises, or simply joined their clients' exodus. The lack of food markets and playgrounds particularly affected faculty families with young children. During all these years, Columbia never considered the possibility of mixed-use, multi-purpose buildings that would provide institutional facilities, housing, and essential needs for urban life, such as stores, laundries, and perhaps playgrounds.

The Morningside Renewal Council brought together the heterogeneous groups living on Morningside Heights with those in Manhattan Valley below 110th Street and in West Harlem east of Morningside Park. These groups all shared the fear that urban renewal meant the destruction of their neighborhoods and homes, comparable to what had happened to the area north of 123rd Street. This apprehension fostered rapport and united diverse ethnic factions, creating a sense of community that bridged the Park, which Columbia had considered a convenient natural barrier against an alien world.

The image of Morningside Park as an impenetrable no-man's-land was nurtured by the institutions on the Heights. Faculty and students were warned of criminals lurking in the bushes and behind rocks. Described as dangerous, ugly, dirty, and "no good," it became an

---

26. *Crisis at Columbia: The Cox Commission Report of the Fact-Finding Commission Appointed to Investigate the Disturbances at Columbia University in April and May 1968* (New York: Vintage Books, 1968), 39.

out-of-bounds territory to be avoided. Unproven stories of attacks on people and of pickpockets hiding in the caves under the balconies along Morningside Drive were avidly circulated.

In the 1950s, Morningside Drive between 113th and 123rd Streets was residential in character. A few families living there questioned the hearsay about the Park and promoted improvements that would lead to the use of this open space at their doorstep. Mothers petitioned the Parks Department and Morningside Heights Inc. to build ramps at strategic points to allow access for baby carriages and bicycles, as well as to provide guards within the Park at least during certain play hours. The response to these suggestions was sympathetic, but unproductive. The only improvement was the installation of sandboxes in some of the balconies. The decision to terminate the residential character of the blocks between Amsterdam Avenue and Morningside Drive had already been made by Columbia University, thus eliminating, from the institutional viewpoint, any need for enhancing use of the Park.

In 1954, the university Board of Trustees commissioned the architectural firm Harrison & Abramovitz to prepare a comprehensive plan for development of the campus east of Amsterdam Avenue, from 115th to120th Streets. The City agreed to the creation of a unified campus that obliterated two cross streets from the established grid. As mentioned, 116th Street between Broadway and Amsterdam became part of Columbia's domain, although it continued to be open for pedestrian access; 117th Street, between Amsterdam Avenue and Morningside Drive, disappeared as a city street. A block-wide elevated pedestrian bridge over Amsterdam Avenue united the main campus with the superblock of the planned East Campus. It was one of the least attractive additions to the campus, of little use above, and sinister and ugly below. The first building constructed (1959–1961) was the Law School, which acquired the sobriquet "The Toaster," at the corner of 116th Street and Amsterdam Avenue. Further buildings within the East Campus complex extending to 118th Street would comprise a graduate student residence hall (1965) and the School of International Affairs on 118th Street and Morningside Drive. The historic Casa Italiana, designed in 1926 by McKim, Mead

& White, and the President's House on the corner of 116<sup>th</sup> Street and Morningside Drive were spared from the resulting demolition.[27]

The buildings of the East Campus along the edge of Morningside Park formed a virtually impenetrable "cordon sanitaire." Access was from the campus side on the west, while blank-walled buildings faced Morningside Drive. Their architectural design was undistinguished, to say the least, and pedestrian circulation between the buildings and over the bridge to the campus west of Amsterdam Avenue proved awkward.

Prime scenic real estate was dedicated to institutional facilities in a financially unwise move that was detrimental to sane planning for the Heights. Morningside Drive could have been developed as a pedestrian-friendly boulevard with buildings combining faculty as well as community housing, stores, and eateries. This urban blunder significantly enhanced ill feelings among those living below the Park and facing a formidable bulwark above the escarpment.

By 1965, the effect of the removal of tenants—primarily faculty families—to accommodate the East Campus development could be assessed by glancing at the few remaining side streets near Morningside Drive, now deserted except for the uniformed guards hired by Morningside Heights Inc. to patrol where families had formerly provided life and a sense of security. The well-being of families affiliated with the institutions received scant attention. Removing them from the area near Morningside Park had destroyed a sense of neighborliness that had encompassed families from West Harlem and Manhattanville as well. One might suspect that Columbia was glad to put an end to these contacts.

To compensate for the loss of faculty housing, two high-rise residential towers were built in 1964 and 1967 at the northern end of Riverside Drive and 124<sup>th</sup> Street.

Resembling the public housing on Manhattan's Upper East Side, these buildings rose isolated from the campus and any urban amenities remaining on Broadway. Garages were located beneath the faculty apartments, but no thought was given to providing pedestrian access for families.

---

[27]. Bergdoll et al., *Mastering McKim's Plan*, 102–103.

An overview of institutional policies prevailing on Morningside Heights demonstrates Columbia's resistance to acknowledging the existence of other cultures beyond the Ivy League enclave, and the possible value of being located in a teeming metropolis of international renown. This narrative acknowledges this "other" world, and the complex reality of the "community" and its relationship to urban space.

Despite the reputation fostered by the institutions on the Heights, Morningside Park was never the deserted no-man's-land it was reputed to be. Although the steepness of the terrain made crossing the park rather difficult, picturesque stairs and walks made up for the inconvenience. Because of various work shifts, employees and patients traveled on foot between St. Luke's Hospital and 114th Street in West Harlem at all hours, and students as well as workers at the other institutions often reached their destinations via the Park from the 8th Avenue subway station at 116th Street.

People walked for pleasure and exercise in Morningside Park. In the early morning, dog walkers from the surrounding neighborhoods would greet one another as they made their daily rounds, chatting while their dogs played. Most of them took the "goat walk" high up to the west between 116th and 118th Streets, with the upper meadow near 113th Street as their destination. This path was particularly pleasant on sunny winter mornings when it was sheltered and warm along the retaining wall. A grey-haired gentleman of striking athletic appearance would frequent this route from his home in Harlem, proceeding at an energetic pace, slowing down only to exchange greetings. The owner of a Dalmatian dog once began setting bulbs along the path, "so we can all enjoy spring flowers." She commented that parts of the Park reminded her of the Alps.

After a heavy snowfall, the sledable slopes would fill with youngsters. For many children living west of Morningside Park, these were among the few occasions on which they joined their peers from West Harlem. The expanse of the snow was hard to resist, and it allowed people to forget their fears and prejudices. The children on the slopes shared sleds, and even mittens. Irwin Edman nostalgically describes winter fun on those slopes facing Morningside Avenue, where he lived as a child many years earlier: "it was not necessary to go far afield for diversion. Right close by, in Morningside Park, there was coasting in winter."[28] With the melting of the snow, the children living on the Heights retreated to the western periphery, while Harlem youngsters freely roamed the Park, taking advantage of its exciting topography. They scaled rocks, climbed trees, and improvised shelters with fallen branches.

The level areas in Morningside Park along Morningside Avenue underwent considerable change over the years. In 1955, a playground with a small field house was constructed at 123rd Street, across from Public School 125. Under the direction of Mrs. Gloria Lynch, and with the help of mothers from both sides of the Park, a preschool playgroup was sponsored by the Parks Department, with Morningside Heights Inc. contributing financial support. The narrow stretch below the steepest section of the bluff, extending from 116th Street to 119th Street, was converted to paved recreation facilities in 1957. The basketball courts and playgrounds, although unimaginative, conformed to the approach of that time, and were welcomed and extensively used. High fences surrounded and cut them off from the rest of the Park. Their only access was from Morningside Avenue to the east, thus enhancing the "Park as barrier" concept.

These structured intrusions impaired Olmsted and Vaux's design and their intention of preserving a rare example of Manhattan's original nature. The visual impact of the wooded embankment was impressive from West Harlem as it formed the western terminus for the streets from 110th to 123rd. Viewed from tenement windows, sitting on stoops, or walking to the corner store, the Park contributed a sense of place to a neighborhood in need of an uplifting element.

Columbia's Bicentennial year, 1954, was the beginning of fourteen years of escalating threats that would affect the ethnic diversity on Morningside Heights, as well as in the adjacent communities, and would culminate with the events of 1968. Within the context of racially motivated decisions, Morningside Park emerged as a focal point. As urban

---

[28.] Edman, *Philosopher's Holiday*, 165.

planning issues bore upon the Park, it would become a prime issue of concern uniting the surrounding communities, as well as alerting devotees of Olmsted parks and advocates of the environmental movement. The Park drew the attention of Columbia University's faculty and students gradually. The Board of Trustees and the university administration, in conjunction with various departments of New York City, might have anticipated the repercussions generated by the urban events they set in motion. In retrospect, these repercussions gravitated toward "a storm foretold."

There was a consequential step in 1954 when Columbia President Grayson Kirk began discussions with Robert Moses, then Commissioner of Parks of New York City, regarding the possibility of constructing an athletic field on five acres of level ground at the southern end of Morningside Park. Public and private educational institutions were permitted to use the city's public parks for their recreational programs by signing up in advance to reserve available playing fields for certain hours. What Columbia proposed, however, was a different and, as the Department of Parks described it, a "noteworthy arrangement."[29] *The New York Law Journal* of April 9, 1969, summarized the implementation of this arrangement in a report on Forster, Jr. vs. The Trustees of Columbia University: "In 1954 and 1955, upon the agreement of community leaders, Parks Department officials, and Columbia University representatives, extensive plans were formulated for the physical improvement of Morningside Park. A public hearing was conducted on the plans in December 1955, and the Board of Estimate approved the subject permit that same month [on December 29, 1955.]" Under this "permit," which was revocable at the discretion of Parks Commissioner Moses, Columbia University was granted permission to construct, at the cost of $200,000, an athletic field with the proper drainage network, a field house, toilet facilities, and a wooden running track.[31] Title to the buildings and improvements was to be held by the City of New York, and the Department of Parks was responsible for the maintenance. The institution was to pay insurance (fire and liability) and worker's

---

[29.] New York City Department of Parks, *Thirty Years of Progress, 1934–1964*, 26.

compensation, and to conduct and supervise an athletic program for neighborhood children, providing staff and equipment. Columbia was to have exclusive use of the facilities and the field for Columbia College[30] student activities, including those of the Naval Reserve Officers Training Corps (NROTC), annually from October 1 through May 31 between 8 a.m. and 6 p.m. From June 1 through September 30, and during weekends and university holidays the rest of the year, the athletic field would be open for public use "by organized community teams." The Parks Department considered this "a most satisfactory arrangement, one which benefits both the students and the residents of the adjacent community."[31]

However, three rows of eight-foot, iron-link fence around these facilities, and locked gates, removed a large segment of a city park from public access, except under the specifications of a private entity. There was little overt community opposition to "Columbia's ball field" as it was usually referred to, although the ethics of taking over a major portion of the scarce level area in the Park was questioned. Columbia's contention that the field was previously swampy and unfit for playing was vigorously denied by State Senator Basil Paterson and others who grew up nearby and played on it as youngsters. Senator Paterson described it as one of only three softball fields available to Harlem children. He, as well as a Senator Warren from the Bronx, had as youngsters participated in citywide athletic contests conducted on this field by the Parks Department. Senator Paterson insisted that the area saw much more use before Columbia undertook to improve it and fence it in.[32]

An autumn 1963 special issue of the alumni magazine *Columbia College Today*, entitled "Athletics: Lion in a Rusty Cage," commented quite differently: "Moses was worried because Morningside Park was woefully underused; hardly any white families had entered it in nearly a decade

---

[30.] Columbia College is the division of Columbia University for male undergraduates.

[31.] New York City Department of Parks, *Thirty Years of Progress, 1934-1964*, 26

[32.] Cox Fact-Finding Commission Transcript, Rare Books & Manuscript Library of the Columbia University Main Library, testimony by Basil Paterson, 2,999–3,002.

and Negro families were not especially attracted to rock-climbing. Dr. Kirk was worried about Columbia's serious lack of space for recreation and exercise, and its relations with the surrounding community."

The regulations regarding the use of the athletic field not only restricted its availability for the community: the facility was for the exclusive use of students of Columbia College, at that time all male. Neither graduate students, which included women, nor faculty and their families were permitted its use. Local journalist Roger Starr describes the implications of this restrictive arrangement: "The Columbia-Community Athletic Field is off-limits to everyone who does not actively participate in its programs. The programs, furthermore, are only open to those boys, and young men who either belong to a team, or are stable enough to join one and remain with it, after presenting themselves for a tryout. The players, though most of them come from poor or nearly poor families, are not the delinquent or pre-delinquent Children of Harlem; they are, rather, its future middle-class citizens."[33]

Columbia has claimed that the idea to plan a gymnasium in Morningside Park developed out of the success of the community athletic program, which "encouraged President Kirk to discuss with Commissioner Moses in April 1958, the possibility of constructing a gymnasium next to the playing field—an indoor extension of the outdoor joint City-University program."[34] Ralph Furey, formerly Director of Athletics and Physical Education at Columbia College, stated in a private interview that informal discussions were held within the university as early as 1952/53 on the possibility of using Morningside Park for both an athletic field and an adjoining gymnasium.[35]

The Trustees had formed a Gymnasium Committee some time prior to the discussions with Robert Moses, and various sites had come

---

[33] Roger Starr, "The Case of the Columbia Gym," *The Public Interest*, no.13, Fall 1968, special issue: The Universities, p. 108.

[34] *Columbia College Today*, Fall 1963, "Athletics: Lion in a Rusty Cage."

[35] Ralph Furey interview with Richard M. Wolfe, January 21, 1970. Reported in Richard M. Wolfe, "Columbia 's Morningside Park Gymnasium: A Case Study in Park Encroachment," unpublished thesis presented to the Faculty of Architecture, Columbia University, February 1970.

under consideration. Among these were the block bounded by 115th and 116th Streets between Amsterdam Avenue and Morningside Drive, and a location on Broadway between 112th and 114th Streets. The costs involved in acquiring a site large enough to accommodate a gymnasium and the problems involved in relocating tenants were forbidding. The university tended to stress that the desire to provide recreational facilities for the community guided the final choice of situating the gymnasium in Morningside Park next to the athletic field, although this had other major and self-evident advantages.

The original McKim, Mead & White plan called for siting the gymnasium in the center of the campus behind Low Library. A partially constructed building located there, University Hall, contained the athletic facilities at the time. Expanding the so-called University Hall northward toward 120th Street was considered in 1941. Plans published in *The Columbia Alumni News* of February 7, 1941, proposed a gymnasium for the entire student body, including those not only from Columbia College but also from the professional schools and graduate faculties. This building would have balanced the layout of the campus, effectively complementing Low Library and the newer Butler Library. (*Mens sana in corpore sano:* A healthy mind in a healthy body.) However, the project was shelved until 1948, when Dwight D. Eisenhower, then President of Columbia University, received a report compiled by University Comptroller Henry McA. Schley and a committee of eleven deans, "Study of Present Campus: Morningside Heights Looking Toward Future Expansion." Among suggestions for the entire campus, the report called for partial demolition of University Hall and construction in its place of a new gymnasium with playing fields on its roof. The Board of Trustees received the Schley report in February 1949, but nothing has been heard of it since.[36]

The decision to locate the Columbia gymnasium in Morningside Park was affected by financial and political influences that involved members of Columbia's administration, alumni, and Board of Trustees, and that preceded President Kirk's discussions with Robert Moses in

---

[36.] The Schley report is discussed in greater detail in Wolfe, "Columbia 's Morningside Park Gymnasium: A Case Study in Park Encroachment."

the summer of 1958. Only then was it announced that the new School of Business would be built on top of University Hall. Two brothers involved in New York real estate, Harold and Percy Uris, were donating $3,000,000 toward the $8,500,000 cost of the building. Preliminary construction of the School of Business had actually begun in the spring of 1957, ruling out the possibility of locating the gymnasium on the campus. It is notable that Percy Uris, an alumnus of Columbia's School of Business (1920), had been named special advisor for new construction to President Kirk in 1957 (he joined the Board of Trustees in 1960).

The influence of the Uris Building Corporation did not earn the School of Business building academic esteem.[37] Criticism of the architectural design of recent buildings on the campus and the absence of comprehensive planning peaked with the design and placement of the School of Business. At the official groundbreaking ceremony for Uris Hall in April 1962, protesters from the School of Architecture picketed with slogans reading "We Protest Bad Design, Ban the Building" and "No More Uglies." The physical growth of the campus, its impingement on the surrounding cityscape, and the university's relations to the surrounding communities were increasingly critically reviewed in the media. Among others, Ada Louise Huxtable's articles in *The New York Times* were particularly cogent. Her friend and colleague George R. Collins, a faculty member of both the School of Architecture and the Department of Art History at Columbia, exchanged letters with Huxtable and provided her with local news, clippings, and illustrations from the *Columbia Daily Spectator*. Huxtable's extensive May 1968 article, "Strike at Columbia Architecture School Traced to Anger over Exclusion from Planning," summarizes her views on the architectural "disasters" on the campus.[38]

Unwelcome notoriety became a concern for President Kirk and the Trustees as it might affect fund raising efforts. Besides Percy Uris, another

---

[37.] Bergdoll et al., *Mastering McKim's Plan,* 104–116, is an astute and well documented description of the rise of student activism in relation to new buildings and the expansion of the campus.

[38.] Ada Louise Huxtable, "Strike at Columbia Architecture School Traced to Anger over Exclusion from Planning," *The New York Times*, May 20, 1968.

Columbia alumnus and trustee, Harold F. McGuire, was intimately associated with the proposed gymnasium. A graduate of Columbia College (1927), he was chairman of the Trustees' Gymnasium Committee as well as chairman of the Gymnasium Site Subcommittee. In his testimony to the Cox Fact Finding Commission, McGuire declared that Robert Moses first proposed the "cliff site" to the Gymnasium Committee, but that the latter initially considered it unwise to become involved with public parkland.[39] In his autobiography, Parks Commissioner Moses relates a different version of the initial negotiations regarding placement of the gymnasium in Morningside Park: "The fact is that President Grayson Kirk of Columbia begged us to provide air rights for his gymnasium and for a ground-floor gym for the neighborhood, that he delayed, temporized, and ran out on his agreement, that he let Commissioner Hoving denounce us and rouse the Negro neighborhood against an alleged 'giveaway,' and that he lost everybody's respect in the process."[40]

It is likely that the initial idea for the gymnasium in Morningside Park did, indeed, come from the university, and could have been received favorably by Moses because it fitted his enthusiasm for high-intensity use of public parks. There is additional documented evidence that the project originated within the university. Ira Silverman, who became one of the editors of the neighborhood newspaper *The Morningsider*, and later news editor of the "6th Hour News" for NBC television, was at that time working for the Office of Development of Columbia College, from which he had just graduated. He remembers being sent out to take photographs of what was destined to become the gymnasium site in Morningside Park—*previous* to any meetings with city officials. Silverman recalled being told specifically to take the photographs while standing on the athletic field and at an angle that showed the "rocky cliff" but not the wooded plateau above. Silverman was later present at a meeting where the photographs were shown to McGuire, James Cahill

[39.] Cox Fact-Finding Commission Transcript, testimony by Harold F. McGuire, Columbia University Trustee, 396–400.

[40.] Robert Moses, *Public Works: A Dangerous Trade* (New York: McGraw Hill, 1970), 37. Thomas Hoving was Parks Commissioner from January 1966 to March 1967.

from the Columbia College Council, and various university officials. This meeting preceded conversations with city officials—except perhaps unreported, private contacts.[41] Because the photographs showed the gymnasium site only from the plain below and from the southeast, they may well have persuaded those unacquainted with Morningside Park that nothing would be lost by replacing the "useless rock escarpment" with a "useful" building.

One of Columbia University's original intentions was to buy a piece of the Park and provide a comparable site elsewhere for a public open space as a land swap. Although no swap site of comparable size was ever mentioned, if available space could not have been found on Morningside Heights for the gymnasium, an alternative land swap could have been arranged east of the Park in West Harlem. This scheme would have involved the removal of housing and pushing an "undesirable" neighborhood further away from the academic domain, the Park, and the gymnasium. A similar suggestion was rumored to have been made by Skidmore, Owings & Merrill in their study for Morningside Heights Inc., presented in 1959. This plan, which has not been seen since, proposed that institutional buildings occupy most of Morningside Park, and that the lost parkland be replaced with an open area east of Morningside Avenue. The neighborhoods responded to this suggestion with angry resentment; West Harlem residents feared that the gymnasium was the first step toward the institutions absorbing all of the Park, shifting dense Harlem further eastward, and separating the institutions from it with a wide, insulating strip. This fear among Harlem residents familiar with the proposal outweighed any possible advantages of a relocated public park, even if it were topographically more suited for active recreation.

The Parks Department would not agree to the land-swap plan or to selling public parkland, but was willing to consider a long-term lease of the air rights above a facility constructed for community use. New York City's public parkland is legally under the jurisdiction of the State of New York. It was therefore necessary for Mayor Robert Wagner and the City Council to send a home rule message to the state legislature

---

[41.] Author's conversations with Ira Silverman, held on several occasions between 1968 and 1971.

requesting passage of an act enabling the city to lease the parkland to Columbia University. While the legal aspects of this first step were being worked out, the Parks Department and Columbia began drafting the lease. The two parties also discussed specifications for the community portion of the gymnasium. Initially, there was apparently no consultation with neighborhood leaders on these details or on the percentage of the overall space to be allotted for community use.[42]

On February 2, 1960, a bill authorizing New York City to lease part of Morningside Park to the Columbia University Board of Trustees was introduced to the New York Senate by James L. Watson, a Democrat representing the Morningside/West Harlem area. A companion bill was introduced to the Assembly by John Brook, also a Democrat.[43] Although the first bill was supposedly drafted by Senator Watson, an Afro-American, the true author and originator of the bill has been identified as Senator MacNeill Mitchell, a Columbia alumnus. Later conversations with Senator Watson indicate that he was at that time under the impression that the space in the projected gymnasium was to be shared on a much more equitable basis than turned out to be the case.

Only a month later, on March 1, 1960, the City Council's Committee on State Legislation, with the concurrence of the City Council, recommended that Mayor Wagner send a home rule message to the State Legislature requesting passage of Senator Watson's bill. The bill's title reads: "An Act to amend the administrative code of the City of New York, to empower the City of New York to lease a tract of land, constituting a part of Morningside Park in the City, County and State of New York, to the Trustees of Columbia University in the City of New York for construction at its own cost and expense, of a building, a part of which building is to be for the exclusive use of the Trustees of Columbia University in the City of New York, and a part of which

---

42. Letter from Stuart Constable, Executive Officer of the Parks Department, to Ralph Furey, Director of Athletics at Columbia College, dated July 30, 1958. A copy of this letter is among the "Exhibits" attached to the Cox Fact-Finding Commission Report testimony by Harold F. McGuire.

43. Cox Fact-Finding Commission Transcript, testimony by Harold F. McGuire. Starr, "The Case of the Columbia Gym," 110–112.

building is to be sublet or reserved for the exclusive use of the City of New York." This act became law on April 14, 1960, with the approval of Governor Nelson Rockefeller. It passed in both the State Senate and the State Assembly by two-thirds votes.

Over the next year, the details of the lease, the sublease, and the agreement regarding the use of the gymnasium, as well as preliminary architectural plans were worked out between the City of New York and Columbia University so that they could be presented to the Board of Estimate for approval. The architectural firm of Eggers & Higgins was retained by Columbia for this project. In a complex legal arrangement, the Trustees of Columbia University became the "Tenant" of the City of New York, referred to as the "Landlord," and were permitted to lease approximately 2.12 acres in Morningside Park (public parkland!) for the construction of a gymnasium. Then, the "Tenant," Columbia University, was to sublet part of the building to the "Landlord," the City of New York. Each party had separate appraisals made to determine the rent to be paid by Columbia University. The unusual circumstances of the case, which required taking into account the terms and conditions set forth in the lease (see below), made it extremely difficult to set a fair rent. The rent agreed upon was suggested by the city appraiser and set at $3,000 per annum. This was $500 higher than the amount arrived at by the firm of A. White & Sons, asked by Columbia for an appraisal.

One of the major community objections to the gymnasium in Morningside Park centered on the "insufficiency" of the rent to be paid by the university for 2.1 acres of land in Manhattan. The considerable financial obligations that Columbia was entering into with regard to the construction of the building, and the running of the athletic program in the community gymnasium, were never publicized sufficiently to offset the popular contention that "Columbia was getting something for nothing."

The lease, sublease, and gymnasium agreement between the City of New York and the Trustees of Columbia University in the City of New York are lengthy documents couched in legal terms. The major points are as follows:

The "initial term" of the lease was to be fifty years; thereafter, the Tenant (Columbia) would have the privilege of renewal for five successive periods of ten years each. Thus, the arrangement could conceivably continue for 100 years. At each renewal time, the rental would be renegotiated, but not set below the initial $3,000 per annum to be paid during the first fifty years. The construction of the building was to commence within six years from the date of the drawing up of the lease, a stipulation that would produce considerable aggravation for the university. Preliminary plans for the gymnasium were attached to the lease, to be followed by more comprehensive "intermediate plans" prepared by the architects within the next six months. The final plans, not to differ substantially from the first two sets, were to be ready within five and a half years of the date of the lease. Further changes could, however, be approved by the Landlord. If the Tenant, Columbia University, should be unable within the next five years to raise the necessary funds for the construction of the building, the Tenant could terminate the lease by giving thirty days notice to the Landlord. Should the Tenant fail to complete the building within five years of commencement of construction, the Landlord could terminate the lease by giving thirty days notice.

One section of the lease specifies requirements that would gain major importance within the coming decade. These stipulations address the possibility that the projected gymnasium in Morningside Park might not become a reality but rather remain "unbuilt": "if the Tenant shall commence construction of the building and fail to complete construction of the building as in this lease prescribed, the Tenant shall, at Landlord's option, be required, at Tenant's cost and expense, to demolish the uncompleted building and restore the premises substantially to their condition as it existed immediately prior to the commencement of the construction of the building; provided further, however, that Tenant may, at its option, substitute landscaping for rock."

Regarding the use and occupancy of the gymnasium, the lease specifies: "The Tenant's portion shall be for the exclusive use and occupancy of the Tenant, which shall use and occupy the premises as a gymnasium, as a Naval Reserve Officers Training Corps drill hall, for classrooms, for office space, and for any other purposes not inconsistent with Tenant's function as an educational institution, or for any one or more of such purposes." The classrooms and office space included in the language of the lease were criticized as inconsistent with the function of an athletic recreational facility for which public parkland had been "usurped."

The lease required Columbia to maintain the exterior and interior of the Tenant's section and provide insurance, liability coverage, and worker's compensation. The sublease specified that, upon completion of the building, the City of New York would, at no cost, sublet that part of the building to be used by the general public. In the city portion of the gymnasium, Columbia was obligated to provide substantial facilities as well as heat free of charge. Over the ensuing years, the facilities in the city portion were substantially modified from the preliminary plans.

The Gymnasium Agreement between the City of New York and The Trustees of Columbia University in the City of New York documents the provisions for setting up the city's portion as a community gymnasium for the general public. Columbia agreed to provide in the building an extension of the outdoor program on the adjacent athletic field for organized teams of male teenagers. The Gymnasium Agreement does not provide information on programs conducted by the Parks Department for supplementing the restricted schedule proposed by Columbia.

In the spring of 1961, the proposed lease and the preliminary plans for the gymnasium building were submitted to various city departments for consideration. The Municipal Arts Commission, which was charged with approving all plans for buildings to be erected in public parks, passed the plans for the gymnasium. On July 27, 1961, the Board of Estimate held an open hearing on Columbia's plan to build a gymnasium in Morningside Park; it was Calendar No. 817 on the agenda. Calendars for public hearings conducted by the Board of Estimate were announced only a couple of days before taking place. Ingenuity and determination were necessary to find out when a calendar item of particular interest would come up for discussion. In spite of this hindrance, several organizations sent representatives. The stenographic transcript of the hearing on Calendar No. 817 shows that many civic organizations of reputable standing did not view the proposed gymnasium in Morningside Park favorably.[44]

---

[44.] Cox Fact-Finding Commission Transcript, exhibit attached to McGuire testimony, 396–400.

No grassroots neighborhood groups were represented at this time. They had not been consulted by either the Department of Parks or Columbia University on their recreational needs. Though the negotiations had not been conducted entirely in secret, they had received little publicity in the communities surrounding Morningside Park. It was therefore not surprising that the two organizations that might be called "community groups" in attendance at the Board of Estimate hearing favored the gymnasium—and may have been invited by Columbia University. They were "The Grant Houses Tenants" from the low-income housing project at the northern end of the Park and the "Morningside Civic Group," said to represent 1,600 people working and living on Morningside Heights. Neither group was ever heard from again. There was no community input representing West Harlem or Manhattan Valley at the hearing, although the gymnasium's racial implications were beginning to draw attention.

The voices of opposition at the July 27 hearing tended to stress aesthetic arguments and conservationist objections to park encroachment as a matter of principle. One of the first speakers was Albert S. Bard, representing the Fine Arts Federation of New York. He asked that decisions be postponed until the architectural firm of Eggers & Higgins could present a scale model of the proposed gymnasium building. In his opinion, the city should not approve the lease until the design was satisfactory to all concerned. This request was not granted.

Harmon H. Goldstone, speaking as President of the Municipal Arts Society, opposed the project on grounds of both park encroachment and aesthetics. "Parkland is a public trust to be held for primary park uses," he said, and "leasing of public parkland to private users, no matter how worthy and deserving in this case, creates an extremely dangerous precedent for future policy." He emphasized that the proposed structure would obstruct the view of the Cathedral Church of St. John the Divine. The preliminary plans for the gymnasium building showed a 50- to 60-foot rise above Morningside Drive street level at 112th to113[th] Streets east of the cathedral apse. Goldstone suggested modification of the design so that the side of the gymnasium facing Morningside Drive should not rise above it, and provision of a landscaped terrace on top of the building to compensate the City for lost park acreage. (A final version of the building design did indeed reduce the elevation above Morningside Drive, but it did not include the roof terrace, although it presumably was promised.)

The Park Association of New York, through its representative Daniel Chase, voiced its opposition to the diversion of parkland from primary park purposes and to the erection of any structures in parks except to fulfill primary park needs, which even then should be inconspicuous. This was actually in keeping with the early attitude regarding buildings in Morningside Park held by Olmsted. He had even preferred to eliminate the modest shelter and comfort station shown on the preliminary plans, and suggested using the caves under the balconies for public comfort stations and storage of maintenance equipment. The gymnasium architects had used an old plan of the Park, without erasing the "Existing Comfort Station" on the upper level at approximately 114th Street. This small building had disappeared long before Columbia became interested in Morningside Park.

George Hallet Jr., Executive Secretary of the Citizens Union, explained that he had learned of the public hearing only the previous day. He was, however, well informed on the case. He objected to the gymnasium because it was going to bisect the Park, as well as destroy the impressive view of the Cathedral Church of St. John towering above the cliff. The cathedral's legal counsel had submitted a statement on this same point and requested a modification of the plan. Hallet explained that the Citizens Union had held discussions with Columbia University and had been assured that the plans would be modified, yet this had not been done. The Citizens Union was not, on principle, opposed to the use of parkland for a building if the building were designed to fit the conditions of the site, and equivalent park area were made available elsewhere.

The Executive Director of St. Luke's Hospital, Dr. Lloyd Gaston, voiced concern regarding the traffic and demand for parking that would be created by a large building across Morningside Drive from the hospital. At the hearing, he was assured by the architect in charge of the design, R. Jackson Smith, an Eggers & Higgins partner, that the students would walk from the campus to the gymnasium. This was probably true, but it was quite laughable that no mention was made of alumni, parents, and guests likely to arrive by car to attend athletic events, especially as there was no subway stop nearby on Morningside Heights. Gaston also objected to the height of the building, which would obstruct the view for patients and convalescents in the east galleries and balconies of the hospital.

Through George Hallet, the Citizens Union was the first to voice concern publicly over the allotment of a mere ten percent of the total space of the gymnasium to the community, a point stressed repeatedly by the city's Deputy Comptroller—identified only as Mr. Cohen in the transcript—during the testimony of Parks Commissioner Newbold Morris, who had succeeded Robert Moses in 1960. At the hearings, Morris was the chief defender of the gymnasium project agreed to by his predecessor. After praising Columbia's leadership in unspecified "neighborhood improvements," the Parks Commissioner compared the proposed "community recreation center" to a gymnasium and swimming pool built in 1936 in Astoria Park, one of Robert Moses' public works. Deputy Comptroller Cohen objected to this comparison, because the facility in Astoria Park was run entirely by the Parks Department for the use of an average 5,000 youngsters. He stated, " I just want to get some of the plain simple factors. I know about all the good that Columbia does and that sort of business, but what I am really inquiring about is about the amount of space that is actually left for the community, and that is the great concern." He questioned Newbold Morris at to whether it was true that nine-tenths of the gymnasium was going to be for Columbia's use, and one-tenth for the public. Morris replied, "That is a fact!" Pressed hard on the space allotment, the Parks Commissioner gladly turned to showing the photographs supplied by Columbia of the site's "useless rocky cliff." He also brought up the matter of safety in Morningside Park, and how the gymnasium with its correlated activities would contribute to making the Park a safer and better place. As an example of existing conditions, he related an incident in which thirty men were allegedly found hiding out in one of the "catacombs" under a Morningside Drive balcony and conducting forays to mug the innocent inhabitants of Morningside Heights. This was another example of how myths regarding the dangers of Morningside Park beclouded the facts.

Morris was elaborating on an incident reported to him by Columbia professor George R. Collins, who exchanged several letters[45] with the Parks Commissioner about the lack of Park maintenance (which was exploited by Columbia officials for their own ends). On election day in November 1960, when several families, including the Collinses, had gathered on the terrace-balcony of Morningside Drive at 118th Street to air their young and their views of the election, smoke began to emerge from the cracks in the pavement. It came from the cave beneath the terrace, originally intended as a storage place for park equipment, but long vacant and disused. As the volume of the mysterious smoke increased, somebody alerted the fire department. The sizable gathering of adults and children watched the firemen carry hoses down the stairs into the Park and direct a stream of water into the cavern. With a police car now on the scene, a solitary figure suddenly emerged from the cave—wet, bedraggled, groggy, and confused. Apparently, he had fallen asleep in his park-side dwelling, and his cigarette had set his bedding on fire. When he was searched by the police, several tools, but *no* weapons, were discovered on him, and he was taken away in the police car. The entrances to the caves were walled up soon after this incident.

Although Commissioner Morris' tale was vastly exaggerated, his argument that busy athletic activities related to the gymnasium would enhance security in the neighborhood was popular with local residents and storekeepers. He made no mention of maintenance conditions in the park.

Smith, the project architect, described his background, which included a longstanding interest in sports and the proper design of athletic facilities. He proceeded to elaborate on the plans and sketches for the building, which had to fit, in his words, "an extremely unusual site in the City of New York." Questioned on the accommodations for the community, he replied that the design followed exact specifications supplied by the Department of Parks. Asked if there was to be a

---

[45.] Correspondence between George R. Collins and Newbold Morris, November 1960 to December 1961, CCC Collection, Schomburg Center, Box 8, #2.

swimming pool in the community portion of the gymnasium, he replied that there was not.[46]

Columbia University was represented at the Board of Estimate hearing by its legal counsel John W. Wheeler, an alumnus of Columbia College. He reviewed the legal steps that had preceded the hearing and explained the major points of the lease, sublease, and gymnasium agreement under consideration. Wheeler stressed Columbia's past contributions to the neighborhood, including supervised, athletic programs that would be extended indoors. "The youth of the community are going to be served," he predicted. It was true that the community portion of the gymnasium was only one-tenth of the total space, but this portion of the building was going to cost in excess of $700,000, with annual operating costs estimated at $24,000, to be paid by Columbia. Wheeler bypassed Deputy Comptroller Cohen's question as to the additional sum of $14,000, which the City would contribute annually. According to Wheeler, another benefit to the community at large would be Columbia's expenditure of $200,000 for facilities to support the university's Naval Reserve Officers Training Corps, a program he described as "vitally important ... at this particular moment in our history."

On the basis of this hearing on July 27, 1961, the Board of Estimate unanimously adopted Calendar No. 817, authorizing the lease of 2.12 acres of land in Morningside Park to Columbia University for construction of a gymnasium. The legal transaction that granted Columbia the right to build on public parkland was worked out with great care. There were no loopholes, and the correctness of the legal terms would be stressed repeatedly by university officials in their later defenses of the project, as if the legality made it ethical. Architect Harmon Goldstone, a Columbia alumnus who spoke at the hearings, and who later became Chairman of the Landmarks Preservation Commission, described the arrangement in a letter to the editors of *The New York Times* dated May 26, 1968: "From the start, Columbia's plans have struck me as financially astute, legally impeccable, administratively stupid, architecturally monstrous and morally indefensible. If this view is correct, it follows that

---

[46.] See later chapters for more on the matter of a swimming pool for the community.

the university has failed in the very fields—of wisdom, sensitivity and social responsibility—in which the community that supports it looks, or should be able to look, for leadership."

When Goldstone wrote this letter in 1968, he was a member of the City Planning Commission. These were astute and perceptive comments uttered at a time when tensions on the campus and in the surrounding communities were coming to a head. Although he mentioned the "community," Goldstone did not (specifically) refer to the African American and Hispanic neighborhoods surrounding Morningside Heights. Neither did those in opposition to the gymnasium at the public hearing seven years earlier call attention to the fact that Columbia's action represented a racist affront to minority citizens. Considering the growing attention focusing on the Civil Rights Movement and both its African American and white advocates, it is astonishing that Columbia's Board of Trustees, administration, and faculty—with few exceptions—remained oblivious to or preferred to ignore the racist implications of many of the university's decisions.

Unconcerned, Columbia began a fund drive to raise the $9 million needed for the construction of the gymnasium in Morningside Park as soon as the legal matters were cleared in July 1961. In the surrounding neighborhoods, the proposal seemed far away and somewhat unreal, even for those actively involved in community affairs. Interest in Morningside Park and awareness of its deterioration were, however, steadily increasing.

# 3

## THE SCHOOL ON THE ROCK
### 1961–1964

In 1961, the Parks Department installed gates at all entrances to the Park along Morningside Drive. They were padlocked at sunset and opened at 7 a.m. An article in the *New York Herald Tribune* of December 4, 1961, reported that residents on the Heights "had been agitating for years to have gates built," to prevent purse snatchers and muggers from using the stairs into Morningside Park as an escape route. Commenting on the slowness with which the project was carried out, the *Herald Tribune* informed readers that after their construction, "it took more than seven months before the gates were locked for the first time on November 10. Several Heights residents are convinced that the City Administration had dragged its feet purposely because it feared that locking the gates before Election Day might alienate Negro voters." In addition to the gates, a new iron-paling fence was installed atop the cement balustrade along Morningside Drive. These innovations interrupted pedestrian transit between Harlem and the Heights for more than twelve hours daily for all except those agile enough to climb over these hurdles. The article in the *Herald Tribune* admits that it was a hardship for those accustomed to walking home through the Park after work on the Heights, as well as for Columbia students using the Eighth Avenue subway to and from the 116th Street station.

The locking of the gates continued until the fall of 1967, and contributed greatly to the hostility of the Harlem community toward the institutions above the Park. In addition, there was considerable inconvenience to Heights residents and to the employees of St. Luke's Hospital and the Columbia Faculty Club, located at Morningside Drive and 117th Street, particularly when the gates were locked early in the evening or opened late in the morning, as was frequently the case. Thus, the locked gates were a significant annoyance to those living on the Heights, and those who were supposed to be prevented from "escaping" into the Park from Morningside Drive simply continued to do so by vaulting fences, thus leaving their pursuers, usually policemen in squad cars, obliged to take the long way around the Park.

Many residents on the periphery of Morningside Park were disturbed by the locked gates, which were considered a sinister, as well as useless, alternative to a sound program of rehabilitating the Park. Physical maintenance and police surveillance were at a low point. It was suspected that the deterioration was allowed to continue unchecked, despite community protests, in order to foster public support for the agreement between the City and Columbia University regarding the athletic facilities. It seemed an obvious financial advantage for the Parks Department to be able to rid itself of the responsibility for a large segment of its holdings on the pretext that they were not favored by the public. However, the neglect of Morningside Park was not taken lightly in the surrounding neighborhoods. Even before attention began to focus on the issue of Columbia's gymnasium in 1965/66, there were many grassroots efforts to redeem the Park and its reputation.

In the fall of 1962, the monthly newsletter of the Morningside Citizens Committee included a report by the chair of its Park Subcommittee, Doreen Mocha. She vigorously campaigned for more intensive use of Morningside Park: "A false atmosphere of disinterest in Morningside Park has been created ... people should reappraise their views of it."[47]

That same month, responding to local pressure, Morningside Heights Inc. hosted a luncheon meeting with city officials to discuss

---

[47.] *The Morningside Citizen*, New York, October 10, 1962.

rehabilitation of area parks. As the luncheon guests and hosts walked the entire length of Morningside Park, the general neglect, the rubbish, and the erosion threatening trees and shrubs impressed them all. However, maintenance did not improve, except for the installation of mercury vapor lights that cast an eerie light at night. The city did allocate funds to the Parks Department for a three-stage rehabilitation of the Park to be completed in five years. For the first stage, $100,000 was dedicated to a study of needs and design, as well as some construction. Two years later, this money had not been spent by the Parks Department, ostensibly because there were no personnel available to carry out this task.

In the interim, Morningside Park had fallen prey to a remarkable case of encroachment. It was another instance in which the more neglected a public open space, the greater the danger of invasion by worthy projects mustering popular support by promising "improvement." A park abandoned by those entrusted with its maintenance becomes a mere "open space." The very negativism of this term, implying the absence of something, is an invitation to put something new in place rather than address the needed repair.

The "School on the Rock" was located in the northwest corner of Morningside Park as a result of community clamor for additional school space. For several years, local political leaders, parents, teachers, and the Morningside Heights institutions had pressured city authorities to fund a new public school in the Morningside/Harlem area to relieve the crowded conditions of Public School 125. This school was located on the north side of 123rd Street, across from the tip of the Park. Construction funds were granted in 1962, and the search began for a site entailing a minimum of relocation of residents as well as ensuring an integrated student body.

Attention soon focused on the northwestern corner of Morningside Park between 122nd and 123rd Streets, diagonally across from the existing school building. "One site, although perhaps not perfect, was available without destruction or relocation: the *unused* [author's emphasis] corner of Morningside Park known as 'The Rock'," reported the newsletter published by the Riverside Democrats, attempting to make the bitter pill palatable to those who saw a dangerous precedent in construction of schools in public parks.[48]

"The Rock" was favored by, among others, Manhattan Borough President Edward R. Dudley, the City Commission on Human Rights, and the Riverside Democrats, as well as the parents and teachers of PS 125. Several local community groups, including the Morningside Citizens Committee, were opposed. Within the city government, objections were raised by the head of the City Planning Commission, architect William F.P. Ballard, and by Parks Commissioner Newbold Morris, who had recently defended with enthusiasm the use of the other end of Morningside Park for Columbia's gymnasium.

An alternative location favored by those opposing the site on "The Rock" also involved encroaching upon a park, but would actually have increased the overall acreage of parkland. This proposal called for placing the school on a wedge of Riverside Park at the head of Tieman Place, which was cut off from the main body of the park by Riverside Drive East. It would have placed the school about five blocks west and uptown from PS 125. Obvious advantages would be gained by closing Riverside East to traffic and incorporating it into the parkland surrounding Grant's Tomb and the projected school. Nearly two acres would have been added along with increased pedestrian accessibility. The institutions on Morningside Heights strongly favored this proposal because of its proximity to the high-rise faculty housing units called Prentis Hall that Columbia University was constructing a block north of the Tieman site.[49]

Members of the community were suspicious of the Heights opposition to "The "Rock" site, considering that Columbia University was planning to build a private athletic facility at the southern end of the same park. It also looked as if the institutions were opting for a "lily-white" location for the school that would have greater appeal to faculty for their children. The ambivalent attitude of Parks Commissioner Newbold Morris, supporting one park encroachment and opposing another,

---

[48.] Riverside Democrats newsletter, New York, October 1963.

[49.] In later years Columbia University changed the use and name of the building several times.

enhanced these suspicions, as well as undercut the opposition to the "Rock" site by genuine park advocates.

In the spring of 1963, the State Legislature passed an enabling act that allowed the City to "demap" the 1.35 acres forming the northwest end of Morningside Park. A year later, in February 1964, the Board of Estimate voted to remove these 1.35 acres from the parkland map and reassign them to the Board of Education. The main force behind this move was Borough President Dudley, whose primary interest was to get the school built fast and at a location promising to maximize an integrated student body. The City Commission on Human Rights had recommended "The Rock" site after a study comparing its integration possibilities with the alternate Tieman Place location.

The Board of Estimate overruled the recommendations of the City Planning Commission, which had submitted a report stating its opposition "to pre-empting park lands in densely developed residential communities for other than park purposes." The report continues, "We believe that appropriate sites for public improvements can be found without taking parkland, although at times it seems a difficult task. It is no less difficult to find appropriate sites for parks that are sorely needed, and parks are certainly no less an important element in community development than are schools or other public improvements. The great threat to parklands is not that they will be pre-empted for unworthy purposes. It is rather that worthy causes pose a threat as they tempt us into sacrificing parkland by way of an urgent need of the moment . . . ." This comment obviously referred to the case of Columbia's gymnasium in Morningside Park, which, as the report noted, never came before the City Planning Commission for any official action.[50]

Opposition to the School on the Rock did not go beyond a heated debate at the Board of Estimate hearing and letters and articles in the press. Members of the community who opposed the use of parkland for anything except unstructured public recreation were reluctant to take a strong stand if this meant siding with the institutions and against "maximum integration." Columbia Vice President Chamberlain was privately

---

[50.] New York City Planning Commission Report No. 18205, January 29, 1964.

approached by George Collins with the suggestion that the university or Morningside Heights Inc. should take this opportunity to extend a gesture of goodwill toward the residents of the neighborhood by providing an alternate site for the proposed school that would suit all parties concerned. Such a possibility was a location across from "The Rock" on the south side of 122$^{nd}$ Street where buildings had been vacated and were slated for demolition to make way for Columbia's School of Pharmacy (discussed in the next chapter). Instead of this option, Columbia chose to assist two private schools to establish themselves on the Heights as far away from Harlem as possible. In 1963, the university granted Bank Street College of Education and its laboratory elementary school a long-term loan that enabled it to move to 112$^{th}$ Street between Broadway and Riverside Drive. Similar aid was extended to the Episcopal School of St. Hilde and St. Hugh so that it could move to 113$^{th}$ Street west of Broadway. Columbia's policy of aiding additional institutions of its choice to take up sites on Morningside Heights, while emphasizing its own needs for expansion as the reason for real estate acquisition, accompanied by the eviction of tenants, did not sit well with the community. Indeed, moving of these two private schools entailed the demolition of several large residential buildings and the removal of their tenants, a clear example of a policy with racial overtones that increasingly stirred up anger in the neighborhoods surrounding Morningside Heights and beyond.

Preparations for the construction of Public School 36 began in 1964. The blockhouse situated on the rocks at the northern tip of Morningside Park had been erected as part of the city's defenses during the War of 1812, and served, it is told, as an observation point for General Washington during the Battle of Harlem Heights. The remnants of this historic landmark were blasted away, together with the dramatic outcropping and more of the Park, though it is commendable that the architects succeeded in preserving a considerable portion of the unusual features of the site. The result is one of the most distinguished modern school buildings in New York City. The new public school was ready for use in 1967. Designed by A. Corwin Frost and Frederick G. Frost Jr. (see Figure 8 for site plan), it is a complex of three classroom units connected to a central service-administration unit by means of bridges. Irregularly shaped play terraces surround the buildings, and the entrance has an attractive sitting area that forms an inviting plaza off Morningside Drive.

The controversy over the School on the Rock was undoubtedly observed with interest by Columbia University as it provided a sort of trial balloon for the gymnasium project. While public attention was absorbed with the wrangling over the location of P. S. 36, the university undertook another trial balloon in 1962 when members of Columbia's administration began negotiations with the Parks Department regarding construction of ten tennis courts in Riverside Park on a level area below 120th Street. They were to replace the courts formerly located in an area known as "The Grove" on the lower campus. This charming small park and the tennis courts had given way to the new Seeley W. Mudd Building housing the School of Engineering.

Secrecy shrouded the arrangements that preceded the actual installation of the tennis courts in Riverside Park. There were apparently no public hearings or discussions in connection with the Board of Estimate's approval.[51] The Parks Department agreed to bear the maintenance cost for the all-weather courts, while Columbia paid for the construction. Initially, the facilities were open to the public during the months of June through August, and on weekends during the rest of the year. Eventually, the courts were shared by the institutions and the general public on a more equitable basis.

The area selected for the tennis courts was not much frequented by neighborhood families, who might have objected. Columbia's choice was an open field used for informal ball games by teenagers living north of 125th Street and even further away. This field below Riverside Drive stretching north from 120th Street was one of the few areas available in Manhattan for games by non-teams and non-scheduled groups. It also had the advantage of being isolated from the rest of the Park, so that soaring balls did not endanger other park users.

Irving A. Thau, a lawyer actively concerned with park matters (and who would, in 1968, handle the taxpayers' law suit against the leasing of Morningside Park acreage to the Trustees of Columbia University), was

---

[51.] George Weiser, articles in *The Westside News*, New York, October 17 and November 21, 1963. Also, *New York City Record*, February 21, 1963, 1,899–1,900.

the author of a letter on the subject of the tennis courts that appeared in *The Morningsider* for January 23, 1964. In his letter, Thau contended that the tennis courts, Columbia's athletic field, and the projected gymnasium were all part of a coordinated threat to public parkland in New York City. He was convinced that park encroachment could only be stopped by legal means that would prevent such acts before they could damage the parks.

The School on the Rock episode and the construction of tennis courts in Riverside Park took place almost simultaneously at the northwest and northeast corners of Morningside Heights, and they heightened people's awareness of these parks. In the fall of 1963, a Parks and Piers Committee was established by the Morningside Renewal Council, in the belief that the rehabilitation of parks in urban areas was as important as the rehabilitation of buildings. Under its chairman, Frieda Feldman, the Parks and Piers Committee chose Morningside Park as its pilot project. A list of recommendations was compiled and sent to the City Planning Commission in January 1964.[52] In view of the advanced state of deterioration in certain areas of the Park, the committee decided that only a crash program of physical rehabilitation and educational work among those using the Park would be effective. Dramatic improvements were needed to halt vandalism because experience had shown that well-maintained facilities were less subject to vandalism than those in a state of neglect.

In spite of the dedication and enthusiasm of the Parks and Piers Committee, only a small fraction of these plans was realized. However, the proposal for an educational program brought involvement of neighborhood churches and schools, drawing people from West Harlem and Morningside Heights together, with the Park as their "common" ground.

One grassroots action was a George Washington's Birthday party in February 1964, sponsored by fourteen neighborhood groups as an ironic thank-you gesture to City Hall for a promised $90.00 (yes!!) in the next year's capital budget appropriation for the rehabilitation of Morningside Park. The afternoon event started at the Church of the

---

[52.] Parks and Piers Committee of the Morningside Renewal Council, memo re Morningside Park, December 27, 1963.

Master at Morningside Avenue and 122$^{nd}$ Street. The fun and enter-
tainment did not detract from the serious intent of the occasion. West
Harlem resident Ethel Greer expressed community concerns by saying,
"People have been so busy fighting about schools and housing, that we
haven't done anything about neglect in other areas. . . . Harlem has not
been watching what is being done to it and City Hall considers this a
'safe' and complacent neighborhood politically, an area where you can
get away with things you wouldn't dare attempt elsewhere. We'll be
watching much more closely from now on."[53] Note that this warning was
sounded in February 1964—four years before the spring 1968 wake-up
call that changed awareness of civil rights on the Columbia campus, at
City Hall, and elsewhere.

A fortnight later, representatives of the community made another
attempt to persuade the City Government to reinstate the sum of
$170,000 in its budget for Stage II of the rehabilitation of Morningside
Park; this amount had been cut by the Board of Estimate because the
funds allocated for Stage I had not been expended. On March 2, 1964,
Manhattan Borough President Dudley and other city officials met with
local residents in the field house at the northern end of the Park. The
buffet lunch served included sushi, rice patties, and Japanese seafood
prepared by Suki Ports, one of the organizers of the event. The most
important activity was a tour of Morningside Park. On the previous day,
tipped off about the visit by the top brass, the Parks Department had
sent a contingent of seventy men to help the usual crew of nine with
a clean-up so that the Park would look presentable for the occasion.
However, the years of neglect, the erosion that had been allowed to
damage the roots of the trees, and the broken steps were all too obvious.

While walking the entire thirteen blocks of the Park in the warm
spring sunshine, Borough President Dudley listened to grievances about
Park conditions expressed by local residents. Among them, Wilhelmina
Lewis of the 112$^{th}$ Street Block Association in West Harlem spoke angrily
about the locked gates on the Morningside Drive side of the Park that
had been constructed at a cost of $20,000, which could have been spent

---

[53.] *The Morningsider*, New York, February 20,1964.

on Park rehabilitation. Several residents of the Heights suggested that ramps would improve accessibility, increasing the use of the Park and thereby its safety. There was a need to encourage a more positive attitude and less fear among those who dwelled on the Heights, and the Borough President's office was urged to contribute.

The "Picnic in the Park" succeeded in persuading the Borough President to apply his influence to get the Board of Estimate to reinstate the funds for Stage II of the restorative work on Morningside Park.[54] The Parks Department prepared a map that presented the improvements envisioned for the three stages.[55] The first stage was to begin in the summer of 1964. The Parks and Piers Committee had made specific recommendations to the Parks Department, based largely on the ideas of residents in the adjacent neighborhoods, who knew the Park and its problems intimately. Others not so knowledgeable showed a surprising insensitivity regarding Olmsted's concepts as well as the needs and desires of the surrounding neighborhoods. As a result, the greater part of the work involved the repaving of surfaces, and—horrors!—the installation of eight-foot high chain-link fencing along the "goat path" that followed the Park's upper edge and extended almost the entire length of the Park. As there was no danger of anyone stumbling off the ledge, this offensive disruption to Olmsted's open landscape design served no purpose except to create an additional physical and psychological barrier between the African-American and white communities. Members of the communities were convinced that the fences were installed to hinder access between the Heights and the Plain except at the controllable "checkpoints" at 116th and 120th Streets, where longitudinal walkways met the stairs descending into the Park. The suggested ramps from Morningside Drive were not included in the proposals. Some "restorative" changes were fortunately not carried out, for instance, moving the bear and faun monument to "a more conspicuous location in the Children's Zoo." It was not clear how removal of the only sculptural monument in the entire Park would have contributed to its improvement. The work of the sculptor Edgar Walter, one of the fountain sculptors for the great 1915

---

[54.] Ibid., March 19, 1964.
[55.] New York City Parks Department, M-L-56-113, February 27, 1964.

San Francisco world exposition, the bear and faun drinking fountain/ monument was given by Alfred Lincoln Seligman in 1914. Fortunately, it remains at the entrance to the Park from Morningside Avenue at 114th Street.

Stage III proposed further elimination of vegetation and increased the paving. It also intended the leveling of a large rock outcropping in the middle of the Park between 121st and 122nd Streets. This rock formation had been preserved in Olmsted's original design because it contained a glacial groove about a foot deep, a geological feature unique in Manhattan.

In spite of its shortcomings and crude blunders, the so-called rehabilitation did bring some improvements. The field house at the northern end was upgraded, some grassy areas were reseeded, and playgrounds were refurbished. Unfortunately, the educational program suggested by the Parks and Piers Committee was not followed up by the Parks Department.

In June 1964, the indefatigable Parks and Piers Committee, in conjunction with the Parks Department, organized a highly successful "work party and picnic" in the Park that brought together families from the surrounding neighborhoods. On an intensely hot Saturday, about seventy adults and at least one hundred children spent the morning gathering trash accumulated in the Park landscape. The collected trash, including much glass, was piled up near the entrances at Morningside Avenue where trucks from the Sanitation Department were expected to remove it. An afternoon of picnics and games followed the cleanup with hundreds of neighbors from around Morningside Park flocking to the green, bringing the "no-man's-land" splendidly alive.

Unfortunately, the piles of collected trash were never removed, apparently because the Sanitation Department would not collect refuse from the grounds of city parks, nor was the Department of Parks prepared at the time to gather up the trash. The organizers of the work party were even threatened with a summons for "unauthorized cleaning." In the following days, the large, orderly heaps of debris were blown by the wind back over the Park landscape. Though this pioneering community venture almost ended in disaster for some participants because of the summonses, happily, in succeeding years such cleanup parties became common and acceptable.

The building of the School on the Rock and the spring and summer events of 1964 described above mark a memorable turning point in community/Columbia University relations, particularly because they coincided with a rise in awareness of the African-American community and its latent power. Community bonds formed among African-American, Hispanic, and white communities of Morningside Heights and West Harlem in 1964 as they wrestled with School on the Rock and Morningside Park issues—and began, perhaps unknowingly at the time, to lay the groundwork for a united resistance to the urban manipulations of the Heights institutions that would result four years later in a "storm foretold."

# 4

## Morningsiders United!
### 1962–1965

At the time of the School on the Rock controversy, another crisis was in the making close by. The wedge-shaped site bounded by the curved tip of Morningside Drive, 121st Street, and Amsterdam Avenue, directly south of the new school, became the focus of one of the most embittered battles between an academic institution and its tenants. In November of 1962, it was announced that Columbia University's School of Pharmacy would move from its location on west 68th Street to a new building to be constructed on this uptown site. Though financially independent, the School of Pharmacy had academic ties to Columbia, comparable to those between Columbia and Barnard College and Teachers College. The reason given for the School of Pharmacy move was that it wished to enhance its reputation by establishing closer ties to the Columbia campus on Morningside Heights. To make room for this project, Pharmacy had acquired six fully occupied apartment buildings to be emptied and razed.

To counter what the residents described as a "cold war" (i.e., a "no-heat" approach) to evict them from attractive and structurally sound housing, they formed an organization called the "Morningsiders Six," named for the six threatened buildings. With the aid of several lawyers and under the tenacious leadership of Marie Runyon, a number of the tenants refused to move. Many, however, did leave, and two of the buildings were demolished. Some forty of the original residents signed a pact *in blood* that they would not leave, and they did belligerently remain in the semi-abandoned apartment houses, where maintenance was kept to a bare minimum.

Frustrated by the intransigent tenants, the School of Pharmacy gave up, and ownership was transferred to Columbia University in 1966. However, the "Pharmacy Buildings" and their grim-lipped tenants gained renown for their survival in the face of hostile landlord actions. Following their example, other tenant groups formed on Morningside Heights when threatened with eviction from their apartments in the wake of institutional real estate acquisition.

In response to the prevailing atmosphere of urban crisis and the need for community participation in planning decisions, an open meeting was held at Riverside Church in January 1964. It was attended by over 500 members of the community and, remarkably, also by a number of notable individuals who spoke at the gathering. These included Congressman William F. Ryan (D), Metropolitan Council of Housing Chair Jane Benedict, author Paul Goodman, and members of the various tenant associations. The speakers repeatedly called upon the institutions to plan together with the community for a diversified, safe, and "human" neighborhood.[56] Alarm was expressed that Morningside Heights would become, in the words of Marie Runyon, "an academic ghost town."

Congressman Ryan urged Columbia University to reveal its intentions to the city government, so that a comprehensive plan for the area could be developed with input from the local community. Ryan had held several meetings with city and university officials to discuss institutional policies toward tenants and the numerous small shop owners in his district, who were gradually being forced out of the area. (Over the years, he became convinced that no amount of persuasion would steer the institutions from their disastrous course.) Paul Goodman reproached the university for its efforts to create an ivory-tower utopia insulated from reality. He and his brother, Percival Goodman, a member of Columbia's School of Architecture faculty, had been sounding this warning for

---

[56.] *The Morningsider*, January 30, 1964.

some time—a number of years earlier, their remarks about Columbia's architectural and planning policies had been stricken from a university radio series in which they had participated.

Paul Goodman attended the meeting at Riverside Church as an associate of the University Seminar on the City, which gathered interested intellectuals from the New York area for monthly lectures and discussions. The City Seminar was one of several Columbia professional resources totally ignored by university administration decision makers.

The audience at Riverside Church included officers of Morningside Heights Inc., representatives of several institutions, and a few faculty members. They refrained from entering the debate, with the exception of Stanley Salmen, Columbia's Coordinator of University Planning. Refuting a charge made by one of the speakers, Salmen insisted that Columbia had no intention of expanding south of its 114th Street border. A shocked silence followed Salmen's words because several people present knew very well that this statement was untrue, as subsequent events would prove.

A significant outcome of this community meeting was the formation of an area-wide tenant organization, Morningsiders United for a Diversified, Integrated Community. (Figure 9 displays a flyer from about 1962 that calls for residents to join this group.) This was a step recommended at the gathering by Jane Benedict during her impassioned description of the Strycker's Bay activists in the area of Manhattan Valley south of Morningside Heights.[57] Morningsiders United soon counted a membership of over 500. Despite its constructive aims and its expressed desire to work with the institutions toward positive solutions, the institutional response was disheartening.

At the hearings held by the Cox Fact Finding Commission in the wake of the spring 1968 crisis on the Columbia campus, several Columbia officials remarked that relations with the community had been so difficult because they did not know with whom they should talk. The fact is that they had never tried to talk to anyone but local elected officials. With few exceptions, political figures serving at the behest of their

---

[57.] *Columbia Daily Spectator*, February14, 1964.

local-party clubs were at this time unresponsive to or even apprehensive of any grassroots sentiments.

Morningsiders United consisted of the non-institutionally affiliated (e.g., non-faculty or student) tenants of the buildings on the Heights, plus a few from the surrounding neighborhoods, and included African-American, Hispanic, and white members. Efforts to interest faculty families were unsuccessful, and only a few felt it appropriate to join.

Heights shop owners put up little or no resistance to the "expansion" that eliminated their premises, some of which they had occupied for over half a century. Relocating within the area was rarely convenient, and most folded their tents and disappeared. In part, this may have been because they did not reside on Morningside Heights, and hundreds of their customers vanished. In the 1950s, Amsterdam Avenue from 110th to 125th Streets, and parts of Broadway, were virtual bazaars of small, multi-ethnic shops and eateries. By 1966, these streets had turned into a Jane Jacobs nightmare, and faculty members had to hike for many blocks to satisfy even their most basic household needs.[58]

Morningsiders United asked for "full discussion with all institutions and community groups toward constructive neighborhood planning which will consider all interests, and discriminate against none." It was obvious that the concern was directed against racism. It had emerged from Columbia's veiled position into one openly discussed within the neighborhoods, particularly in West Harlem. It was obvious that Columbia's ambition was to convert Morningside Heights into an "ivory" (e.g., possibly gated white) enclave. It is astonishing that the university failed to recognize the danger of this position while the civil-rights movement was gaining strength and acceptance nationally. The university also disregarded the fact that its reputation as an intellectual center was diminishing, and students and alumni were losing faith in their alma mater.

---

[58.] Although the struggle on Morningside Heights was comparable to those Jane Jacobs was involved in when confronting Robert Moses' urban renewal projects in lower Manhattan, there was never any direct contact with her. The author was well acquainted with Jane Jacobs' publications and idealism, and, in retrospect, considers it an oversight that she was not contacted.

Along with the Morningside Renewal Council, local political leaders, and the city government, Morningsiders United were asking the institutions, in particular Columbia University, for *urban planning* and for disclosure of their future intentions. It was a request for something that, unbeknownst to the community and to a good part of the institutional "family," apparently did not exist. Strange as it may seem, Columbia University, with its outstanding School of Architecture and Planning and internationally recognized faculty in other fields, had no master plan for either its academic or physical future.

The greatly respected university Vice President Lawrence Chamberlain called attention to this situation in a speech before the Alexander Hamilton Medal dinner on November 21, 1963. The university's second-highest official courageously described the decentralized system of fundraising, decades of "drift," and absence of focus and plan. The *Columbia Daily Spectator* published Chamberlain's speech in its entirety, including his proposal that "Columbia should lead the institutions in the metropolitan area in a joint plan." This was a bold proposal, considering that the university had been unable to make a plan for itself.[59]

Instead of an urban plan, and under the key word "expansion," the university followed a policy of real estate acquisition with the only objective being the removal of undesirable tenants, a policy that was surely racist. The random and persistent purchase of properties on the Heights directed by university treasurer William Bloor's office could hardly be considered an advantageous investment approach. Once the renters had been removed, the buildings often remained empty, were razed, or were occupied by university offices—which violated New York City codes. There was no return or profit from the purchases, except for provision of randomly improvised office space. (It is interesting to note that, later, during the 1970/71 furor over the university's investment portfolio, this random real estate acquisition was never mentioned.) The lack of a true need for "expansion" was also indicated by the university's invitation to other institutions to relocate to Morningside Heights, in some cases with encouragement in the form of providing prime building

---

[59.] *Columbia Daily Spectator*, November 27, 1963, "Drift and Mastery. Chamberlain's Speech," CCC Collection, Schomburg Center, Box 8, #3.

sites or financial assistance. In addition to the Episcopal School of St. Hilde and St. Hugh and the Bank Street College of Education, those relocating during this period included the Morningside House for the Aged. When the Julliard School of Music moved to Lincoln Center, Columbia encouraged the Manhattan School of Music to take over the vacated building. In a case where Columbia might have encouraged residential use of an existing building, when St. Luke's Hospital put the old Women's Hospital on the south side of 110th Street on the market, the site was instead occupied by a Consolidated Edison power substation.

It was difficult to determine who was responsible for the reasoning behind these haphazard moves, and who might be considered "in charge" of Columbia's planning, particularly in the absence of a master plan, whose lack was disparaged not only by critics of the university. It gradually became a concern for the administration, as indicated in Vice President Chamberlain's speech. In March 1966, President Kirk appointed a committee of "administrators and deans to formulate plans for the University's expansion and to define Columbia's purpose and direction in the next decades."[60] Notably, the term used was "expansion," not plan. Jacques Barzun, Dean of the Faculties, who was not known to be a friend of the local communities, was chosen to head the group.

From November 1956 until June 1967, the position of Coordinator of University Planning was held by Stanley Salmen. He had formerly been director of the Atlantic Monthly Press and vice president of the publishing firm Little, Brown. He had no training or experience related to architecture or planning. It appears that decisions regarding the purchase of real estate were, as mentioned, actually made by the university's treasurer, William Bloor, whose actions were said often to be unknown to other members of the administration.[61] From the point of view of the investor, any sort of publicity is, of course, damaging in real estate, and in this case, Bloor's talent for acting in secrecy may have been admirable. Acquisition of property followed a predictable course. Anything that

---

60. *Columbia Daily Spectator*, March 7, 1966.

61. Faculty Civil Rights Group at Columbia University, "The Community and the Expansion of Columbia University," December 1967, CCC Collection, Schomburg Center, Box 20, #1, especially pp. 11–13.

became available was picked up, even if the site was of no foreseeable use to the university. Such an approach cannot be called reasonable urban planning, and it totally ignored the human factors in city life. The dislocation of people and the disruption of the urban fabric of an entire district was apparently condoned or even encouraged by the trustees and administration, not only of Columbia University but also of the other institutions involved in Morningside Heights Inc. If there were exceptions, they were not sufficiently vocal, or did not carry enough weight, to stem the course.

One member of Columbia's administration caught between his personal convictions and official institutional policy was Vice President Lawrence Chamberlain. Once described by a local tenant as "the only member of the Columbia administration with a heart," he did try to establish relations with community groups. In an interview reported by Michael Drosnin in the *Columbia Daily Spectator* of April 28, 1964, Chamberlain said: "I think it would be unhealthy to drive the community out. A neighborhood composed solely of the institutions and their staffs would be intolerable. Columbia has both an interest and a responsibility to maintain a large non-University population here." As Columbia's delegate to the Morningside Renewal Council, he was well aware that tension between the community and the white institutions was increasing alarmingly and was damaging not only the climate on Morningside Heights but also Columbia's reputation. His efforts toward resolving the conflict and maintaining a dialogue with tenant groups and members of the West Harlem community were admirable. However, they were not backed by university policy and thus were unproductive; eventually, he capitulated, and left Columbia in the summer of 1967, a deeply disillusioned man.

Before his departure, however, he achieved a remarkable feat by inviting Martin Luther King Jr. for an official dinner at the Faculty Club on Morningside Drive and 119th Street. Only a few members of the faculty were invited to meet King and hear his talk, including the author and her husband George Collins. President Kirk did not attend. Other than the waiters and kitchen staff, King was the only African-American present, and most likely the only one who had ever entered Columbia's Faculty Club as a guest. It is not clear whether King knew about the racial tensions brewing on Morningside Heights and in the surrounding neighborhoods. (Unfortunately, the author does not recall what was discussed.)

Although the policies and actions of educational and religious institutions are generally not closely examined, they are expected to provide ethical leadership and to be ethical in their conduct. Thus, Columbia's scholastic renown shielded its expansion-without-plan purchase of properties that threatened an estimated 10,000 people with loss of their homes without any concern for where they might find other places to live. This policy was at odds with the ideals of the religious institutions on Morningside Heights, but was not vigorously questioned by the members of the Morningside Urban Renewal Council, which included the Episcopal Cathedral of St. John the Divine, Corpus Christi Roman Catholic Church, Riverside Church, Jewish Theological Seminary, and Union Theological Seminary.

The case of the "Bryn Mawr Hotel," however, brought significant reactions from the religious contingent. The building was located at the corner of Amsterdam Avenue and 121st Street, facing the School of Pharmacy site. Once a respectable apartment building, it had been allowed to deteriorate. Its owner had converted it into SROs with scores of city-code violations. Many of the tenants were welfare cases and beset by social problems of every conceivable kind. The Bryn Mawr was described, perhaps unjustly, as "a den of inequity and crime," a haven for drug addicts and prostitutes.

Early in 1964, Gena Tenney Phenix, who lived across Amsterdam Avenue from the Bryn Mawr, called a meeting to discuss the plight of residents living in this building and other similar SROs, and to determine how people of conscience could assist them. No city or neighborhood agency was doing anything to improve their lot. The meeting, held at nearby Corpus Christi Catholic Church, was attended by people connected to the religious institutions, other local organizations, and Teachers College, where Phenix's husband was on the faculty. Fear was expressed that Columbia would buy the Bryn Mawr and simply move out the tenants and their unresolved problems. A committee was set up to study the problems of SRO tenants in general, and find possible solutions.[62] The committee began working with Bertram Weinert, who had been appointed Columbia University Director of Neighborhood Services in late 1963, and with Dr. Joan H. Shapiro of the Community Psychiatric Division of St. Luke's Hospital. In the meantime, Remedco, the real estate arm of Morningside Heights Inc., whose president was university treasurer Bloor, had bought the building in July 1964.

In October 1964, Weinert presented the group organized by Phenix with a "Proposal for the Bryn Mawr" in which he called for an "innovative approach." It included four steps: 1) intervention, 2) relocation of tenants, 3) rehabilitation of the building, and 4) repopulation with former tenants. This proposal did not please Remedco or Columbia University, and the university dismissed Weinert in December 1964. According to Vice President Chamberlain, it was because "he wasn't doing his job," and "our views of the duties and responsibilities of the Office of Neighborhood Services do not coincide.[63] Weinert was replaced by Ronald Golden, who managed to keep his personal conscience from interfering with the duties he carried out under treasurer Bloor's orders.

The religious institutions had hoped to make the Bryn Mawr a model case and Weinert's feasible proposal a pilot program for other residential buildings. However, Remedco began to evict the tenants in November 1964. Speaking for Remedco, Salmen and Chamberlain stated publicly that the takeover of the Bryn Mawr was not dictated by the need for expansion but rather to eradicate a trouble spot.

The Bryn Mawr issue achieved considerable notoriety, and public pressure forced a stay in the eviction of tenants. The remaining residents of the building, aided by some members of the Phenix committee, as well as by the "Morningside Six," initiated their own rehabilitation program, which proved quite successful. Eventually, Remedco succeeded in buying off enough tenants until those who remained were too few to resist

---

[62.] Notes on this meeting taken by the author, who attended, may be found in the CCC Collection, Schomburg Center, Box 8, #2, and other notes were placed in the vertical files of the Columbia University Office of Religious Services in Earl Hall.

[63.] *Columbia Daily Spectator,* December 4, 1964.

eviction. The Bryn Mawr was razed as soon as it was vacant. Barnard College later purchased the site to construct Plimpton Hall Dormitory.

The Bryn Mawr case came to be regarded as the quintessential example of Columbia's policy regarding minorities. Although not all people displaced from Morningside Heights were African-American or Hispanic, they constituted the majority and had the greatest difficulty finding adequate housing. However, the program of tenant removal affected non-minorities as well. Bob McKay, African-American and one of those evicted from the Bryn Mawr, told the author that it was a revelation to him that white tenants were treated as badly as blacks. It was the Bryn Mawr experience and the resulting alliance with the "Morningside Six" resisters that motivated Bob McKay to become a leading activist in the grassroots opposition to Columbia's racist strategies.[64]

Once the Bryn Mawr was vacated, there were almost no African-Americans or Hispanics left living on the Heights except for those working as live-in superintendents or maintenance personnel in institutional buildings. Although this eradication policy was apparently agreed upon by the other members of Morningside Heights Inc., it was primarily connected to the name of Columbia University. In the first weeks of 1964, Columbia's "expansion" was the subject of an inquiry by the City Commission on Human Rights in response to a complaint filed by Margaret L. Cox (Democratic District Leader, 13th Assembly District West). Commission Chairman Stanley H. Lowell informed the press that the matter of Columbia's policy of real estate acquisition and how it affected the racial makeup of Morningside Heights would be investigated.[65] Months later, in December 1964, members of the Commission on Human Rights met with Vice President Chamberlain and Coordinator of University Planning Salmen. The latter afterwards chided the human rights commissioners for being poorly informed regarding Columbia's

[64] Bob McKay became a personal friend of the Collins family. He would join the family for supper, engaging their sons in lively conversation, acquainting them with his eloquent and expressive way of speaking.

[65] *The New York Times*, February 18, 1964. *Columbia Daily Spectator*, February 28, 1964.

contributions toward the well-being of the community.[66] However, the purpose of the meeting, as far as the Human Rights Commission was concerned, centered on the case of the Bryn Mawr building being emptied at that time, while the university's representatives were expecting an investigation of Columbia's policy in general. Chamberlain declared that the matter of the Bryn Mawr was not the responsibility of Columbia, but of Remedco. There were rumors that no report would be forthcoming and that the Commission was cowed by Columbia's prestige. Then, about ten months after the investigation began, Commission Chairman Lowell released a letter addressed to Chamberlain, making the contents of the letter public before the recipient had a chance to appraise its impact.[67]

Based on the Commission's ten-month investigation, the letter was sharply critical of Columbia's urban policies and contained several recommendations for improving them. There was some speculation that this letter, although highly critical, provided Columbia a chance to change its ways before the final report was completed, possibly even preventing its publication. "It's the policy of the Commission," Lowell declared, "that if things can be worked out, a public judgment is not always necessary."[68] The steps recommended to Columbia University by the Commission, according to *The New York Times* of January 4, 1965, were: "Seize the initiative in developing social rehabilitation programs and encourage government and private agencies to support these programs. Provide substitute housing for persons evicted from dwellings needed by the University to expand its teaching facilities. End its 'policy of near-total reliance upon tenant removal as a solution to social problems' in the University's Morningside Heights area. Seek to maintain the multi-racial character of the area." The letter also commented favorably on the effort at rehabilitation of the tenants of the Bryn Mawr Hotel, an action Remedco had already cut off.

About a month later, Lowell wrote to the *Columbia Daily Spectator*, commenting on an editorial that had appeared in this student daily. The

---

[66]. *Columbia Daily Spectator*, December 18, 1964.

[67]. *The New York Times*, January 4,1965. *Columbia Daily Spectator*, January 5,1965.

[68]. *Columbia Daily Spectator*, January 5,1965.

letter, dated February 10, 1965, and published on February 17, concludes: "You should know that the Commission is acting with respect to the charges of discrimination brought against Columbia University as it does in every housing complaint situation. If by conciliation and discussion the matter can be resolved, we do not make a judgment on 'discrimination.' It is for this reason that we have no present plans to release our report." Perhaps the Commission hoped that the unpublished report could be used as leverage to compel Columbia to change, or at least modify, its policies. On January 16, 1967(!), a brief notice in the *Columbia Daily Spectator* suggested that the report was being updated and would be released after all; it has, however, never appeared.

It may have been as a result of the inquiry or perhaps even as part of an agreement with the City Human Rights Commission that the rehabilitation of the Bryn Mawr tenants was allowed to proceed for a while, and some efforts were made to relocate the remaining residents. However, these were small concessions within the total picture. Acquisition of properties and the removal of tenants even seemed to accelerate, and relations between Columbia University and the neighborhood steadily worsened.

In January 1965, University Chaplain John M. Krumm called a meeting of local ministers and clergy to discuss Columbia's neighborhood policies, particularly with regard to the Bryn Mawr and the firing of Bertram Weinert, a case with which Krumm had been particularly involved. Krumm had been criticized by Columbia's administration for letting neighborhood groups meet in Earl Hall, where the campus religious offices were located.[69] It also did not sit well with the administration, headquartered in Low Library, that the religious staff in Earl Hall had circulated a statement to university faculty in May 1964 urging each individual to speak out on civil rights issues, and to pressure the United States Senate to pass the Civil Rights Bill.

In spite of the somewhat strained relations between Low Library and Earl Hall, Chaplain Krumm was able to arrange a May 1965 luncheon meeting of the clergy of Morningside Heights with Vice

---

[69.] Telephone interview with the author, February 10, 1971.

President Chamberlain "to discuss Columbia's relationships to her neighborhood."[70] An impressive group of twenty clergymen accepted the invitation. Krumm phrased the main topics to be discussed with Chamberlain in the form of questions: "If there has to be an extension of the University on the Heights, how can we prevent an institutional ghetto? Are real allowances for other groups made in University planning? What plans are there?" [71] Chamberlain replied that the university wanted a balanced community, but that anticipation of a thirty to fifty percent expansion of the student body over the next fifteen years would entail physical expansion as well. (This plan was not actually implemented.) He emphasized that Columbia did not want to become a "commuter college" and that no buildings "across the river" were being considered. High-rise buildings might be possible, and if zoning laws changed, these could be of mixed usage.[72] Krumm later expressed the opinion that Chamberlain was under considerable restraint during the discussion, and seemed to be vague and evasive in order to comply with the administration's official policy. Although Krumm insisted that his decision to leave Columbia University was not directly related to frustrated efforts to improve town and gown relations, he did leave Earl Hall at the end of 1965 to become the Rector of the Church of the Ascension at Fifth Avenue and 10th Street in Manhattan. (He later became bishop of the Diocese of Southern Ohio.)

Another departure from Columbia in 1965 was that of Department of Psychology faculty member William McGill—who would return in 1970 to become President of the University. He was asked in a 1970 interview if university-community relations had influenced his leaving for a position in California. McGill replied: "My main discontent was with the Psychology Department, but I'd seen a number of things at Columbia in the last several years that had disturbed me. Columbia's expansion program into the community around it didn't seem to be handled very well. There was a hostility springing up between the

---

[70.] Letter from Dr. John M. Krumm inviting clergy to attend the luncheon on March 24, 1965, Earl Hall files.

[71.] Minutes of the meeting held March 24, 1965, by the religious staff of Earl Hall and the Morningside Heights clergy, Earl Hall files.

[72.] Ibid.

community and Columbia that I thought the University was handling very badly. . . . Columbia's troubles with the community around it have gone far beyond anything I expected at the time and, of course, there's very little that I can add except that I knew that was coming."[73] Indeed, Columbia/community relations had reached a point of no return in the spring of 1965, in the wake of the Board of Estimate hearing that resulted in approval of the revised Morningside General Renewal Plan. As McGill indicated, persons affiliated with the University were beginning to take note of the situation, as were elected political figures.

The *Columbia Daily Spectator* of March 15, 1965, reported, "in a tense meeting that lasted more than ten [10] hours, Congressman William F. Ryan (Dem. 20 C. D.) led the combined political-tenant opposition to the plan against an institutional defense headed by Maurice T. Moore, Chairman of Columbia University's Board of Trustees, and Jacques Barzun, Provost and Dean of Faculties." Manhattan Borough President Constance Baker Motley, a graduate of Columbia Law School and a former state senator, sharply attacked the removal of black and Puerto Rican tenants from Morningside Heights for the purpose of institutional expansion. Applauded by a large audience of people from the community, she demanded that "the expanding institutions must maintain the present residential character of the neighborhood."[74] This same Morningside Heights neighborhood was described by Dean Barzun as unsafe, beset by vice and crime, "uninviting, abnormal, sinister, dangerous," in which students and professors were subjected to an environment that required the perpetual qui vive of a paratrooper in enemy country." Barzun spoke not only as a high-ranking academic administrator but also as one of Columbia's top intellectuals and the "humanist" among scholars. In front of Mayor Wagner, the Borough President, members of the Board of Estimate, and an audience that included many political leaders as well as local residents, he described the ideal academic village that the university was hoping the urban renewal would create: Columbia would welcome into its neighborhood, he said, "the steady and peaceable people of every kind, ethnic

---

[73.] *Columbia Owl*, November 12, 1970.

[74.] *Columbia Daily Spectator*, March 15, 1965.

group, occupation or income group," but not "the transient, foot-loose or unhappy people."[75]

Dean Barzun's remarks received considerable publicity and criticism in the press. Shortly afterward, he was confronted in his office by a group of community residents. "No one, especially an educated man like you, has the right to talk about people the way you did. You insulted me," he was told by William Stanley, a graying African-American building superintendent from West Harlem. Margaret McNeil commented that, as the author of *Race: A Study in Superstition* (1937), he should know better. Barzun apologized for his poor choice of words.[76] However, statements made in public are not easily mitigated by an apology. The public view of the university's intellectual and human values, long mistrusted, suffered further damage.

Final approval of the revised General Neighborhood Renewal Plan followed the public hearing by about a month. (In Figure 10, the large dark rectangle at lower center of a 1964/65 Morningside Heights map marks the existing Columbia University campus at the time. Other shaded areas illustrate Columbia's "Early Acquisitions Proposals" dated 1968, including expansion south of the campus. Not shown are additional proposed acquisitions that reached east into West Harlem.) Section 3 of an April 22, 1965, Board of Estimate Resolution imposed a moratorium on future expansion, stating "that there be no expansion of Columbia University or any other existing institutions on Morningside Heights within the next ten (10) years other than the proposed expansion plans shown on Map entitled, 'Morningside GNRP Tentative Institutional Projects,' made by Morningside Heights, Inc., dated April 1, 1965, and marked Exhibit 'H'." According to Columbia University, the inclusion of Section 3 was based on a misunderstanding, and an agreement with the city regarding this map was emphatically denied. A letter from the trustees of Columbia University and President Grayson Kirk to the

---

[75.] Faculty Civil Rights Group at Columbia University, "The Community and the Expansion of Columbia University," quoting a May 1965 issue of *The Amsterdam News*, and *The New York World Telegram and Sun*, March, 17, 1965. Frances Bromley, "Columbia University vs. the People," *Rights and Review*, Winter 1965, vol. 2, no.1.

[76.] *The New York Times*, May 4, 1965.

Board of Estimate, dated December 13, 1965, reads: "It has . . . become necessary for us to make Columbia University's position unequivocally clear with respect to Section 3 of your Resolution. Columbia University has not consented and does not consent and will not consent to Section 3 of your Resolution, either as a condition of your further support of the Morningside Neighborhood Renewal Plan, or otherwise . . . . [We] regard the continual growth of Columbia University as vitally important to our Nation, State and City and regard it as [our] duty to continue our development program subject only to validly applicable laws." They also invoke Section 112 of the Housing Act of 1949, as amended in 1959 (42 U.S.C.A., Sec. 1466), which recognizes the special status of universities in urban renewal projects and seeks to provide, among other things, "a cohesive neighborhood environment compatible with the functions and needs of such educational institution[s]."

While Columbia was protesting its "gentleman's agreement" on the moratorium as invalid, community groups regarded the inclusion of the Project Map in the GNRP as a conspiracy against them by the city and the institutions. In an article entitled "Heights Sellout," community activist George Weiser called it a "hoax."[77]

In the spring of 1965, the last shreds of trust and goodwill harbored by the non-institutional residents on the Heights toward the academic establishment were crushed. There was also growing resentment against a city administration that did not seem to protect the rights of citizens. Despite the so-called moratorium, not considered legally binding by Columbia, Morningside Heights Inc., or Remedco, or other member institutions continued to buy up properties and empty them of tenants in the name of "expansion." Anger and fear helped to unify the hetero-geneous neighborhoods. As former Bryn Mawr resident Bob McKay commented to the author: "I thought only poor blacks were being evicted, but here all these white people were just as powerless."

Surprisingly, perhaps due to an oversight, the gymnasium in Morningside Park did not figure in the Project Map. Although it had not received much attention in the neighborhoods when it was first

---

[77.] *The West Side News* and *The Morningsider,* May 1965.

announced in January 1960, the gymnasium was now beginning to relate in people's minds to the general pattern developing on the Heights, extending the University's jurisdiction even into Morningside Park and beyond into West Harlem. The projected gymnasium assumed the character of a bastion fortifying academia against the "undesirable" neighborhood below, with the entrance to the community portion of the building located on Morningside Avenue—facing away from the community it was meant to serve. See Figure 11, the site plan for Columbia's gymnasium adjacent to the existing athletic field.

Under the agreement with the city, the university was to begin construction of the gymnasium by August 1967. However, two years before this deadline, the fund drive had not proceeded as well as hoped. In the fall of 1965, the *Columbia Daily Spectator* published a "Special 1965 Gymnasium Supplement" containing an "honor role of contributors to the gym fund" and the news that a total of $5,000,000 of the $9,000,000 goal had been received in gifts and pledges.[78] It is not clear whether the site selection or the architectural design of the building was questioned by prospective donors and influenced the paucity of gifts. The *Spectator* supplement contained pictures of the building model (on public display in Low Library) and drawings of the interior. Although preliminary plans for the gymnasium had been provided by the architectural firm of Eggers & Higgins in 1961, to be "locked into the lease," it was only now that they could be appraised by the general public. What the people saw, they did not like, and it was obvious that the fortresslike structure did not belong in Morningside Park. In a column entitled "How not to build a symbol," *New York Times* architectural critic Ada Louise Huxtable, would later write:

---

78. *Columbia Daily Spectator*, October 14, 1965. The campaign among alumni had been launched by the generous gift of $1,000,000 from Francis S. Levien, a graduate of Columbia College (1926) and of Columbia Law School (1928). *Columbia Chronicle*, published on behalf of the university's $200 million campaign, vol. 2, no.1, January-February 1968, lists other large donors to the gymnasium fund, including trustees under the Will of Morton H. Meinhard and the Henry Meinhard Memorial $1,000,000, Brookdate Foundation $1,000,000, Hayden Foundation $2,000,000, Benjamin Buttenwieser $50,000, and the Jacob R. Schiff Fund $250,000 for the University's community athletic program.

> It is certainly not going to be a particularly sensitive
> building. . . . the huge masonry bulk will never blend
> with its rustic setting. It is in conflict just by being
> there. . . . Attempts have been made to minimize
> mass. . . . But you can't disguise an elephant or a
> building in a park. While thought and care have
> gone into the architectural treatment, the result
> cannot be characterized either as inspired or sym-
> pathetic to the site.[79]

Columbia University spokesmen assured the public that "the building will be constructed on a steep, unused rocky hillside at the southern end of Morningside Park."[80] The site selected was variously described as "the rock ledge," "a rocky escarpment neither used nor usable for ordinary park purposes," "a huge rock outcropping where almost no trees or grass will be disturbed," "the useless rock escarpment," and "an otherwise completely wasted cliff."[81] These statements suggest that those responsible for them had never made a firsthand inspection of the Park, or that there was a deliberate attempt to mislead the public about the topography and nature of the site to be preempted.

In reality, the gymnasium was projected to occupy 2.1 acres of the most scenic as well as the most "useful" area of Morningside Park. It extended from Morningside Drive to Morningside Avenue in an irregular shape about the width of two city blocks between 112th and 114th Streets. While the Columbia Athletic Field, as it was called, surrounded by high fencing, had separated the Hispanic community in Manhattan Valley to the south of the Park, the gymnasium site would bisect the open parkland in a manner that cut off West Harlem from the Park and the neighborhood on the Heights. The gymnasium was to be placed on

---

[79] Ada Louise Huxtable, "How Not to Build a Symbol," *New York Times*, March 20, 1968.

[80] Columbia University news release, May 17, 1962.

[81] *Columbia College Today,* Fall 1963. Columbia University news release, May 24, 1962. *Columbia College Today,* Fall 1966. Columbia University, Office of University Relations, official release to the university community by Wesley First, Director, February 9, 1966, CCC Collection, Schomburg Center, Box 8, #3.

the only area in Morningside Park south of the "School on the Rock" that was accessible on a level, without stairs, from Morningside Drive.

The gymnasium site, directly opposite St. Luke's Hospital, was the place where the historic Bloomingdale Road had turned down the hill, and where the wooden blockhouse had been located. A moderate incline formed a meadow with large trees and shrubs, and an esplanade with benches gave it the aspect of a gentile English park. Patients in the private wing of the hospital enjoyed peaceful views of the trees and eastward over the rooftops of Harlem. The "upper meadow," as it was called by those who frequented it, provided a natural play area for children from the neighborhoods that converged at the southern tip of Morningside Park. Rope swings hung from the trees, and there were tree houses among the branches. The mound where the blockhouse had stood invited exploration, and the roots exposed by erosion provided holds for climbing the steeper parts of the embankment. It was an area "used" by adults and children from the adjacent areas for informal recreation and enjoyment. Early in the morning, dog walkers chatted while their dogs raced about. A conservatively dressed Oriental gentleman regularly faced the rising sun to practice *tai chi chuan,* an ancient Chinese form of moving meditation, while others improved their karate skills. A small vegetable garden carefully tended by an elderly woman survived for two seasons. Guitar players and actors often performed under the trees.

To the north, the meadow opened onto the Park's 116th Street path and its flow of pedestrian traffic. To the southeast, the meadow ended in a dramatic escarpment descending about 100 feet to a level area below. Youngsters exploring the crevices had worn a lacework of passages between the rocks. Bob McKay, one of the leading figures in the growing opposition to the gymnasium, remembered how, as a kid, he used to crawl into the caves in the rock formations to cool off on summer days and watch the traffic on the streets below in West Harlem. Adjacent to the Columbia Athletic Field in the lower level of the Park, the bear and faun fountain guarded the entrance to a young children's playground, where unimaginative play equipment presented a sharp contrast to the natural environment on the upper meadow.

Even a cursory overview of the topography of Morningside Park and its relationship to the surrounding communities demonstrates that the gymnasium site had been selected for its convenient access to the Heights and its proximity to the athletic field. The urban layout and social fabric of the area had not been considered, but rather was either ignored or intentionally disregarded. It was suggested that the gymnasium site be shifted north to a location between 116th and 118th Streets, where the structure could be built into the cliff and supporting wall. Thus, the building would sit well above the Park without destroying it, and might even expand it with a landscaped roof terrace. According to Columbia, this proposal was not taken into consideration because too much money had already been invested in the existing plans.

Granted that an athletic facility of the size required by Columbia College could not easily be accommodated by anything but a large structure, an imaginatively designed, community-sensitive building could conceivably have been adapted to a park site and might have received wider acceptance. Or Columbia could have responded to criticism voiced by those viewing the model displayed in Low Library. A major objection was the comparative space allotment to non-affiliates vs. university use, relating not only to size but also to its situation within the building. The community section was located at the bottom of the building, in the basement, so to speak, and hermetically sealed off from the upper area. At a public hearing in 1968, John Wheeler, legal counsel for Columbia University, made the dramatic (if late) revelation that the prime reason for this ironclad separation was the location of facilities for the NROTC program in the floors above. Because weapons and training manuals for their use were to be stored in the offices and classrooms, these were not supposed to be accessible to "outsiders." Records did show that a Columbia news release of May 24, 1962, mentioned the inclusion of a NROTC Armory for a unit of 250 to 300 men, including a Combat Information Center, sonar equipment, classrooms, offices, a library, and storage facilities. It is surprising that even then, prior to the outcry against campus NROTC training, the Parks Department did not question the legitimacy and recreational value of placing an armory on public parkland. The NROTC space was located on the southern end of the third floor, overlooking West Harlem and the Columbia Athletic Field, and adjacent to the upper portion of the community gymnasium.

The entrance to the community section of the building was on the ground level facing east, establishing it as a West Harlem facility, segregated not only from the university's portion of the gymnasium, but also from the western, mostly white, neighborhood, as well as from Hispanic Manhattan Valley to the south, for whom the entrance was virtually inaccessible because of the need to circumnavigate the athletic field. The placement of this entrance was vigorously protested by the surrounding communities, who demanded entrance from three sides, and access to and through the university portion of the building. There was never any reaction or effort by the architects or the patrons of the building to accommodate the design to the needs of the local groups. Neither the architects nor the university administration acknowledged a fact included in any first-year architecture curriculum: the entrance to a building is not only a functional element but also carries a symbolic meaning. Reactions to placement of the community gymnasium entry were bitter, despite Columbia's assurances that it was located at the bottom of the hill for the convenience of Harlem residents. Its placement contributed significantly to the impression that the layout of the community gymnasium exemplified institutional racism. While the project was acquiring ominous racial overtones, those backing it were confident that Harlem would "learn" over time to appreciate what was being offered, and that once the building was completed, opposition would subside. Columbia's understanding of the racist implications appeared to be limited to the belief that athletics was an appropriate way for African-American males to "make it" into the white establishment.

As anti-Columbia sentiment intensified throughout the area, the gymnasium in Morningside Park evolved as an icon of institutional racism, and the hub of the opposition gravitated to West Harlem, with activists from the Heights and the other neighborhoods forming part of what became "The West Harlem Coalition for Morningside Park." This informal grassroots group met at the headquarters of the West Harlem Community Organization on 116th Street. The voices of those at the core of the group—particularly Bob McKay, Joe Monroe, Margaret

McNeill, and, among others from Morningside Heights, Suki Ports and Marie Runyon—will be heard further on in this narrative. The author was imbedded in this loosely formed group and was its trusted record keeper, collecting documentation and ephemera pertaining to a unique grassroots movement opposing the urban manifestation of racism.

Remarkably, Columbia University remained oblivious to the alarming and bitter racial overtones attached to the gymnasium in Morningside Park. The university administration concentrated loudly only on the carefully constructed legality of leasing public land for the site, brushing aside the opposition's argument that citizens had innate rights to public land and to determining its use. The university's contention that the choice of the site avoided the relocation of residents did not hold much water in the face of the continuously rising number of tenant evictions on Morningside Heights.

It was against this background that Parks Commissioner Thomas P.F. Hoving entered the drama.

# 5

## A FUNERAL UNDER THE TREES
## AND OTHER FOREBODING EVENTS

### 1965–1967

After his election in November 1965, Mayor John V. Lindsay appointed Thomas P.F. Hoving to succeed Newbold Morris as Parks Commissioner. Though Hoving is best known as the long-time director of the Metropolitan Museum of Art, a position that he would assume in March 1967, during art history studies at Princeton University, he developed a particular interest in parks designed by Frederick Law Olmsted. He wrote his senior thesis on Olmsted, and considered Olmsted's parks to be landmarks that should be preserved and in the public domain.

During Lindsay's mayoral campaign, Hoving headed a task force that prepared a white paper on the city's parks. This paper was critical of the projected Columbia gymnasium in Morningside Park on the basis of three general principles of park policy:

1. The immediate neighborhood should largely determine for itself how best to use its parklands.
2. Open areas, being few and precious, should not be built upon.
3. Park property should not be allowed to go to private use.[82]

---

[82.] "White Paper on New York City Parks," cited in *Crisis at Columbia*, 78–79, CCC Collection, Schomburg Center, Box 8, #3. Ironically, The Metropolitan

These principles reflected ideas about community advocacy and participatory planning that were attracting increasing attention in urban planning circles. In the 1960s, the environmental or "green" movement in the planning community tracked the concerns of advocacy groups like the Sierra Club and the Audubon Society, among others.

In the white paper, Hoving called attention to Olmsted, reflecting an incipient, but rising, interest in his role in the American park movement, parkways, and their relation to urban development. The debate regarding Morningside Park, Columbia's athletic field, the gymnasium, and other encroachments had hardly mentioned Olmsted and his principles. This was true even of the School of Architecture and the Department of Art History at Columbia University; it was rather comical that it took a graduate of Princeton University to alert Columbia's constituency that Olmsted landmarks surrounded Morningside Heights on three sides.

Hoving's brief tenure as Parks Commissioner coincided with a critical phase of the opposition to the gymnasium. He voiced publicly the political and social aspects of park conservation, and gave them official sanction by virtue of his position and personal presence. He was erroneously accused of inciting the neighborhoods to oppose the gymnasium—although Robert Moses remarks in his memoirs that Hoving "roused the Negro neighborhood against an alleged 'give-away',"[83] this frequently cited interpretation ascribed inordinate influence to a white art historian upon a diverse grassroots movement. This opinion, founded on the belief that local residents, particularly those living in West Harlem, were incapable of taking a stand on their own without the guidance of political and civic leaders, was also expressed by Trustee Harold McGuire in his comments to the Cox Fact Finding Commission in June 1968.[84]

Shortly after taking office, Hoving told the *Columbia Daily Spectator* that had he been in office at the time, he would not have approved the lease of public parkland to a private institution, and that looking into the matter of the Columbia gymnasium was one of his "highest

---

Museum of Art in later years encroached upon Central Park.

[83] Moses, *Public Works*, 37.

[84] Cox Fact-Finding Commission Transcript, 451–452.

priorities."[85] Disturbed by the public position taken by the new Parks Commissioner with impressive academic credentials, university officials arranged to meet with Hoving at his headquarters in the Arsenal building in Central Park. Those attending were President Kirk, Trustee McGuire, and the architect Jackson Smith of Eggers & Higgins. On January 25, 1966, *The New York Times* reported on the meeting, citing a university spokesman saying that there had been "no particular outcome." During his appearance before the Cox Fact Finding Commission, Hoving related that it was at this meeting that those present calculated the percentage division of space in the projected building—apparently for the first time.[86] Based on architectural drawings brought along by the visitors, it was calculated that the community share of the gymnasium would be 12.5% and that for the college students 87.5%. The *Times* cited Hoving as saying that President Kirk's explanation of Columbia's position "convinced me in the opposite direction. . . . I told him the university was getting an extraordinary deal. . . . The more I saw the community's slice of this particular pie, the more disturbed I was at the thinness of the slice. . . . It is absolutely ridiculous! To palm this off as a significant contribution to community needs is—I just can't believe it."[87]

Hoving's opinions regarding the Columbia gymnasium received considerable publicity. A number of citizens and civic groups from the immediate environs of Morningside Park got in touch with him. He was applauded for using his official position to bring about a reevaluation of the project and for his support of orderly community protests.[88] His thoughts about participatory planning were echoed among urbanists in the 1960s and were particularly welcome in West Harlem.

The University's immediate response to the charges made by the Parks Commissioner was a news conference in February given by President Kirk and his top administrative aides and advisors: Dean David Truman of Columbia College, Trustee Harold McGuire, and Capt. Harold N. Poulson, commanding officer of the University's Naval Reserve Officers

[85]. *Columbia Daily Spectator*, January 4, 1966.
[86]. Cox Fact-Finding Commission Transcript, 3,569.
[87]. *The New York Times*, January 25, 1966.
[88]. Cox Fact-Finding Commission Transcript, 3,569.

Training Corps. Without direct mention of Hoving's criticism, Kirk tried to clarify the university's position, particularly regarding the 12.5% community portion of the building. Previous Parks Commissioners Moses and Morris then released letters supporting the lease of public parkland to a private institution. In addition, a lengthy memorandum was sent to all connected with the university, and an abbreviated version was published in the *West Side News*. The memo outlined the shortcomings of the athletic facilities available to Columbia students and described the history and success of the athletic field in Morningside Park as the basis for the agreement with the city for constructing a gymnasium at an adjacent site. The projected gymnasium's facilities were also described, concluding: "Nothing has been hidden . . . it was entered into in good faith by all concerned."[89] See Figure 12 for the first and second floor plans of the projected gymnasium that show the community section, including the community swimming pool added in 1967.

According to West Harlem Community Organization spokesman Bob McKay, it was the tone of this university memorandum, containing phrases like "the useless rock escarpment," "the otherwise completely wasted cliff," "the upper floors—naturally the main part of the building—are for Columbia programs," that, as McKay expressed it, "put West Harlem into battle position."

A group of advocate architects had responded to the threats posed by urban renewal on Morningside Heights and in the surrounding neighborhoods by forming the Architects' Renewal Committee in Harlem (ARCH) in October 1964, under the leadership of C. Richard Hatch, a white architect active in civil rights causes. The group's aim was to improve the environment through self-help community actions. ARCH grew by acquiring foundation support, a staff of three, and volunteers who were primarily interested university students and teenagers from HARYOU (Harlem Youth Opportunities Unlimited), financed by federal anti-poverty funds.[90]

---

[89]. Release from Wesley First, February 9, 1966.

[90]. Andrea Lopen, "Harlem's Streetcorner Architects," *Architectural Forum,* vol. 126, December 1965.

Under Hatch's direction, ARCH investigated the area's urban problems and studied and critiqued the effects of Columbia's policies. Local misgivings about the group's white-architect composition were eventually overcome, particularly when ARCH was joined by J. Max Bond Jr., the first African American to receive architecture degrees from Harvard (BA, 1955; MA, 1958) and other blacks, some of whom were not trained in architecture or planning. ARCH empowered the people of West Harlem by helping them to formulate their voice in the planning process. Bob McKay of the West Harlem Morningside Park Coalition explained the resulting approach this way: "We don't need well-meaning do-gooders to ask us questions. We need qualified technicians and professionals who know more than we do, whom WE will ask questions."

From its beginning, ARCH had opposed the gymnasium in Morningside Park, and the group welcomed Hoving's stand in a letter to *The New York Times* signed by Hatch as Executive Director of ARCH.[91] "As officialdom laments the scarcity of park land in Harlem," he wrote, "Columbia persists in its policy of expansion by encroachment. We hope that Mr. Hoving will be . . . tough."

Hoving's opposition to the gymnasium in the Park put pressure on the university to schedule ground breaking by August 1, 1967, as specified in the lease, rather than trying to negotiate an extension with a Parks Commissioner hostile to the project. Yet, the fund drive was lagging, and by February 1966 only $5.3 million of the $9 million goal had been raised. At the trustees' meeting on February 7, 1966, members decided to proceed with ground breaking as soon as possible, perhaps as early as October of that year, by means of a loan from the university's general endowment fund.[92] (In the end, Columbia did have to ask for two extensions of the deadline, so that ground breaking did not take place until February 19, 1968. As Hoving was appointed director of the Metropolitan Museum of Art on December 20, 1966, he was no longer Parks Commissioner when the extension requests were officially presented, having been succeeded by August Heckscher.)

---

[91.] *The New York Times*, February 24, 1966.
[92.] *Columbia Daily Spectator*, February 24, 1966.

The year 1966 had opened auspiciously for those opposing the gymnasium in Morningside Park, which was "basking in the renaissance of civic attention," as the *Morningside Citizen* put it.[93] The press was eager to report on the controversy that pitted a charismatic public official with intellectual credentials against one of the city's leading academic institutions, giving the dispute the spin of a personal conflict.

Although the *Columbia Spectator* remained neutral regarding the gymnasium until April 1968, a series of articles written by reporter Leigh Dolin and published in February 1966 commented perceptively on neighborhood sentiment about Columbia, directing students' attention to community matters that included the gymnasium.

In January 1966, the Parks and Playgrounds Committee of the Morningside Urban Renewal Council arranged for a special meeting of the member organizations opposing the gymnasium in Morningside Park. In response to this initial attempt to organize community opposition, twenty-seven of thirty member organizations, including seven of the nine from Harlem, sent representatives. This first meeting was chaired by Walter South, a sociologist by profession, here representing a neighborhood tenant organization. A second gathering was chaired by local Democratic district leader Amalia Betanzos, who became the first chair of the Ad Hoc Committee on Morningside Park that resulted from these meetings. Patrick Crossman, local Republican district leader and a member of the steering committee of the Morningside Renewal Council, was chosen as vice chair.[94] Encouraged by the Parks Commissioner's interest in the gymnasium, the Ad Hoc Committee invited Hoving to its first protest demonstration, which was planned to take place on the site of the projected building in Morningside Park on April 24, 1966. It was this event that Trustee McGuire charged Hoving with having organized in his testimony to the Cox Fact Finding Commission two years later.[95] However, fliers announcing the rally as well as subsequent news reports provide conclusive evidence that it was a grassroots endeavor sponsored

---

[93]. *The Morningside Citizen*, February 7, 1966.

[94]. Patrick Crossman is erroneously referred to as Patrick Cronan in *Crisis at Columbia*, 79, 202.

[95]. This information was then also reported in *The New York Times*, May 21 and June 2, 1968.

by the members of the Ad Hoc Committee on Morningside Park.[96]

On a drizzly Sunday, more than a hundred people, mostly from the adjacent neighborhoods, gathered on the upper meadow in Morningside Park. The area leased by Columbia University had been marked off with white crepe paper, as was the actual footprint of the projected gymnasium building, so that it resembled the marking of a burial plot according to the custom in some rural regions. In addition, an impressive cardboard tombstone leaned against a tree, displaying the inscription: "Requiescat in Gymnasium. Morningside Park 1870–1966. Erected in Loving Memory —G. Kirk."

The Parks Commissioner interested in the preservation of parks for people had sent flowers to the "funeral in Morningside Park"—a large arrangement of gladioli that was placed next to the tombstone. Several of the organizers wore black armbands, yet the mood on the meadow was animated and festive. It was really beyond the belief of those gathered that this large and scenic area was doomed to destruction. While children climbed on the rocks and played hide-and-seek in the bushes, speakers, frequently interrupted by barking dogs, expressed a variety of reasons for opposing the gymnasium.

Standing with Amalia Betanzos next to the tombstone and the gladioli, Commissioner Hoving promised to do "all in my power to prevent construction of the gymnasium." If the contract for the lease could not be repealed, he advised the community to push for a larger share of the facility.[97] State Senator Basil Paterson reminisced about playing in the Park as a child. Pointing out that he was speaking also as a representative of the NAACP, he compared the recreational needs of 25,000 Columbia students with those of 80,000 residents in Harlem. This was actually

---

[96.] At that time, this loose coalition included the following member organizations: ARCH, Ascension Church, Bank Street Tenants Association, Club de Madres, Columbia University CORE, Manhattanville-Morningside Neighborhood Council, Morningsiders Republican Club, Morningsiders United, NAACP, Pleasant Homes Inc., Puerto Rican Committee on Housing, Riverside Democrats, Riverside Park and Playgrounds Committee, West Harlem Community Organization, West Side Block Association, and 116th Street Block Association West Harlem.

[97.] *The New York Times*, April 25, 1966. *The Morningside Citizen*, May 6,1966. *The Westside News*, April 28, 1966.

a misconception frequently made by both sides of the controversy. In reality, the gymnasium was planned for the use of only the approximately 2,780 undergraduate students of Columbia College plus 630 in the School of Engineering—3,410 in all—to the exclusion of students from other divisions of the university, faculty, and staff. Paterson ended his address on a prophetic note: "Columbia shall not build a gym in this Park. Let the first bulldozers come here and you'll know what I mean."[98]

A plea to the Parks Commissioner to take steps to correct the neglected character of Morningside Park that made it vulnerable to encroachment was made by Rev. William Robinson of the West Harlem Mission on Manhattan Avenue. Significantly, two among the seven speakers were associated with Columbia University. One was a member of the religious staff, Rev. Henry A. Malcolm, Protestant student counselor, who repeated Earl Hall's often expressed concern over deteriorating town-and-gown relations in the Morningside Heights area. The other was the president of the Columbia University Student Council (CUSC), David Ment. The Council consisted at that time of delegates from seventeen schools within the university and represented a total of 25,000 students. It was primarily through concern about Columbia-community relations within the framework of Morningside Urban Renewal that CUSC became interested in the gymnasium controversy. In April 1965, CUSC had completed an evaluation of the Morningside General Neighborhood Renewal Plan and requested acceptance as a member of the Renewal Council, a request that was initially refused because it was thought that the student organization would further "institutionalize" the council. (CUSC was later accepted as a member, in the fall of 1966.)

The Morningside Renewal Council passed a resolution opposing the gymnasium on March 7, 1966, "because it involved the use of parkland for a non-public purpose."[99] Two days later, CUSC voted 14 to 11 to request that the University "suspend all efforts to construct a gymnasium in Morningside Park, and that discussions with community

---

[98]. *Columbia Daily Spectator*, April 25, 1966. *The Westside News*, April 28, 1966. *The Morningsider*, April 28, 1966.

[99]. Cox Fact-Finding Commission Transcript, testimony by Rev. Dwight Smith, Chairman of the Morningside Urban Renewal Council (elected 1965), 2,547.

groups be instituted immediately, in order that any decision on the site and functions of the gymnasium be the joint agreement of institution and community groups." CUSC President Ment told the *Columbia Daily Spectator*, "We are neither opposed nor in favor of the gym. We simply want open discussion and compromise."[100] A small notice about the CUSC resolution appeared in *The New York Times*[101] Immediate reaction by University officials was to declare the CUSC resolution of no consequence. Stanley Salmen asserted that the students' move would "make little practical difference," and no discussions with community leaders were planned because "there is nothing more to say."[102]

Daniel Pellegrom, who succeeded David Ment as CUSC President in 1967, told the Cox Fact Finding Commission that the response by the university administration was "disheartening." As Columbia felt no responsibility to "open consideration" of the project for which all legal steps had been cleared, and as its recommendation had been "flatly turned down," CUSC consequently decided to participate in the "Funeral in Morningside Park" community protest on April 28, 1966.[103]

Notably, it was a member of the Columbia chapter of the Congress of Racial Equality (CORE) who introduced the March CUSC resolution. CORE had made contact with ARCH during efforts to organize a community action committee in the fall of 1965 to oppose the urban renewal encroachment in West Harlem. The Columbia chapter of CORE was represented on the Morningside Renewal Council and had also become a member of the Ad Hoc Committee on Morningside Park. CORE took a more active position against the gymnasium than CUSC, including picketing a gymnasium fund benefit staged by members of the Columbia College faculty and distributing fliers on campus asking, "Must the natural beauty of Morningside Park be destroyed so Columbia jocks have a bigger playpen?"[104] It was the beginning of greater visibility for African-American students on campus and their emergence as a voice

---

[100] Ibid., transcript of testimony by David Ment, 66.

[101] *The New York Times*, March 11, 1966.

[102] *Columbia Daily Spectator*, March 14, 1966.

[103] Cox Fact-Finding Commission Transcript, testimony by Daniel Pellegrom, 67–69.

[104] *Columbia Daily Spectator*, February 24, 1966.

to be heard. Initially, their liaison with the community had been tentative, but soon it would become an important aspect of events escalating toward the spring crisis of 1968.

Ascribing the upsurge in opposition to the gymnasium in Morningside Park to Hoving certainly was an oversimplification. Almost as if on cue, yet independent of each other, a range of organizations and individuals were joining the fray in the spring of 1966. In an interview at this time, Congressman William F. Ryan (Democrat, 20th District) declared that the controversy "could not be separated from the larger problem of urban renewal on Morningside Heights." He urged further consultation between the university and the community to correct the "flaw in understanding and planning."[105] Also, Hugh Ferry, Democratic district Leader (78th Assembly District), announced his opposition to the gym, while David Dickens, state assemblyman for the same district, was in favor of it.

A strong letter of protest written by the chair of the Morningside Renewal Council, Rev. Dwight C. Smith, appeared in *The New York Times* on May 20, 1966. It pressed the basic issues involved in the form of a question: "Has any institution the right to claim special privileges for its own members in the use of public parkland?" The letter concludes, "An aroused community resents this appropriation of public park space for essentially non-public, non-park use." Smith also sent a carefully worded letter to each member of Columbia University's Board of Trustees, noting tensions between Columbia and its neighbors, and objecting to the placement of the gymnasium in the park. No reply was ever received, although his letter (see Figure 13) bore the letterhead of the MRC and listed the members of the council's steering committee, which included individuals with impressive religious and political affiliations.

In early February 1966, lawyer Irving Thau, President of the Riverside Park and Playgrounds Committee, had announced he would initiate a taxpayer suit "to enjoin Columbia from actually beginning construction." Columbia legal counsel John Wheeler declared Thau's chances of succeeding "virtually nil," and said that he was "not afraid

---

105. Ibid., April 29, 1966.

of a taxpayer's suit."[106] At the request of Parks Commissioner Hoving, a group of city lawyers was at this time studying Columbia University's lease in an effort to find grounds for cancellation or modification of the agreement between the institution and the city. By the fall, Parks Department counsel declared that the result of the investigation showed "this particular contract [to be] beyond recall."[107]

In another legal action, in May of 1966, State Senator Basil Paterson and Assemblyman Percy Sutton (later Borough President), both Democrats, introduced parallel bills in Albany to repeal the 1960 law that gave New York City the right to lease 2.12 acres of public parkland to Columbia University. Neither Paterson nor Sutton made it clear that community pressure was needed to persuade the City Council or Mayor Lindsay to send a home rule message to Albany, and that, without this step, the legislature would not consider a bill concerning an internal city matter. Lacking the home rule message, the Paterson-Sutton Bill was not considered in the current legislative term and died automatically with the adjournment of the session on July 7, 1966. A second anti-gymnasium bill was proposed the following fall by Paterson and Charles Rangel (Democrat), who was then running for the position of state assemblyman. The Paterson-Rangel Bill was introduced in January 1967, but by March had failed to get out of committee.

In his testimony to the Cox Fact Finding Commission, Paterson declared that his first contact with university officials, initiated by them, came after the first bill had been unsuccessful but word had gotten around that a second try would be made.[108] It was Columbia's concern that legislative action might block the project that prompted the University's approach to Senator Paterson, rather than a response to mounting tension in the neighborhood. This is substantiated in a memorandum by Stanley Salmen, dated October 14, 1966, about a lunch meeting he had with Senator Paterson on October 7. The ostensible purpose was to introduce Paterson to Wesley First, director of Columbia's Office of University Relations. However, the real purpose of the meeting was to

[106.] Ibid, February 14, 1966.
[107.] Ibid., October 19, 1966.
[108.] Cox Fact-Finding Commission Transcript, 3,638–3,639.

determine Paterson's position regarding the gymnasium in Morningside Park. Salmen writes in his memo: "During lunch, he informed us that he was going to re-introduce his bill in the Senate to revoke the lease in Morningside Park. He told us that the only reason the bill did not pass last time was that it had not received a Home Rule message. It had advanced through the committees far enough so that if the message had been received before the session ended, the bill would have come before the houses for passage. It is true that Senator Marchi had promised me that it would not be passed through the Senate without the Home Rule message and Travia had told Mr. Cahill that such a message would be a prerequisite to passage in the House. These delaying tactics worked because Senator Patterson's [sic.] bill was introduced only a month before the session adjourned. It is altogether unlikely that we should be able to keep the bill bottled up through a whole session. Patterson [sic.] is well liked by his associates, and he and the man from Brooklyn control the seven Negro votes in the Senate which are sometimes necessary for the passage of other legislation. The gymnasium is not the kind of thing that would prevent a deal in order to obtain these votes."

It is notable that Senator Paterson's name is misspelled throughout Salmen's memo and also that the last name of Amalia Betanzos is spelled "Petanoz." Both were members of the Morningside Renewal Council, personally known to university officials, including Salmen, who attended the council's meetings. If names were misspelled, so conversations may have been misinterpreted, and Salmen's memo may not reflect the truth of this important occasion. This is obviously the case with the following passage in the memo, which maintains that Senator Paterson was introducing the bills "to establish a negotiating base with Columbia University" that would lead toward assignment of a 50% share of the projected gymnasium for community use. Bowing to Senator Paterson's political standing and reputation, the memo concludes, "It looks, therefore, as though he were in a position to stop the gymnasium in the Park unless we negotiate with him before July 1st and arrive at some solution which will satisfy him but which would not be a contractual obligation on the part of the University."

On May 31, the *Columbia Daily Spectator* reported that the CUSC resolution on the gymnasium had reached Albany, and had been seen by Senator John Marchi, chairman of the committee reviewing the Paterson-Sutton bill. The *Spectator* further reports that "to off-set the effect of the CUSC resolution," a petition in support of the gymnasium was circulated among the students, gathering 1,200 signatures. Word of this petition reached Senator Marchi, and may have contributed to the bill's continued lingering in his committee.

University officials were disinclined to act upon any suggestions emanating from CUSC, but they were beginning to view with some alarm the signs of opposition to the gymnasium coming from within the Columbia "family." Although the Columbia Republican Club continued to support the project, the Columbia-Barnard Democratic Club voted to oppose it. The letter signed by the students in favor of the gym in Morningside Park seemed to vindicate Dean Truman's comment that those in favor "were never heard from."[109] During the Cox Commission Hearings, however, a signed statement was submitted by Emily C. Moore, a research associate at the Population Council, and witnessed by Rev. William F. Starr, declaring that in the spring of 1966, when she was employed as an administrative assistant to university planning coordinator Salmen, the text of the "student petition" in support of the gymnasium had been dictated to her by Salmen. He then contacted a specially selected undergraduate student to claim authorship of the letter. When Moore questioned her boss on this procedure, he replied that it was quicker and more efficient to prompt the students into action this way. Thus it was, in the spring of 1966, that the voice of the "silent majority" was heard on the gymnasium question. Another boost to the morale of those supporting the athletic facility came in the form of the announcement that Harold McGuire, one of the six alumni trustees on the university's 24-man board, had been elected Life Trustee of Columbia University.[110]

While the Parks Commissioner was attending the funeral under the trees in Morningside Park and the gymnasium was receiving

---

[109]. *Columbia Daily Spectator*, May 4, 1966.
[110]. *Columbia College Today*, Spring 1966.

unprecedented attention in the press, a three-way tug-of-war between the city, the Morningside Urban Renewal Council, and Columbia University was taking place—much of it behind the scenes. The council had decided to oppose the city's acceptance of Federal Survey and Planning funds for the Cathedral Parkway Urban Renewal Project that comprised areas 1A, 1B, and 1C of the General Renewal Plan until certain community needs had been guaranteed. The community, through the council, was determined to block urban renewal altogether unless provisions were made in the immediate neighborhood for the relocation of displaced tenants. The community was also asking for a firm commitment on the part of the city government to hold the institutions to the expansion "project map" presented in April 1965.[111] Though the details of the intricate negotiations between City Hall and Low Library are beyond the scope of this chronicle, it is certainly clear that the city officials were in an uncomfortable position—under pressure from the federal government and community groups, as well as in some instances from their political leaders, yet reluctant to take a firm stand against the institutions whose influence on the political scene of New York City was considerable. As a result, in May 1966, the Survey and Planning funds for the Cathedral Parkway Project were approved after a public hearing of the Board of Estimate, during which a statement by Mayor Lindsay was read that promised to take whatever action necessary to enforce the guidelines for institutional expansion voted by the Board of Estimate the previous spring.

The institutions were miffed and openly resentful of the Morningside Urban Renewal Council, which had thwarted their desire to use "urban renewal" to create an academic enclave on Morningside Heights surrounded by a cordon sanitaire, a buffer and barrier of "renewed" blocks. It is perplexing how divorced from contemporary urban reality the academic institutions were. Patrick F. Crossman, Republican District Leader, 69th Assembly District, and a member of the Morningside Urban Renewal

---

[111.] A detailed account of these developments can be found in *Columbia and the Community: Past Policy and New Directions,* a report of the Columbia College Citizenship Council Committee for Research by Marc Rauch, Bob Feldman, and Art Leaderman, 1968, 41–59.

Council Steering Committee, addressed their stance in a bluntly worded statement:

> It is of course absurd to try to produce an integrated neighborhood renewal plan with one large element in the community considering itself totally exempt from the renewal guidelines voted on by the majority of the Council and accepted by the Housing and Development Board. If the institutions continue to isolate themselves from the community resolutions, the Renewal Plan will probably make drastic changes in the now unilateral institutional plans.[112]

After the trying spring of 1966, Columbia officials had good reason to be relieved when the summer brought a lull to the campus and Morningside Heights. Although the University had scored a point when the Paterson-Sutton bill failed to get consideration, the "gym in the Park" was gaining importance as a controversial political issue, and it was beginning to concern the student body. In a maneuver intended to cut off further controversy and in the belief that bad feelings would disappear once the building was a reality, Columbia announced that ground breaking would take place in November, before frost set in. However, in October, ground breaking was postponed until early 1967, because of "technicalities." The final Eggers & Higgins plans were not ready until the end of the summer, and the approval of these plans by the Parks Department was required for construction to begin.[113] While the university was protracting the presentation of the plans to a Parks Commissioner publicly opposed to the project, Hoving was offered the directorship of the Metropolitan Museum of Art, a position too attractive to refuse.

During his brief term as Parks Commissioner, Hoving had done much to further interest in and enjoyment of city parks. His vigorous questioning of Columbia's plans for the gymnasium in Morningside Park had boosted the morale of those opposing this project. However, it was disappointing that Hoving was unable to actually put a stop to it.

---

[112.] *The Morningside Citizen*, May 20, 1966.
[113.] *Columbia Daily Spectator*, October 18, 1966.

The Parks Department disappointed the community in other ways as well. Many among those opposing Columbia's Park encroachment were anxious and willing to work to restore the Park as a truly "alive" outdoor recreation area. "If Columbia University, the Department of Parks, and the citizens of the Morningside Heights area were to cooperate in re-thinking and replanning the function of Morningside Park, a great step would have been taken in the process of communication . . . these three groups have it in their collective power to make Morningside Park a vibrant cultural and recreational part in the lives of those around it," wrote Deborah W. Callard in *The Morningside Citizen*.[114] But neither the Parks Department nor the institutions were interested in supporting this proposal, although it might have been a wise move for Columbia officials to combine their zealous determination to build the gymnasium with an effort to cooperate with the community toward rehabilitating the total Park. It certainly would have been in Columbia's power to persuade the Parks Department to embark on a dramatic program of improvements.

Indifference toward, and perhaps ignorance of, Frederick Law Olmsted's accomplishments as America's paramount landscape architect among the decision makers at the institutions on Morningside Heights, which was surrounded by three of his major creations, is quite astounding. The name Olmsted was never mentioned in the discussions pertaining to the gymnasium or urban planning in general, and in the rare cases where his name appears in memos or reports, it is misspelled. Columbia's apathy toward the unusual natural attraction and recreational possibilities of Morningside Park reinforced the community's ill feelings regarding the impending encroachment.

By the end of 1966, the threat of the gymnasium was looming as a reality, and it seemed that the only possible action was to press for a larger share for community use. This "settlement," however, failed to address the primary issues of the controversy: the taking of public parkland for private non-park use, and eliminating the building as a symbol of Columbia's racism.

---

[114.] *The Morningside Citizen*, May 20, 1966.

# 6

## NEVER LOOK A GIFT HORSE IN THE MOUTH
### Fall/Winter 1966–1967

Columbia's attitude toward its surrounding neighborhoods and the realities of the 1960s was now to be challenged from an unexpected angle, catching many, particularly members of the university administration, by surprise. The annual Columbia University Charter Day Dinner held on October 31, 1966, was designated "A Night for History" by the organizers, who couldn't have anticipated the truth that resided in that phrase. On the occasion, a three-year campaign to raise $200 million for Columbia University was officially announced, and the Ford Foundation had already pledged $35 million toward this goal. Of this sum, $10 million were to be used, in the words of Ford Foundation President McGeorge Bundy, "for the support of new efforts in the field of urban and minority affairs."[115] Speaking to the assembled guests at the Charter Day dinner, Bundy stressed the serious implications of the grant: "Today, the great university in a metropolis must have a special and urgent concern for the future of the city and the future of those in our cities who lack full equality of opportunity. The great university on Morningside Heights is neighbor of one of the greatest problems and opportunities of American life—the problem and opportunity of Harlem." He envisioned that the urban grant

---

[115.] Quoted by Fred M. Hechinger in "Questions of Town, Gown and the Dollar," *The New York Times*, November 6, 1966.

would be used for "study, teaching and action."[116]

It was a gift Columbia could ill afford to refuse, yet it presented a direct challenge—even affront—to its cherished position as a cloistered Ivy League institution, forcing upon it the role of a proactive urban university and threatening to unleash problems that the university was hardly willing to confront or solve.

The philosophy behind the urban grant also presented a conflict with Columbia's allocation of $75 million of the $200 million fund drive for physical expansion, which would involve further destruction of the neighborhood and displacement of people supposedly benefiting from the Ford grant. These plans included the construction of a new "South Campus" from 114th to 112th Streets between Broadway and Amsterdam Avenue—a long contemplated move that Salmen had expressly denied at the public meeting in Riverside Church two years earlier. Predictably, it would threaten countless people—described by Bundy as "lacking full equality of opportunity"—with losing their homes.

To introduce the $200 million campaign, the university had prepared a handsome publication entitled *The Progress and Promise of Columbia University in the City of New York*.[117] In glowing terms and using handsome photographs, it reports on Columbia's accomplishments and outlines needs for expansion. It is dated July 1967. One is tempted to suspect that the last chapter, "Toward the Twenty-first Century," was added, or altered, in response to the Ford Foundation grant. At the end of the chapter, it is noted that "ten million of this [35 million] was an outright appropriation to finance Columbia's study of urban environments and ways to provide equal opportunities for minority groups in cities."[118] The tone of this sequel differs markedly from an earlier chapter, "The University and the City," which describes Columbia's encouraging the creation of Morningside Heights Inc., "to cleanse and restore the neighborhood" under the slogan "To promote

---

[116.] *A Night for History*, a report on the 1966 Columbia University Charter Day dinner held Monday, October 31, 1966, in the New York Hilton Hotel.

[117.] *The Progress and Promise of Columbia University in the City of New York*, July, 1967.

[118.] Ibid., 144.

the improvement of Morningside Heights as an attractive residential, educational and cultural area." This chapter promotes urban renewal in the area north of the campus, noting that it has met with opposition from "self-styled political leaders and other quarrelsome elements, often finding allies among professional politicians, [who] have done much to impede the renewal plan." This chapter also mentions plans for twenty additional buildings, and a "spectacular new gymnasium, which will be shared with the Morningside Heights and Harlem communities."[119]

Student and community groups were quick to seize upon the chance to improve town and gown relations, taking the Ford Foundation mandate at its word. Bundy had explicitly cited "action" as part of the urban program, and Champion Ward, a Ford Foundation vice president, announced that it was expected that representatives of the Harlem and Morningside Heights communities would be included in the discussions, although the initiative of inviting them would rest with Columbia.[120] President Kirk refrained from commenting on this open-door policy, and cautiously steered away from committing the university to any program of community action. On the other hand, Rev. Dwight Smith, Chairman of the Morningside Renewal Council, contacted the Ford Foundation seeking further information.

The Columbia College Citizenship Council (CCCC) was more involved with the surrounding neighborhoods than any other segment of the university.[121] Launched in 1960, CCCC was largely the initiative of Lawrence Chamberlain, then dean of the college. By the fall of 1966, the Citizenship Council could count on over a thousand student volunteers, who joined its program for reasons described by Frank Ward, council

---

[119.] Ibid., 27–28.

[120.] *Columbia Daily Spectator*, November 7, 1966.

[121.] Joel Ziff, Chairman of the Columbia College Citizenship Council, described its functions to the Cox Fact-Finding Commission as "an organization of about eleven programs involved in various kinds of community work, ranging from volunteering in hospitals to community organizing, involving about 1,100 students during the course of the year—summer and during the winter." Commission Transcript, 3,376.

chair in 1967: "We are learning a new social geography. I don't want to spend my life just making money and living quietly in the countryside somewhere. I want to be involved in other people's lives. I don't want to escape from the world: I want to join it. And help make it better."[122]

Both the College Citizenship Council and the Columbia University Student Council urged university officials to allow their own organizations, as well as CORE, the faculty, and members of the community, a voice in the planning of the $10 million urban affairs program that envisioned an emphasis on action rather than on research.[123] Columbia dampened the students' commitment to cultural ideals that were inclusive and pluralistic. It was Bundy himself who was obliged to disclose at a meeting with eight community leaders, including the chair of the Morningside Renewal Council, that the community would not be directly involved, and that the program would be primarily educational.[124]

Early in December 1966, the 24-member Columbia President's Council on Urban-Minority Problems was established to "offer advice and counsel to the [urban affairs] program's policy-making group,"[125] and five members of the council were appointed to the President's Committee on Urban-Minority Problems. Clarence C. Walton, dean of the School of General Studies, chaired both groups. The larger council included three students, members of the university's administration, and faculty representing a range of disciplines—but no community representatives. According to President Kirk, outside individuals and organizations were to be consulted, and he declared that "Columbia desires to be a good neighbor to everyone."[126] The contradictions implicit in the Ford Foundation's urban affairs grant to Columbia University at times took on a tragicomic quality; possibly, university officials were secretly wishing it away. While President Kirk was setting up the Urban Affairs Council, the institutional expansion policy was proceeding relentlessly, disregarding the efforts of the Morningside Renewal Council to work toward a

122. "The New Evangelists," *Columbia College Today*, Fall 1966, 42–47.
123. *Columbia Daily Spectator*, November 23, 1966.
124. Ibid., November 22, 1966.
125. *The New York Times*, December 11, 1966.
126. *Columbia Daily Spectator*, December 8, 1966.

comprehensive plan that would avoid isolating the area completely from its urban surroundings.

Democratic District Leader Franz Leichter (69th Assembly District) in an open letter to President Kirk dated November 25, 1966, charged that "the high purposes for which Columbia exists and its integrity as an institution of higher learning have been tarnished by its eviction in the past few years of up to 7500 residents . . . many of them minority members." The letter, as paraphrased in the *Columbia Daily Spectator*, makes the following recommendations:

> That Columbia review its expansion policy and "involve faculty and student representatives in the planning." That Columbia disclose these plans "to the community, other institutions on the Heights and the City." That Columbia "agree to limit its expansion to facilities which must be on the Heights campus and to utilize other sites either in the city or the suburbs for such divisions which need not be here." That Columbia "commit itself to multi-purpose use of sites . . . combining institutional and residential facilities in one building."[127]

Leichter's figure of 7,500 evictions was disputed by Coordinator of University Planning Stanley Salmen, who declared, "There have been very darned few people evicted by Columbia . . . no more than one thousand have been evicted." Seemingly unaware of the tact demanded by the Urban Affairs Program, Salmen added, "We are looking for a community where the faculty can talk to people like themselves. We don't want a dirty group, not a noisy group. We've very nearly achieved that."[128]

The news that $75 million of the fund-raising campaign launched by Columbia was destined to finance its physical expansion was greeted with mixed feelings by the architectural and planning professions. Ada Louise Huxtable wrote in *The New York Times* about Columbia's building

---

[127.] Ibid., November 29, 1966.
[128.] Ibid.

and planning record to date: "Results visible now, after almost a decade of construction are so uncoordinated and undistinguished that they suggest to critics a kind of do-it-yourself planning based on a lack of administrative understanding of urban planning as a process, or a source of superior design. If the present system and standards continue, they predict that the next ten years (an estimated close to $150 million worth of construction) will produce a great deal more of the same." Huxtable described planning as practiced at Columbia as a "purely administrative process with architectural afterthoughts." She concluded, prophetically: "But it is the proven inability of the university to see the environment as a whole and to recognize the need for the highest level of professional vision that threatens its development program, and the Morningside neighborhood, with planning disaster." Criticizing Columbia's recently built or projected buildings one by one, she refers to the future gymnasium as "one of the most controversial . . . under attack as park encroachment and as inadequate for promised community uses."[129]

Though Huxtable's criticism usually addressed architecture, in this piece she focused convincingly on Columbia's lack of urban planning. Her opinion gained notoriety among professional colleagues and caused embarrassment for the university administration in the midst of the university's major fund drive.

Urban planning had emerged in the United States and abroad as a prominent and much debated subject, and in America it was frequently discussed in relation to the civil rights movement. In the 1960s, it became Columbia's Achilles' heel, exposing it to criticism beyond the confines of Morningside Heights and the surrounding neighborhoods.

Stimulated by Mayor Lindsay's concern for the visual quality of what was being built in New York (his) City, Arthur Drexler, Director of the Department of Architecture and Design at The Museum of Modern Art (MoMA), organized the exhibition "The New City: Architecture and Urban Renewal." It opened in January 1967, although planning for it had begun in 1965.[130] MoMA invited teams of architects and city

---

129. *The New York Times*, November 5, 1966.
130. Elizabeth Kassler, Sidney J. Frigand, and Arthur Drexler, *The New City: Architecture and Urban Renewal*, catalog for exhibition held January 23–March 13,

planners from four universities, Columbia, Cornell, MIT, and Princeton, to present their ideas for the renewal of Harlem. Although Harlem had been selected as emblematic of an African- American ghetto, its name was not mentioned in the exhibition title. The catalog includes two extensive essays and an introduction by Drexler, which explains that the assignment presented to the participating teams asked for consideration of "specific social as well as aesthetic goals." One of these goals—"How can we provide housing and other kinds of renewal without relocating the people for whom such improvements are intended"—was particularly pertinent to Columbia's tactics at the time.[131] Similarly pertinent were passages describing New York as having a unique "population mix" and being "a city of minorities" in the essay "A Perspective on Planning" by Sidney J. Frigand, former deputy executive director of the New York City Planning Commission. He notes "the new voice" and "pressure coming from the ghettoes," predicting that "we will see planning for local areas carried out with full citizen participation—with knowledge that resources are available to implement the plans."[132]

Columbia's capital fund drive and the Ford urban affairs grant increased public awareness of Columbia's urban image and racist attitude toward minorities. The *Columbia Daily Spectator* reflected concern for these issues and, within this context, expanded its attention to the gymnasium controversy, featuring it in frequent news items. Significant among these was a sequence of letters to the editors regarding the naming of the community part of Columbia's athletic facility after a donor's family.[133] In 1963, the Meinhard family had contributed $1 million to the gymnasium fund to be used specifically for the community section of the building. The *Spectator* mentioned other sizable donations to the community part of the project: $250,000 from the Jacob R. Schiff Charitable Trust and $200,000 from the Charles Hayden Foundation. The irony of it all was pointed out by Suzanne Crowell, a junior at Barnard College, in a letter explaining that Columbia, while maintaining that the university would carry the cost of the community portion of

---

1967 (New York: The Museum of Modern Art), 48 pp.
[131] Ibid., 22.
[132] Ibid., 4, 7.
[133] *Columbia Daily Spectator*, October 28, November 2, 1966.

its gymnasium, actually was receiving contributions from foundations specifically "to pay for the whole package." Crowell concludes that "the elected State representatives of West Harlem, all the West Harlem community organizations, and the Morningside Renewal Council all oppose the gym."[134] Columbia officials' uneasiness regarding the comments about the financial grants for the gymnasium, and the change in campus mood, effected a prompt reply to Crowell's letter from Columbia College Dean Truman.[135] He called her letter "an interesting compendium of beliefs that are prevalent in the community and in the College itself ... that are contrary to fact." The encroachment of Morningside Park, he said, is deemed preferable to displacing tenants on Morningside Heights, and the building would contribute to the safety of the area. Truman attributed the opposition to the gymnasium to a "campaign of distortion and misrepresentation"—showing how far removed the university administrators were from the social and political realities of the late 1960s.

A few days after the publication of Dean Truman's letter, a half-page paid statement by Columbia CORE appeared in the *Columbia Daily Spectator* (see Figure 14).[136] Entitled "White Man's Burden?" it refuted, with a bitterness and intensity that shook the campus, Dean Truman's statement as a "clumsy and misleading attempt to explain away valid community criticism." With the ring of a wake-up call for action, the ad text concludes by demanding that "Dean Truman and the entire administration give assurance that students and residents of this area will be given a role in deciding the future of Morningside Heights." More than anything else that had happened so far regarding the gymnasium controversy, these three public statements in the *Columbia Daily Spectator* profoundly affected campus opinion. Dean Truman's letter also elicited one of Park Commissioner Hoving's last comments on the Morningside Park gymnasium while he was still in office.

Based on his faculty position in Columbia's Department of Art History and School of Architecture, as well as being a fellow graduate

---

134. Ibid., November 2, 1966.
135. Ibid., November 7, 1966.
136. Ibid., December 1, 1966.

of Princeton, George Collins began corresponding with Hoving when he was Parks Commission in order to keep him abreast of developments regarding the gymnasium in Morningside Park and Columbia's reactions to Hoving's comments. Among Hoving's remarkably frank letters to Collins is the following response to the Truman letter:

> There are many reasons for opposing the project. First, it is completely out of scale for a park of this size. Second, the design lacks distinction of any. . . . Third, the 12% figure for community use is totally inadequate for any alleged "Columbia-community" gymnasium. If, as Dean Truman says, 12% is *more* than the City asked Columbia to provide for the community, my only response is that this proves the proposal was a mere "land grab", with the conniv-ance of politicians and bureaucrats who did not serve the Harlem community . . . . Fourth, the proposed plans provide for segregation between the Columbia and the community facilities.[137]

Perceiving a new awareness on Campus of the controversial aspects of placing the Columbia gymnasium in Morningside Park, several faculty members sought an occasion to precipitate discussion of the matter at a meeting of the Columbia College faculty, which had not previously entertained any formal consideration of this athletic facility for its stu-dents. They hoped that discussing the issue at a faculty meeting might persuade the university to reconsider and modify the project before it was too late. The only fall 1966 meeting of the Columbia College faculty was scheduled for December 19. This was the last chance before the groundbreaking date as it was scheduled at the time. The following resolution was presented to the meeting:

---

[137.] Letter signed by Thomas P. F. Hoving, on Department of Parks stationary, to Professor George R. Collins, dated November 16, 1966, CCC Collection, Schomburg Center, Box 8, #5.

1. That we express serious reservations about our University employing public lands, and in particular park land, for the construction of its own facilities. 2. That we urge the Administration and the Trustees to renegotiate the arrangement with the City for the use of land in Morningside Park for the Columbia University Gymnasium, in order that: a) A full 50% of the physical plant be available for the use of the City and the community; and the University, in turn, not be responsible financially for the construction or maintenance of other than its own portion. b) That this gymnasium and all other facilities that the University has constructed in the Park be available for *any* community use (subject to a proper controlling body) and not just for "organized youth activity." [138]

The resolution was received with total indifference. Although the predominantly "liberal" faculty members and their families, many of whom lived on Morningside Heights, supported civil rights causes in general, they recoiled from becoming involved in a real situation with political overtones on their doorsteps. As far as most of them were concerned, the pursuit of knowledge conferred on the university a status of virtual eminent domain. The moral and legal rights of Columbia to proceed arbitrarily with the so-called "plan" of expansion went unquestioned by the majority of the faculty until the crisis in the spring of 1968 engulfed the campus. The gymnasium controversy, which might have caused a stir in the hearts of academic nature lovers, was considered hopeless as an issue and not worthy of their pressuring the university for alternatives.

Morningside Park was simply not on the radar screens of the majority of Columbia's intelligentsia. At a time when Frederick Law Olmsted's ideas and work were beginning to gain the attention of those concerned

---

[138.] The author of the resolution was Professor George R. Collins of the Department of Art History. Source here is a letter from Collins to Joseph L. Blau, Secretary of the Faculty of Columbia College, correcting the wording of his resolution, CCC Collection, Schomburg Center, Box 8, #5.

about conflicts between natural and man-made environments, neither those at the School of Architecture, nor historians of American culture, nor art historians—all professionals who might have been expected to be involved—paid attention to the threat evolving a few blocks from their offices. (It is interesting to note that a number of art historians devoted considerable energy and funds to saving the treasures of Florence after the floods of 1966. Even allowing for a certain prejudice regarding American art and architecture, their indifference toward a neighborhood landmark was a sad statement on the spiritual and humanistic content of their disciplines. Obviously, there was no esteem to be gained in defending Olmsted's park compared to that to be gained by aiding Florence.) The destruction of Morningside Park for the construction of a gymnasium was an anachronism when it took place in 1968; given the times, it would have been an impossibility a year later.

The belief that so-called "progress" justifies the destruction of historic landmarks continues to be quite prevalent in the academic world, and it was not unique to Columbia University in the 1960s. In his book *The Modern American City*, Christopher Tunnard examines changing attitudes toward the historic past in urban planning. He notes how in their battles to stave off destruction of the valuable evidence of the historic past, "Save-the-Park committees and Historic Preservation Trusts discovered that, besides the ignorance and venality of local and state administrations, destruction of cherished buildings and sites was being blithely undertaken by their own favorite institutions: the universities, the churches, and the country clubs. All were either moving or expanding, and as one university president put it, 'My institution must put education of new generations before the preservation of the monuments of the past,' apparently not perceiving any relationship between the two concepts."[139]

In a 2009 article, Ada Louise Huxtable comments: "For a maverick movement begun by little old ladies in tennis shoes fighting bulldozers in the urban renewal demolition wars of the 1960s, historic preservation has achieved some astounding successes, from the passage of landmark preservation laws and the establishment of the National Trust for Historic

---

[139.] Christopher Tunnard, *The Modern American City* (Franklin Watts Inc., 1968), 95.

Preservation to the recognition, restoration and reuse of an impressive part of this country's architectural heritage. . . . from the monumental to the vernacular—repair first, restore second, rebuild last . . . ."[140]

The moral, ethical, and aesthetic issues behind the opposition to the gymnasium in Morningside Park never penetrated the désengagé position of the faculty, and the whole irritating affair was ignored. The Park, the people who treasured and used it, and the problems it represented were, to borrow Ralph Ellison's phrase, "invisible," as indicated by comments from Diana Trilling, the literary critic and wife of a prominent Columbia professor, who wrote in 1968 about Morningside Park: "I myself, in long years of residence on Morningside Heights, have never known anyone, black or white, who has dared use the Park even for a short-cut, let alone for relaxation."[141]

It should not be assumed that the faculty's tacit approval of the projected gymnasium was prompted by enthusiasm for student athletics; most professors preferred to see a student in the library studying instead of on the gymnasium floor at any time. It was rather that the academic minds on Morningside Heights could not relate, or rather opted not to relate, their (liberal) convictions to a local issue until April 1968, when a storm engulfed their world.

The baffling position, or non-position, of the Faculty Civil Rights Group (FCRG) regarding the gymnasium has never been explained convincingly by members of the organization. FCRG was established at an ad hoc meeting of activists in April 1966 "to investigate the problems of community groups in the Morningside area, and to explore the possibilities of urban renewal plans which might satisfy both the University's needs for expansion and the community's need for housing."[142] The enthusiasm of the group is indicated by the substantial "payroll" tax that the members imposed on themselves to subsidize their local activities and contributions to national causes. The result of the information

---

[140.] Ada Louise Huxtable, "The Beauty of Brutalism, Restored and Updated," *The Wall Street Journal*, February 25, 2009.

[141.] Diana Trilling, "On the Steps of Low Library: Liberalism and the Revolution of the Young," *Commentary*, November 1968, 34.

[142.] Cox Fact-Finding Commission Transcript, testimony by Professor Immanuel Wallerstein, Chairman of the Faculty Civil Rights Group, 2,286.

gathering carried out by FCRG, especially by Professor Peter Haidu, was an insightful report on "The Community and Expansion of Columbia University," issued in December 1967.[143] This twenty-eight-page document was based on relevant publications and extensive interviews with representatives of the university and the community. It explains the meaning of certain key words prevalent in the debates regarding the conflicts brewing in the Morningside Heights and surrounding neighborhoods, using "community," for example, to designate those not affiliated with the institutions, who were usually grouped under references to "Columbia." The meaning of "expansion" as applied to various aspects of Columbia's urban actions has been discussed in previous chapters of this narrative, and the FCRG report devotes several pages to this critical issue in the Columbia-community controversy.[144]

According to the testimony of Professor Immanuel Wallerstein from the Department of Sociology to the Cox Fact Finding Commission, the FCRG, although seriously concerned over Columbia's "oil-slick expansion . . . never at any point made a public statement about the gymnasium." He gave two reasons for this: "1. In the light of expansion, we considered the gym a peripheral issue; it was one more instance of this expansion, a relatively minor one, that took over parkland rather than evicting tenants." While the FCRG was not in sympathy with it and saw it as a "grievous error," it considered the gym "symbolic of the larger issue, and . . . wished to tackle the larger issue directly;" and "2. For our purposes, it was not useful to concentrate on the gym as a symbol," because the FCRG was trying not to antagonize the trustees, administration, and alumni in order not to jeopardize making headway on "other important issues."[145] The FCRG failed to see the encroachment on public parkland and cultural Harlem turf as a symptom of Columbia's urban myopia and racism, as well as another step in its program of building a wall around Morningside Heights. FCRG members did not question the administration's argument that taking parkland was

[143.] Faculty Civil Rights Group at Columbia University, "The Community and the Expansion of Columbia University." See also the author's introduction to this chronicle.

[144.] Ibid., 3–9, and passim.

[145.] Cox Fact-Finding Commission Transcript, Wallerstein, 2,333.

an ethically justified alternative to evicting tenants, nor did they take a position at the December Columbia College faculty meeting regarding the resolution intended to precipitate a wide-ranging discussion of the gymnasium in Morningside Park, although there had been advance assurance of support for the resolution. This select faculty group did not act appreciably differently from their colleagues when it came to the gymnasium. However, one week of events in the spring of 1968 would have a considerable effect on their mindsets.

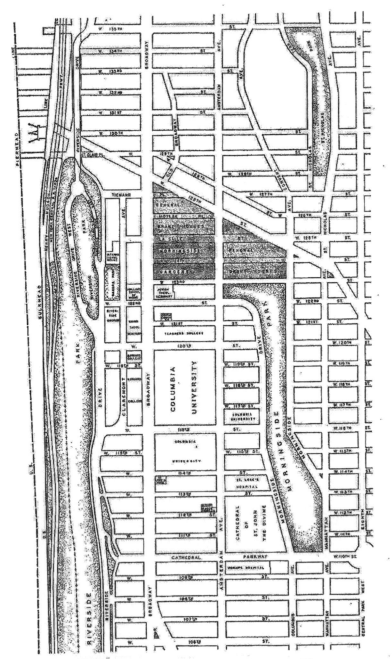

Figure 1a. Overview map of Morningside Heights showing the location of Morningside Park east of the Columbia University campus.

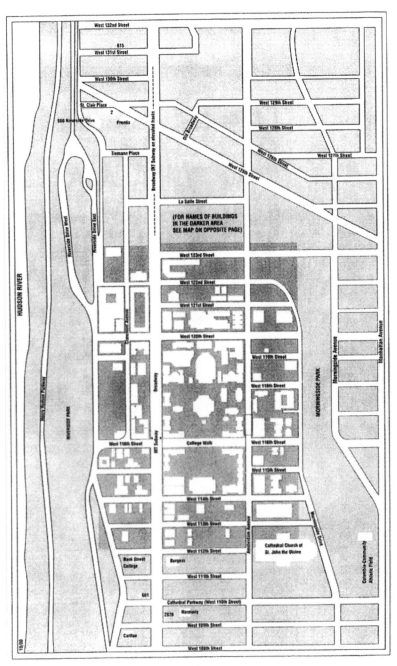

Figure 1b. Campus detail map of Morningside Heights showing the location of Morningside Park east of the Columbia University campus.

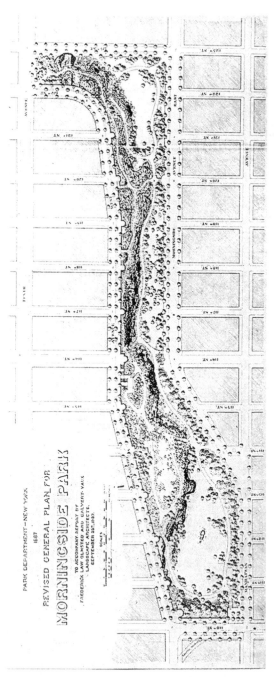

Figure 2. Revised General Plan for Morningside Park of 1887, by Frederick Law Olmsted and Calvert Vaux. (The original plan has never been found.)

Figure 3. A view from "the EL," the elevated train station at 110<sup>th</sup> Street, shows the southern portion of Morningside Park with the Cathedral of St. John the Divine in an early stage of construction and St. Luke's Hospital to the right of the cathedral. Photograph, winter 1903/04, courtesy of New York Historical Society.

Figure 4. "Cathedral Heights," oil on canvas done in summer or early fall of 1905 by Earnest Lawson, painted from the same location as Figure 3.

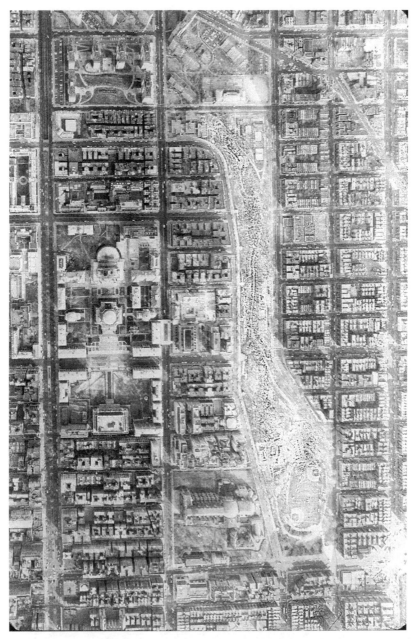

Figure 5. Aerial photograph of Morningside Heights includes Columbia University's campus, with the Cathedral of St. John the Divine at lower center. The university's Morningside Park athletic field is located to the right and downhill from the cathedral.

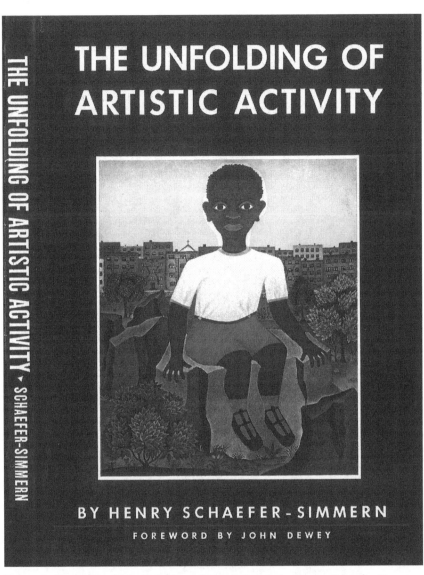

Figure 6. The cover of *The Unfolding of Artistic Activity* by Henry Schaefer-Simmern (University of California Press, 1948) shows a black child sitting on a rock, possibly in Morningside Park. The book's foreword was written by John Dewey.

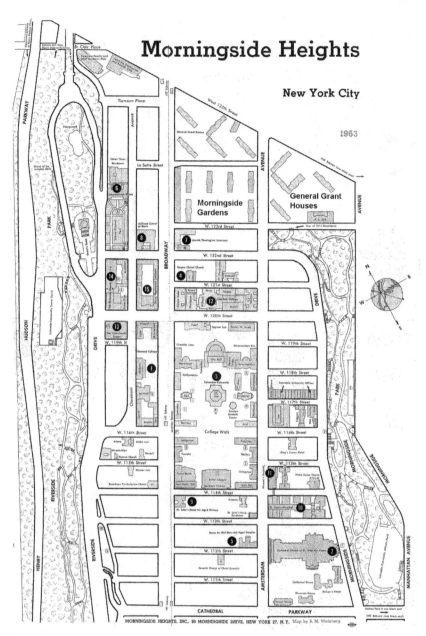

Figure 7. Map published in 1963 in "A Guide to Morningside Heights, New York City." The General Grant public housing is at top right, and Morningside Gardens rental housing is to its left. Morningside and Riverside Parks are to the right and left of the map. Map by B.M. Weinberg, publisher Morningside Heights, Inc.

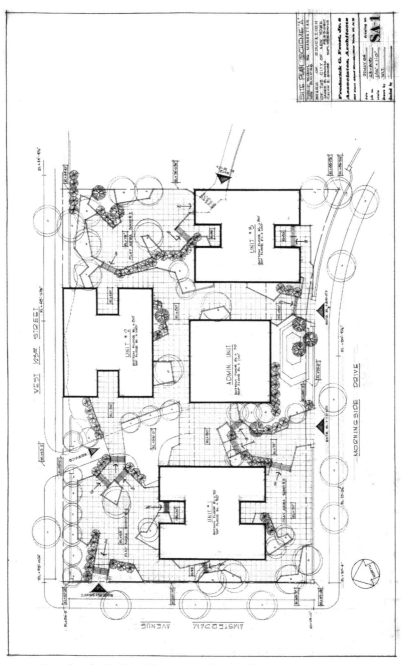

Figure 8. Site plan for Public School 36 by Frederick G. Frost & Associates, 1964. Courtesy of Avery Architectural Library, Columbia University.

# Morningsiders United

## for a diversified, integrated community

***Believing that*** this community needs people, homes, shops, restaurants, schools, lively streets and parks, and not merely a larger mass of non-residential buildings, with isolated streets and depopulated sidewalks

***Estimating that*** 10,000 Morningsiders—inheritors of an acute metropolitan housing shortage—will be displaced within the near future if the recently accelerated institutional expansion continues

***Knowing that*** 15 businesses have closed—one symptom of a dying community—within just 2 blocks during the past 2 years

***Realizing that*** the needs of residents and institutions for space are in direct conflict

## Morningsiders United aims

- ***to bring about*** the house by house, block by block organization of residents, multiplying the voice of the citizen wherever community decisions are made,

- ***to oppose*** demolition of sound housing, and to take all appropriate action to insure the preservation and maintenance of homes,

- ***to bring together*** residents and businessmen, both vital in a diversified neighborhood, for effective representation of their interests and their contributions to the community.

**We ask for full discussion with all institutions and community groups toward constructive neighborhood planning which will consider all interests, and discriminate against none.**

**Morningsiders United,** 1235 Amsterdam Avenue, New York 10027

357

Figure 9. Flyer from about 1962 calls for residents to join Morningsiders United for a diversified, integrated community.

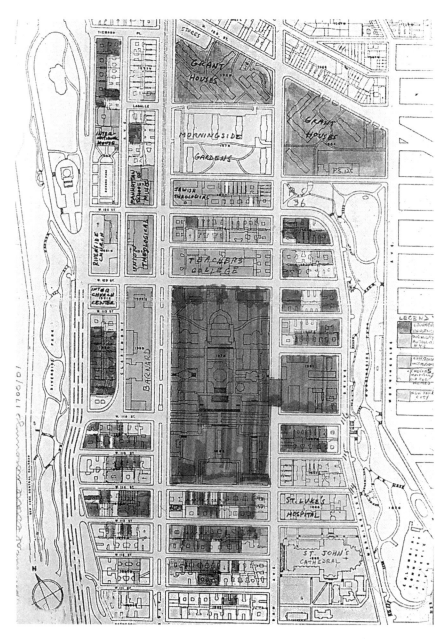

Figure 10. The large dark rectangle at lower center of this 1964/65 Morningside Heights map marks the existing Columbia University campus at the time. Other shaded areas illustrate Columbia's "Early Acquisitions Proposals" dated 1968, including expansion south of the campus. Not shown are additional proposed acquisitions that reached east into West Harlem.

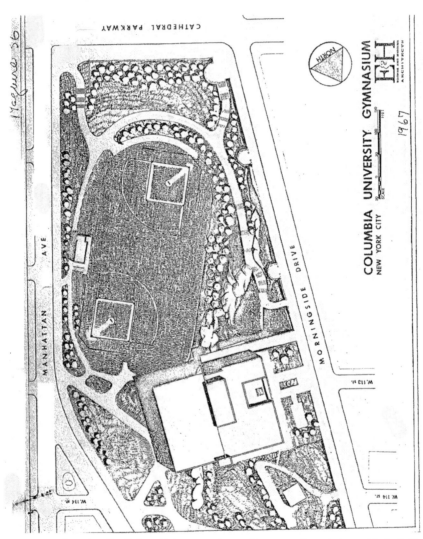

Figure 11. Site plan for Columbia's gymnasium adjacent to the existing athletic field.

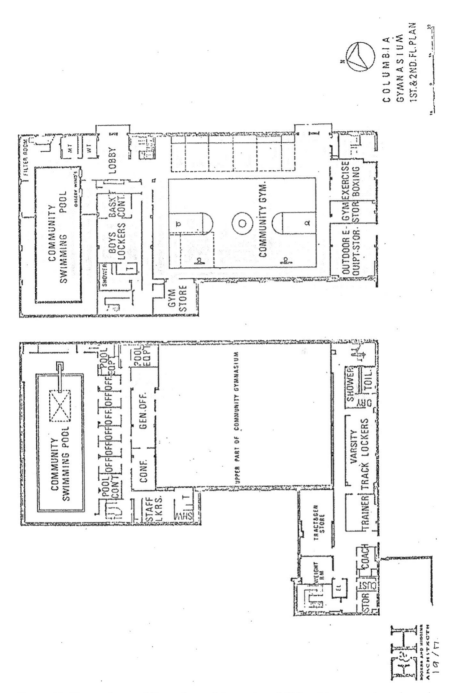

Figure 12. First and second floor plans of the projected Columbia gymnasium show the community section, including the community swimming pool that was added in 1967.

# Morningside Renewal Council

Dwight C. Smith, *Chairman*
114 Riverside Drive
New York 27 — 870-3045

Amalia Betanzos, *Vice-Chairman*
207 West 106th Street
New York 25 — 666-7244

Marion Emerson, *Secretary*
601 West 115th Street
New York 25 — MO 3-1969

Forrest L. Abbott, *Treasurer*
106 Morningside Drive
New York 27 — MO 2-4300

May 16, 1966

STEERING COMMITTEE

Audrey Cooper
*West Harlem Community Organization*

Patrick Crossman
*Morningside Heights Republican Club*

Randolph Dyer
*Union Theological Seminary*

Eugenia M. Flatow
*Riverside Democrats, Inc.*

Aramis Gomez
*Puerto Rican Citizens Committee on Housing*

John Hadden
*Morningsiders United*

Robert Hedges
*Manhattanville-Morningside Neighborhood Council*

Wilhelmina Lewis
*West 112th Street Block Association*

Jesse Lyons
*Riverside Church*

Harriet L. Pickens
*Harlem Neighborhoods Association, Inc.*

Edward Robin
*Riverside Democrats, Inc.*

Walter South
*109th-110th-Columbus Block Association*

William H. Willis, Jr.
*Manhattan-122nd Street Tenants*

As a Trustee of Columbia University you probably know of tensions and conflicts between the University and the neighboring community, particularly as physical expansion by the University reduces area available to residents of Morningside Heights.

This is a matter of concern to more than sixty organized groups and institutions which, with the University, comprise the Morningside Renewal Council. As chairman of that Council, I observe a bitterness and hostility towards the University which are good for neither Columbia nor the community. Some tension is inevitable in a dynamic situation; but these attitudes and feelings are poisoning the very atmosphere between us.

As a resident who has long admired Columbia University, and wishes it well, I deplore this steady erosion of good will in our neighborhood. Of course it is partly due to various misunderstandings. However, I must frankly add that it is partly due to what the community sees as intransigence and insensitivity on the part of the University.

No doubt the advancing of University interests is a primary concern of the Administration and Trustees. But what is intended to accomplish that purpose may in fact deal a serious blow to the University by damaging Columbia's reputation for integrity and concern for human values. A great University must clearly act in accordance with its professed ideals.

The gym-in-the-park is a case in point. It is important that you should not minimize the fact of so much opposition to the project. At the request of our Steering Committee I enclose copies of two communications which may help you understand how a significant part of this community feels on the issue.

Very truly yours,

*Dwight C. Smith*
Chairman

DCS:efp
2 Encs.

Figure 13. Letter from Dwight C. Smith, Chairman of the Morningside Renewal Council, sent to members of the Board of Trustees of Columbia University, May 16, 1966, noting tensions between Columbia and its neighbors, and objecting to the placement of the gymnasium in the park.

120

# WHITE MAN'S BURDEN?

Dean Truman's letter of November 7th concerning the proposed gymnasium in Morningside Park is a clumsy and misleading attempt to explain away valid community criticism. While trying to defend the plan, Dean Truman in fact exposes the truth of the community objections to the proposal.

The Dean dismisses as "irrelevant" the fact that the residents of Morningside Heights and West Harlem will lose valuable park land in return for a small basketball court and wrestling room. From the community's viewpoint and that of many students the Dean's argument that the gym will provide "a facility for an all-weather program" is not convincing since the Morningside Renewal Plan includes plans for a community center with all these facilities and more within three blocks of the gym site. In face of strong community protest it is paternalistic and unjustifiable for Columbia to decide that its proposed gym is more valuable to the neighborhood than parkland.

Columbia University made a similar decision in fencing off a baseball diamond and track also partially available to the community. Contrary to Dean Truman's assertion, this program is widely disapproved of by the neighborhood because it is open only to the use of organized supervised teams which have made reservations for its use. This large area is now fenced off from mothers and young children and, in fact, from the average unorganized kid of West Harlem. It is not the responsibility of Columbia University to teach the children of West Harlem how to play.

Dean Truman expects the community to thank Columbia for taking only their parks instead of their homes. He should hardly be surprised that the community replies "Why take either?" If it is necessary for Columbia to expand in this area, then the University must openly and honestly discuss its expansion plans with the community and attempt to take into consideration the needs of the entire neighborhood. Columbia University has never co-operated in the planning of the gym with the present mayor, with local congressmen, assemblymen or state senators, with the Borough President, with Park Commissioner Hoving, or with the Morningside Renewal Council, all of whom opposed the plan.

We can name the community leaders who are opposed to the construction of the gym in Morningside Park; will Dean Truman name those who are in favor of it? Indeed, his claim that such leaders fear to express approval would merely show the depth of the neighborhood's nearly unanimous opposition to the gym in the park. What kind of community leaders are these who can speak more openly to Columbia University than to the community? It discredits Dean Truman to imply that anti-gym sentiment is the result of a "campaign of distortion and misrepresentation" and find it necessary to resort to the time-worn excuse of dismissing dissent on the grounds that it is fomented by outside agitators and opposed by anonymous "responsible" leaders. We demand that Dean Truman openly announce the names of these supposed leaders or retract his statement. But more importantly, we demand that Dean Truman and the entire administration give assurance that students and residents of this area will be given a role in deciding the future of Morningside Heights. It is bad enough that Columbia University presumes to put itself "in loco parentis" for 20-thousand Columbia students, but we are amazed at their naive paternalism in attempting to do so for 45-thousand Negroes and Puerto Ricans.

*Columbia C.O.R.E.*

Figure 14. This statement by the Columbia University chapter of the Congress on Racial Equality (CORE) was published in *The Columbia Spectator*, December 1, 1966.

Figure 15. Photo of a sit-in in front of the bulldozers at the gymnasium site on February 20, 1968. Participants, from left, are Maria Miller, Justus Poole, Marchall García, Bob McKay (hidden), author Christiane Crasemann Collins with her dog Kim, and Suki Ports. Photo by G.R. Collins.

Figure 16. Bob McKay in the scoop of the bulldozer. *The New York Times,* February 21, 1968.

Figure. 17. Gymnasium protesters, which included both community members and students, carry placards at a gathering on Morningside Drive. Photos by G.R. Collins

Figure. 18. Student and community protestors include Joseph Monroe or William Stanley, who looked much alike, standing in front of the barricades to the left of a policeman. Photo by G.R. Collins

Figure 19. Protestors demonstrate in front of Columbia University President Kirk's house at Morningside Drive and 116th Street. Photo by G.R. Collins

Figure 20. These photographs depict destruction in Morningside Park as work on the gymnasium site began. Photos by G.R. Collins

Figure 21. Rev. Kendall A. Smith of Beulah Baptist Church, Harlem, was arrested for trespassing a public park and resisting arrest and then pushed into a paddy wagon. Photos by G.R. Collins

Figure 22. Left, students pull down the cyclone fence at the gymnasium site. Right, student Fred Wilson is arrested. Photos from the *Columbia Daily Spectator*

Figure 23. Dean Henry Coleman in captivity at Hamilton Hall. Photo by Richard Howard for the *Columbia Daily Spectator*

Figure 24. Black students occupy Hamilton Hall. Photo by Richard Howard for *Columbia Daily Spectator*

Figure 25. Photos show buildings occupied on the Columbia campus. Photos by
Nicolas Collins

Figure 26. Photos that were taken at the gym site after the construction was stopped exhibit extensive destruction of the Morningside Park landscape. Photos by G.R. Collins

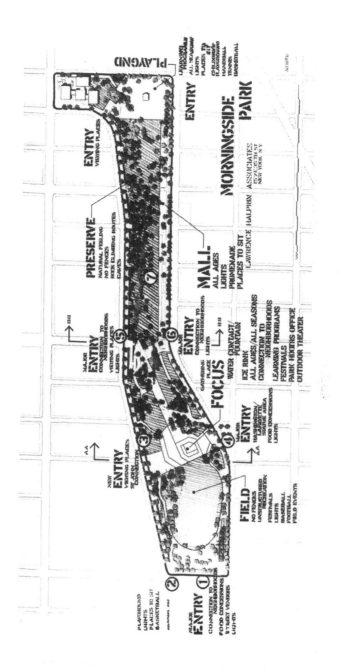

Figure 27. Plan by Lawrence Halprin & Associates for the restoration of Morningside Park, 1974.

# 7

## "GYM CROW"

### 1967

In January 1967, the Paterson-Rangel bill to repeal the enabling legislation permitting the city to lease parkland to Columbia University was introduced into the New York State Legislature. There has never been an explanation for why this move was not accompanied by pressure on the city government to send a home rule measure to Albany requesting that the legislature take action on this measure. Possibly, the authors of the bill did not want to stop the gymnasium altogether, but rather, as Senator Paterson commented at the time, that the bill not "preclude negotiations over the community's share of the structure."[146] By March 1967, the Paterson-Rangel bill had failed to get out of committee.

However, Columbia University at last agreed to hold discussions about the gymnasium, having obtained an extension for the presentation of "final plans" for the building from the Board of Estimate. The discussions that took place in the spring of 1967, presumably in response to political pressure rather than community sentiment, focused primarily on redistribution of space in the projected building. Sessions were held in Borough President Percy Sutton's office, attended by representatives of the university, political leaders, and certain elected officials—but no one from the community.[147]

The Morningside Renewal Council representing sixty community

---

[146.] *Columbia Daily Spectator*, January 16, 1967.

[147.] Cox Fact-Finding Commission Transcript, testimony by Basil Paterson, 3,638–3,639.

organizations, of which forty were located in immediate proximity to Morningside Park, was neither informed nor consulted. Its chair, the Rev. Dwight Smith, wrote on April 26, 1967, to Mayor Lindsay, reiterating the position the council had taken by vote in March 1966: "The Morningside Renewal Council opposes the Columbia University gym in Morningside Park, because it involves the use of parkland for non-park purposes, and requests that the City act to rescind the agreements between Columbia University and the Parks Department with respect to the gym and the Athletic Field." Smith asked in his letter to be kept informed, and concluded, "Indeed, if there are conferences or discussions held in which the opinion and advice of the community might appropriately be sought, you might be assured of our readiness to participate in any such consultation."[148] The reply from the mayor's office, dated May 1, 1967, said, "We shall indeed seek to keep you informed of any developments relating to the gymnasium."[149] On a file copy of this correspondence, Smith noted that this promise was not kept. He also wrote to Borough President Sutton, including a copy of the letter sent to Mayor Lindsay. Referring to the closed-door sessions in the borough president's office, he said, "On behalf of the Morningside Renewal Council, I should like to ask what factors determined the choice of community organizations included in these discussions." The letter continues, "We should suppose that either the Council itself or some qualified representative of the Council might have been invited to participate in conversations which certainly bear on the use of the Park, the life of the immediate community, and the underlying matter of general neighborhood renewal." Sutton's reply was courteous, but not responsive to the questions asked.[150]

Even without grassroots opponents to the gymnasium attending, no agreement could be reached at the meetings in the borough president's office. Mayor Lindsay then moved in early May to host a high-level session at Gracie Mansion. In addition to the mayor and the borough

---

148. Letter from Rev. Dwight C. Smith, Chairman of the Morningside [Urban] Renewal Council, to Mayor John V. Lindsay, April 26, 1967.

149. Letter on official letterhead signed by Deputy Mayor Robert W. Sweet to Rev. Dwight C. Smith, May 1, 1967.

150. Letter from Rev. Dwight C. Smith to Borough President Percy Sutton, May 16, 1967. Response from Sutton, June 5, 1967.

president, this meeting included Congressman William F. Ryan, Assemblyman Charles Rangel, City Councilman J. Raymond Jones, Chairman of the City Planning Commission Donald Elliott, City Corporation Counsel J. Lee Rankin, Columbia University President Grayson Kirk, Vice President Lawrence Chamberlain, and Dean David Truman of Columbia College, as well as Frank Hogan, District Attorney of Manhattan and trustee of Columbia University[151] It was certainly an impressive list, a testimony to the importance ascribed to the gymnasium in Morningside Park beyond the confines of the Upper West Side. Like so many summit meetings, this one resulted only in frustration and disappointment. University spokesmen refused to comment, but Assemblyman Rangel told the *Columbia Daily Spectator* that the session had ended in a "deadlock" and predicted that negotiations might continue.[152]

Although Columbia was presumably anxious to ease tense relations with the city government, there was no noticeable change in attitude toward the people in the surrounding neighborhoods—possibly, the university administration was unaware that many members of the community felt that they were not adequately represented by their elected officials. As a result, the local political leaders attending the sessions in the borough president's office were pressing for a larger share of the athletic facility, while a majority of grassroots people had not abandoned the hope of keeping the gym out of the park altogether, and were fighting for this end. The gym represented a chance—perhaps the last chance—to resist Columbia's expansion. Taking over individual buildings like the Bryn Mawr did not have the drawing power necessary to create a citywide "cause célébre," while the multifaceted gymnasium affair gained attention nationwide from various spheres of influence.

The determination to make the gym in the Park the last desperate attempt to stop Columbia's urban "piracy" bound a diverse group of people from the adjacent neighborhoods together, and within the next twelve months captured the attention of Columbia's students and eventually even the faculty. Many students opted for sharing rented local apartments rather than living on campus, seeking a more relaxed lifestyle

---

151. *The New York Times*, May 14, 1967.
152. *Columbia Daily Spectator*, May 15, 1967.

than permitted in the dormitories. This was an increasing trend in the sixties. As tenants on Morningside Heights, the students faced the same problems community residents had been struggling with for years. They found themselves to be members of a diversified neighborhood sympathetic toward them. Where the students found low-rent accommodations from which previous tenants had been evicted by Columbia, tensions might arise, yet many students living off campus joined tenant groups. As their awareness of the "other side" of institutional expansion policies grew, they became active participants in community action. The similarity between the tenants' powerlessness in their struggle and the students' lack of a voice in university decisions contributed to a unique alliance.

At a neighborhood meeting in early 1967, Stanley Salmen declared that Columbia's academic interests had priority over commitments to the community, and that he doubted an agreement could be reached on the issue of expansion.[153] A few days later, the *Columbia Daily Spectator* ran an editorial on Columbia's "attitude of isolation," noting that Salmen's comments reflected "an unusual lack of sensitivity on the part of the University to the rights and interests of Morningside Heights and the neighborhoods' residents," and stated that the university "must change its basic attitude from one of isolation to one of beneficial involvement."[154] This suggested "involvement" was obviously contrary to Columbia's strategy of surrounding its enclave with a cordon sanitaire that included the gymnasium as a major redoubt against the alien territory to the east.

In May of 1967, the three student members of the Ford program's Advisory Council on Urban-Minority Problems resigned. In a letter to President Kirk, signed by Jay Dobkin, Daniel Pope, and Frank Ward, they called the council a "sham" and "window dressing." They charged that all vital policy decisions were made by the five-member executive committee without council involvement. Suspecting that the consultations with community leaders supposedly held by the executive

---

153. Ibid., March 1, 1967.
154. Ibid., March 14, 1967.

committee had been equally vacuous, the students predicted that no good would come from the Ford urban grant.[155]

Since September 1960, Morningside Heights had had its own forthright neighborhood newspaper. Many of the events discussed in the preceding chapters were brought to the attention of the residents of the area by *The Morningsider*. Its editors were two recent Columbia College graduates, Ira Silverman and Bruce Buckley, who followed an independent editorial policy. Initially, the newspaper had the encouragement of Vice President Chamberlain and of Father Ford from the Earl Hall staff. Hoping the venture would nurture community spirit and bridge the isolation between the institutions and neighborhood people, Chamberlain obtained funding for the newspaper venture. However, the financial predicament of *The Morningsider* was a continuing problem that led to its merger with another newspaper in the spring of 1967, and the combination became *The West Side News and Morningsider*. Editorial policy and content changed considerably, and *The Morningsider* later dropped out. It was rumored that the deathblow was struck by Morningside Heights Inc. objecting to articles critical of Columbia's expansion policy.[156] The gap left by *The Morningsider* was felt most acutely in the summer months when the *Columbia Daily Spectator* appeared irregularly, leaving the community less informed of decisions made behind the ivy walls. This meant that people were doubly suspicious of the institutions during the June–September lull, as they tended to use those weeks to take actions they did not want exposed to public scrutiny.

The summer of 1967 brought unwelcome attention as well as embarrassment for Columbia, when the university accepted a deal with inventor Richard Strickland for a cigarette filter. The Strickman filter supposedly reduced the nicotine content of cigarettes without affecting their taste. The university was to receive substantial royalties in return for having its medical school attest to the safety and health benefits of Strickman's invention. However, doubts were voiced by the medical school, as well as by an editorial in the journal *Science*, and President

---

155. Ibid., May 5, 1967. Also, Cox Fact-Finding Commission Transcript, testimony by Joel Ziff, Chairman of the Columbia College Citizenship Council, 3,402.
156. *Columbia Daily Spectator*, April 13 and October 5, 1967.

Kirk was persuaded to put the "Strickman affair" to rest.[157]

Concurrently with the Strickman unease, there were several changes in university administration staff. The office of the provost was eliminated. It had been held by Jacques Barzun, a vocal advocate for a sheltered academic enclave on Morningside Heights, who was named "University Professor," an honorable non-administrative designation. Vice President Chamberlain left the university, and David Truman, who had gained the respect and good feelings of faculty and students as Dean of Columbia College, took his place. Truman was deeply committed to the gymnasium in Morningside Park and remained devoted until the very end of this ill-fated project. These changes were of no particular significance to the community, as they did not auger a change in urban policy. However, there was wishful speculation upon the termination on June 30, 1967, of Stanley Salmen as coordinator of university planning, a position he had held since November 1956.

The closed-door negotiations on the distribution of space in the projected gymnasium building created a curious predicament for members of the Ad Hoc Committee on Morningside Park. Its chair, Amalia Betanzos, as well as some others, all elected political officials, attended the sessions in Borough President Sutton's office and were bound to secrecy regarding these crucial meetings. According to Bob McKay of the West Harlem Community Organization, "the Ad Hoc Committee had painted itself into a corner," with its chairperson dealing with the distribution of space in the building, while the committee, as well as the people it represented, were opposing construction of the gymnasium in the Park altogether. At the same time as the need for greater West Harlem activism grew more urgent,[158] "people power" was stirring nationwide. It gained strength as a movement, promoting the conviction that people, even those living in a ghetto, had a right to shape their environment and to enjoy adequate housing, as well as open space and parks. The gymnasium in Morningside Park emerged as emblematic of years of Columbia's urban policy of racial segregation, and the responsibility for opposing it began to shift decidedly to the African-American community.

---

157. Robert A. McCaughey, *Stand Columbia*, 432–433.

158. Cox Fact-Finding Commission Transcript, testimony by Franz Leichter, 1,236–1,238.

Disappointment with their elected leaders drove the members of the West Harlem Community Organization to initiate, in June 1967, a West Harlem Morningside Park Committee (WHMPC) co-chaired by Bob McKay and Joseph Monroe. Letters were sent to local organizations on both sides of the Park, inviting them to an informal meeting on June 21, to discuss plans for action. Two further sessions followed this initial one, and a demonstration was planned for Saturday, July 29. A letter written by Bob McKay stated that its purpose was to declare publicly that WHMPC was "totally opposing the construction of the gymnasium."[159] Organizers stressed the peaceful nature of this rally, although West Harlem Community Organization Chair Edith Pennamon intimated that "rioting was definitely possible," and that "the kids are very bitter, and very, very angry."[160]

The leaflets promoting the rally listed eight West Harlem organizations as WHMPC members, as well as noting the support of the Ad Hoc Committee for Morningside Park and several of its member organizations. Every one of the leaflets stressed the segregated character of the projected building. One showed an injured, sneaker-shod crow lying on its back with an inscription reading "Stop Columbia University GYM-CROW in Morningside Park—July 29, 1967."[161] The rally and the GYM-CROW leaflets mark a turning point in the anti-gymnasium struggle, significant for African-American participation and for a sense of citizen empowerment in urban planning. Among the activists, Bob McKay and Joe Monroe excelled for their inspiring and perceptive leadership. Calm and patient, Bob McKay articulated the concerns of many, and endeavored to bring diverse groups together. Under the title "Columbia: Gym Crow," Julie Lewin, writing for *The West Side News* of August 3, 1967, reported that a crowd estimated between 80 and 200 people attended the protest rally. A motorcade of five cars cruised through West Harlem. Speakers included district and community leaders Franz Leichter, Frank Baraff, and Amalia Betanzos, as well as George

---

[159.] Letter by Bob McKay, Co-Chairman of the West Harlem Morningside Park Committee, July 4, 1967.

[160.] Cited in *Columbia Daily Spectator*, July 6, 1967.

[161.] CCC Collection, Schomburg Center.

Hickerson (chair of Morningsiders United), James Latimore (president of Riverside Democrats), and Mike Colen (of Democrats for Peace and Politics). A graduate student in political science at Columbia and a member of the Riverside Democrats, Colen had run for Democratic district leader earlier in the year. Hickerson had signed Colen's nomination petition and urged him to support the tenants' struggle against the university's expansion and the opposition to the gymnasium in Morningside Park. Two students who worked on Colen's campaign did much to bring the gymnasium issue to the attention of Columbia students: Michael Golash, a student in the Graduate School of Engineering, and Daniel Pope, who represented the Columbia University Student Council on the Morningside Renewal Council. Hickerson had also conducted discussions with groups of students from the Citizenship Council and CUSC, visiting them almost weekly over a period of several months, urging the students to come together with the community on local issues. According to Hickerson, it took considerable persuasion to convince students that the urban crisis in their neighborhood was related to the national issues that monopolized their attention: the war in Vietnam and the US military draft. The participation of about 50 students in the GYM-CROW rally may have resulted from Hickerson's efforts.[162]

The rally did not, however, draw the wide support from West Harlem that was expected. Julie Lewin commented, "to oppose the gymnasium, a resident apparently needs to know more than a superficial account of the situation."[163] The gymnasium controversy, which had lasted almost eight years, had indeed become increasingly complex. Not everyone was willing to listen to discussions of the issues behind the offer of a basketball court, locker rooms, showers, and even a swimming pool. As a result, the opposition continued to include primarily those who knew something about Morningside urban renewal and the impact of Columbia's expansion policy.

The GYM-CROW rally took place two days after the Board of Estimate met to discuss an amendment to Columbia's lease permitting alteration of the gymnasium plans to include a $465,000 swimming pool

---

162. Author's conversation with George Hickerson, February 21, 1971.
163. *The West Side News*, August 3, 1967.

for the community. This addition would increase the non-Columbia share to 16% of the total facility. The offer of the community swimming pool emerged from the closed-door session in Borough President Sutton's office as an alternative to pressure from political figures, particularly City Councilman J. Raymond Jones, to allot 50 percent of the building for community use or to work out a timetable designed to effect sharing of the entire gymnasium.[164] Members of the West Harlem Morningside Park Committee and the Ad Hoc Committee on Morningside Park protested in front of City Hall, objecting to both the sharing *and* the pool. Columbia, in turn, termed the proposal for an equitable time-sharing distribution "impossible."

Recent developments had provided new support for the opposition's contention that Columbia was building a "Gym Crow" gymnasium on Harlem's turf. Several political figures involved in the negotiations over the space allotment faced the dilemma of whether they should accept a pool to which their constituents were hostile.[165] As Assemblyman Charles Rangel put it, "We were caught in the embarrassing position to be going down to the Board of Estimate to fight the addition of a swimming pool not because we didn't want the community to share more, but because we didn't want to have anything to do with the whole project."[166] At the July 29 rally, Rangel declared emphatically, "There will be a colored pool and a white pool . . . doesn't Columbia realize that to put in a colored pool is insulting rather than accommodating?"[167]

This comment reflects the intense discussions about and accusations of racial prejudice in the location of public swimming pools built under the direction of Robert Moses in New York City.[168] Presumably,

---

[164.] *The New York Times*, July 30, 1967.

[165.] Cox Fact-Finding Commission Transcript, testimony by Basil Paterson, 3,008, 3,647.

[166.] Ibid., testimony by Charles Rangel, 3,047.

[167.] *The New York Times*, July 30, 1967.

[168.] Marta Gutman, "Equipping the Public Realm: Rethinking Robert Moses and Recreation," and Martha Biondi, "Robert Moses, Race, and the Limits of an Activist State," chapters in *Robert Moses and the Modern City: The Transformation of New York*, Hilary Ballon and Kenneth T. Jackson, eds (W.W. Norton & Company), 2007.

Columbia's administration was oblivious to the fact that swimming pools were hot topics, singled out as exemplary of racism and elitism. Adding a pool for African Americans to be accessed by a separate entrance in a building containing a larger pool for primarily white male students only made the whole Gym Crow situation worse, as did locating the community-section entrance at the bottom of the gymnasium. It is remarkable that not only those making decisions for the projected facility but also the project architects were insensitive to the symbolism inherent in the design and placement of the entrance to the building.

Borough President Sutton, who chaired the session at which the lease amendment was presented to the Board of Estimate, sounded anything but enthusiastic in a letter to President Kirk, dated June 26, 1967, writing, "Please be advised that while I do not believe that the addition of the swimming pool alone is a *resolution* of the problem, as a whole, I do understand it to be an improvement over the initial agreement and the maximum concession Columbia finds itself able to make."

Damning testimony before the Cox Fact Finding Commission indicated that the community pool had actually been contained in earlier plans for the gymnasium but then held back as a concession to be used if needed.[169] If this was truly the case, the swimming pool offer was ill timed. It did not appease the political figures, although the Board of Estimate voted its acceptance. Among community people, it was considered insulting that a separatist pool was being offered as a bribe and to divert attention from the basic issues over which they were fighting. Columbia had once more misjudged the mood in the surrounding neighborhoods. Offered as a gift, the pool was unwelcome and suspect—worse than no gift at all.

The West Harlem Morningside Park Committee (WHMPC) achieved cohesion among the diverse factions that made up the opposition to the gymnasium. Its chairmen used personal consultations, casual meetings, and grapevine communications to keep diverse groups focused on a seemingly hopeless cause. These tactics alerted the Hispanic Manhattan Valley neighborhood south of Morningside Park,

---

169. Cox Fact-Finding Commission Transcript, testimony by Joel Ziff, 3,379–3,380.

which previously had not been an active participant, although the park, approachable from Cathedral Parkway (110th Street) was favored by Latino families. This neighborhood had been little affected by Columbia's expansion policy, although development of the athletic field had confiscated a large level area considered its turf. Amalia Betanzos continued to be a strong voice for Hispanic concerns, participating in meetings and rallies. Within the rising interest among students for community issues, Juan Gonzales emerged as an important leader, and he founded the Latin American Student Association at Columbia. (After the events of 1968, Juan Gonzales continued as a major activist in the Young Lords, a group focused on East Harlem and El Barrio.) Thus, fostered by WHMPC, Gym Crow became a common cause that joined West Harlem and the Hispanic neighborhood.

In addition to local interest, WHMPC received moral and occasionally financial support from individuals and civic groups engaged in the preservation of public parks and landmark buildings. The Central Park Conservancy and The Friends of Prospect Park were established conservationist organizations dedicated to preserving parks designed by Frederick Law Olmsted. They were keenly aware that the takeover of parkland by a prestigious educational institution sanctioned by the Parks Department, the city, and the state government was a dangerous precedent for future encroachment on public parks.

Numerous letters of protest were written to city officials and to members of the Columbia administration. Robert Makla, a New York attorney and longtime champion of Olmsted parks, was an active promoter of this letter-writing campaign. For the old-line conservationist associations, it was a new experience to find a Harlem-based organization joining their campaign for city parks, and they welcomed the newcomers with somewhat mystified enthusiasm. However, the establishment camp remained reluctant to become actively involved in a situation that had strong socio-political and racial implications, and hesitated to participate in open protests and rallies. Had the opposition to the gymnasium in the Park arisen in the 1970s, rather than the 1960s, the movement could have counted on vigorous, widespread support, drawing strength from the ecological concerns that swept the country. However, the events that gripped Morningside Heights and its adjacent neighborhoods took place just before "the environment" became a respectable cause.[170] African Americans in West Harlem pioneered these issues with pride, deep conviction, and no fear, foreshadowing activities nationwide.

In a somewhat later letter to *The New York Times*, when excavation for the gymnasium was underway, Richard Edes Harrison, Chairman of the Save Central Park Committee, expressed his opposition to the gymnasium, citing some fundamental statistics that until then had never been made public.[171] These concerned park acreages by boroughs and their relationships to the publics they served. Harrison reported the following: "The National Recreation Association some years ago established a norm which stipulated that a city should have an acre of park for every 160 inhabitants. By dividing the population (1960 census) by the park acreages (1967 City Directory) we arrive at the following figures: People per acre of park: Staten Island, 37; Queens, 108; Bronx, 210; Brooklyn, 440; Manhattan, 650; citywide average, 210." He concludes: "It should be painfully obvious from these basic data that Manhattan has no park space to spare for gymnasiums, police stables, Egyptian temples, or fire alarm stations."[172]

In retrospect, after decades of public emphasis on climate and ecological concerns, one marvels at the disparaging remarks made by university officials about the "bird and bough fanatics," the "greenswarders," or as Columbia Trustee McGuire called them, "that group who didn't believe in having buildings in public parks," as if they were hopeless romantics incapable of accepting the realities of modern times.[173] Columbia's contempt for environmental and public health concerns in the Gym Crow issue paralleled its cavalier attitude toward people's lungs when considering endorsement of the Strickman cigarette filter for financial gain.[174]

---

170. Leo Marx, "American Institutions and Ecological Ideals," *Science*, vol.170, no. 3961, November 27, 1970.

171. *The New York Observer*, September 26, 1988. Richard Edes Harrison was an internationally known cartographer, described in his obituary as "the master of American cartographers," and the author of several books on his subject.

172. *The New York Times*, March 12, 1968.

173. Cox Fact-Finding Commission Transcript, testimony by Harold McGuire, 448.

174. See Note 157.

Not long after the July 29, 1967, demonstration, Robert C. Weinberg, critic-at-large for architecture and planning at New York Public Radio's WNYC, devoted a critique to "Columbia's Gymnasium in Morningside Park," one of several commentaries he gave on the subject. An architect-planner with a degree from Harvard's Graduate School of Design, Weinberg also lectured at Columbia. He had long been critical of the planning policies and architectural taste of the institutions on Morningside Heights, and he had opposed the gymnasium in the Park since it was first announced. Now he voiced his support for the efforts of WHMPC and urged the Harlem community to "insist that the University not be allowed to build *at all* in Morningside Park. . . . It would be unfortunate," he said, "if the community agreed to accept more space in Columbia's building as a condition for dropping their opposition to the entire scheme. This would only be a short range, temporary solution leaving unresolved the larger problem of whether a private institution should be given any part of our limited, city-owned park land for its own purposes."[175] Weinberg's philosophy was shared by the grassroots, although hardly by their elected officials.

Upon the recommendation of Manhattan Borough President Sutton, a meeting was arranged by President Grayson Kirk in Low Library with "several of the University's neighbors regarding the proposed gymnasium in Morningside Park."[176] As far as Columbia was concerned, the gymnasium issue was settled once and for all at that September 20, 1967, meeting, when President Kirk and Vice President Truman met with about a dozen people from the communities on either side of the Park to present Columbia's position regarding the gymnasium. There was no give-and-take during the two-hour session in which the additional swimming pool was set before those attending as a fait accompli.

Neither deceived nor assuaged by the gesture, the same group of concerned community people, their ranks swelled by others, attended on the next day the Board of Estimate hearing on Columbia's request for an extension of the groundbreaking deadline from November 30,

---

[175.] Robert C. Weinberg on the air at WNYC, Aug. 22, 1967.

[176.] Letter from Grayson Kirk, President of Columbia University to Bob McKay, Co-Chairman, West Harlem Morningside Park Committee, September 14, 1967.

1967, to February 28, 1968, and for approval of the amended plans for the building to accommodate the addition of the community swimming pool. Individuals from the opposition took the occasion to precipitate a discussion of the primary issue of a private athletic facility being built on public parkland. Columbia's representatives took pains to keep the meeting focused only on the addition of the pool, considering all other matters settled.

Eloquent and passionate voices of opposition to the gymnasium were heard first. William Stanley (vice president of the Metropolitan Council on Housing, executive director of the Uptown Tenants Council, and a member of several Harlem organizations) emphasized the critical lack of parkland in Harlem. Wilhelmina B. Lewis (member of the Morningside Renewal Council board of directors and of the West 112th Street Block Association) declared solemnly, "the spiritual enrichment which parks provide cannot be measured in dollars and cents . . . and these intangible values of life, we shall not surrender without a fight." Fears that the gymnasium would divide the communities east and west of Morningside Park by forming a monumental physical barrier between them were expressed by Bob McKay as co-chair of WHMPC and vice chair of Morningsiders United. As Columbia was not in the philanthropic business, he considered its suggestion that the gymnasium was for the benefit of the community to be an insult to their intelligence. Joseph Monroe (the other WHMPC co-chair) called attention to the fact that the community was not even getting a regulation-size gym.

Speaking for the surrounding neighborhoods' Democratic district leaders, Franz Leichter recommended that the Board of Estimate cancel Columbia's contract rather than approve the amendment under debate, which would merely increase the community's share of the proposed building from 12 percent to 17 percent. Commenting on Harlem's rejection of the gymnasium, State Assemblyman Rangel said, "Being poor people doesn't necessarily mean that they are people without pride." Mike Colen of Morningside Independent Democrats predicted that the gymnasium would be a continuing source of antagonism.

These arguments were countered by Columbia University Counsel and spokesman John Wheeler, who stressed the impeccable legality of it all. As he saw it, the opposition had centered on the lack of a swimming pool for the community, and the whole session was on the granting of this wish. He threatened that Columbia would withdraw the offer of the pool if the amendment to the lease was not granted that day. The pool, as noted above, was now being used as bait. The shrewdness and tactical skill displayed by the university on this occasion showed some insight into the sentiments that the opposition had stirred up in the city government. Stressing the benefits for children, which, considered out of context, would obviously gain everybody's approval, Bernard M. Weinberg of Adult-Youth Association Inc., which was sponsored by Morningside Heights Inc., declared, "There is certainly no youth worker who would not endorse the addition of this swimming pool to the community gymnasium, and children will echo the endorsement for all the years to come." The Executive Director of Morningside Heights Inc., Edward C. Solomon, chose to speak as a private citizen and resident of Morningside Heights, because his organization was not taking an official position on the matter. "It is my opinion," said Mr. Solomon," based on years of close observation, that there is strong support among local residents, youth workers, parents and children for the gymnasium."

There were also people from Harlem who spoke in favor of the projected facility, and to whom, in the words of Lucretia Lamb of Citizens Care Committee, the only thing that mattered in the controversy was "recreation for children and the pool." She listed several organizations in agreement with her view, and termed the pool a "small goody," but "a beginning." James Young, Director of Community Activities for Columbia's athletic field, talked about the benefits of his program for the youth of the area, which would soon be expanded in the planned gymnasium.[177]

*The New York Times* of September 26, 1967, reported that on September 25, "a reluctant Board of Estimate voted unanimously" to permit Columbia University to go ahead with plans to build the gymnasium in Morningside Park. The curious wording reflects the confusion and ambiguity hanging over the decision. According to the *Times*, some

---

[177.] Board of Estimate Record of the discussion on Calendar #69, September 21, 1967.

board members, among them Borough President Sutton, were less than pleased over the amount of sharing that had been worked out. Mayor Lindsay called it "not ideal," but added that Columbia was "making every effort to have good relations with the communities."

Actually, the Board of Estimate did not adopt a resolution on the addition of the swimming pool until October 25. On that occasion, a so-called "second amendment" to the lease was passed that allowed for changes in the "final plans" to provide greater sharing of the facilities and the inclusion of the community pool. At the same time, a "third amendment" to the lease was passed that extended the groundbreaking deadline to "on or before February 28, 1968." It should be remembered that the "first amendment," adopted on April 20, 1967, had extended the groundbreaking deadline from July 30, 1967, to November 30 of that year.

There was much bitterness that the city had disregarded grassroots sentiment by continuing to support Columbia's plan to build the gymnasium, quibbling over percentages as if it were a matter of raising transit fares when there were fundamental principles at stake. These frustrations were conveyed to Mayor Lindsay by Morningside Urban Renewal Council Chairman Dwight Smith in a frank letter written after a council meeting in late November. The great majority of the members (more than forty) present at the meeting had voted to reiterate their "emphatic opposition to this invasion of public park space for a facility basically intended to serve the limited clientele of a private institution." The letter continued: "It is a matter of great disappointment to most of the member groups in our Renewal Council that you appear to have acquiesced in agreeing to Columbia's unilateral decision about this area without due regard to the views of those affected by them. Knowing that so large an institution has many ways of exerting pressure, we had hoped that our public officials could be counted upon to act as champions of the citizens who have no such power apparatus. . . . Putting the matter succinctly, the Morningside Renewal Council feels that the public interest in this instance has been betrayed by our public officials."[178] Copies of this letter

---

178. Letter from Dwight C. Smith, Chairman of the Morningside Renewal Council, to Mayor John V. Lindsay, November 16, 1967.

were sent to the borough president, the City Planning Commission, and the state senator and assemblyman for the Morningside area—all of whom were implicated in the decision. A slightly different version of Smith's letter appeared in *The New York Times*.[179]

Dampening Mayor Lindsay's hope that the university would make greater efforts to improve relations with its neighbors, Columbia chose this time to install imposing iron gates at both ends of "College Walk." This is the block of 116th Street between Amsterdam Avenue and Broadway ceded to Columbia on the occasion of the university's bicentennial celebration in 1954. Pains were taken to explain that these gates were designed seventy years earlier, part of the original McKim, Mead, and White architectural plans, though the 1890 design called for ornamental "pylons" rather than metal gates capable of closing off the 116th Street block. A functioning city street cannot, in fact, legally be closed off by private gates. *The Columbia Newsletter* of September 1967 assures the public that "the new gates will not be fully closed at any time, except for those occasions as Commencements and the Spring Carnival. They will allow continued free access by the Columbia community and the public to and through the Campus at all hours." Historically, separation of black and white Americans has been effected through land-use policies and definition of public and private spaces, and Columbia's claim that the purposes of its new gates were primarily for aesthetics and for special-occasion use was hardly convincing.

By now, an image of "Fortress Columbia" was firmly lodged in the minds of its neighbors. Every new building added to the university complex during the previous decade had contributed to surrounding it with an almost impenetrable enclosure, converting an open urban campus into an academic enclave. The architecture had isolated its natural site and shaped a racially segregated place. The Seeley-Mudd engineering building, rising like a bulwark at the corner of 120th Street and Amsterdam Avenue, sealed off the campus on the northeast, while Ferris Booth Hall completed the enclosure at the southwest corner. A wide bridge spanned and darkened an entire block of Amsterdam Avenue, and

---

179. *The New York Times*, November 27, 1967.

117th Street had been pre-empted between Amsterdam Avenue and Morningside Drive. The new gates at the entrances of Campus Walk, however "artistic" their ironwork, seemed to be just one more instance of Columbia's efforts to isolate itself from its urban setting. Some saw in them a fancier version of the gates previously installed at the entrances to Morningside Park. Persistent complaints on behalf of its employees from St. Luke's Hospital about the latter gates blocking access to subway stops west of the Park finally resulted in the gates being left unlooked beginning in the fall of 1967.

Despite the physical and psychological barriers Columbia was erecting, neighbors made their presence felt on campus on several occasions before the end of 1967. On November 11, the West Harlem Morningside Park Committee held a rally at the 116th Street and Broadway gate. A group of school children chanted, "We want the Park, keep Columbia out!" About fifty participants and at least twice as many onlookers watched the burning in effigy of Columbia Trustee Frank S. Hogan. Bob McKay explained that Trustee Hogan had been chosen rather than Trustee McGuire because of all the trustees, as district attorney, Hogan was the one closest to the city government, which had recently given Columbia permission to proceed with the gymnasium plans.

In early November, it was announced that the first $2.7 million of the Ford Foundation grant would be allocated to ten projects, eight to be administered by existing departments of the university, and two by new entities to be established, a Center on Urban-Minority Affairs and a Development Division.[180] Eight of the projects were dedicated to improving educational, legal, cultural, and living conditions in the Harlem community. The largest of them funded Columbia's Teachers College to develop a program of involvement in Harlem public schools. The Student Citizenship Council objected to the choice of projects because the money was channeled to the university for the benefit of faculty and students rather than for the community. Although neighborhood leaders had been consulted, it was clear that their suggestions had no influence on the final decisions made by the university's urban-grant

---

180. *Columbia Daily Spectator*, October 30,1967.

committee. This prompted the Citizenship Council to send out more than 400 invitations to community groups and leaders in Harlem to attend a meeting at Columbia on November 9 to discuss the Ford Urban Minority Affairs program. In the words of Jay Dobkin, Columbia 1968, Chair of the Citizenship Council, the meeting was intended to give members of the community "the opportunity to propose programs and to air grievances against Columbia and the Ford Foundation." Dobkin added, "We will actively support the decisions and plans of action which the community devises, and organize student support . . . . We will present information and chair the meeting but we will seek no role in the policy and decision making procedures."[181] Over 200 attended, representing a cross-section of leaders from Harlem organizations, including NAACP, CORE, Haryou-Act, Morningside Tenants Associations, Mau-Maus, and the East Harlem Community Federation, among others. Jesse Gray, representing the Community Council of Harlem summed up the general impression regarding Columbia's handling of the Ford Foundation grant and its "clinical" attitude toward the neighborhoods east and south of Morningside Park: "We're tired of being studied!" Every one of the speakers stressed Harlem's ability to articulate its own needs.[182]

Neither the Ford Foundation nor Columbia sent representatives to the meeting. When it was over, a caucus passed a resolution disapproving the $2.7 million allocation for the programs selected without citizen participation. It also passed another resolution calling for a demonstration on campus by Harlem groups. University officials quickly responded by contacting Harlem community leaders to reassure them that they would be consulted. Perhaps as a result of this move, the number attending the rally in front of Low Library's locked doors was not impressive. Demonstrators from Harlem were joined by a contingent from Morningside Heights and some students, but the turnout was small. Furthermore, although originally called to protest the Ford Foundation allocations, the demonstration concerned itself mainly with Gym Crow.

The *Columbia Daily Spectator* report on this event contains, however, the first mention of a new participating constituency: "Students for a

---

181. Ibid., November 9, 1967.
182. Ibid., November 13, 1967.

Democratic Society has added its voice, declaring that it respected the right of Harlem residents to choose their own future and that Harlem is not Columbia's 'plantation'."[183] An increasingly broad spectrum of student and community interests came together at this time over issues of common concern. Though some of these involvements were exploratory and cautious, overall they were a portent of things to come.

Another new and more radical element entered the scene when H. Rap Brown, then chairman of the Student Nonviolent Coordinating Committee (SNCC, later renamed Student National Coordinating Committee) spoke on the evening of the same day, November 15, to a crowd estimated at 1,400 in McMillan Theater on the Columbia campus. Brown had come at the invitation of an "ad hoc" committee of African-American students. He defined the role of white students in the blacks' struggle in America not as working within the black community, but rather in organizing among whites. He criticized American universities as "propaganda mechanisms for white nationalism" that were "producing only job-fillers," and he urged Columbia's black students "to apply their education to changing the world and making it better."[184] On this occasion, he made no reference to the university's relationship to the Harlem community or specifically to the gymnasium controversy. A month later, however, Brown attended a meeting in Harlem called by the West Harlem Morningside Park Committee to discuss the nature of further action toward halting ground breaking for the gymnasium, now scheduled for early 1968. The meeting was chaired by Joseph Monroe, and the speakers included Basil Paterson, Edith Pennamon, Charles Rangel, and Bob McKay. Brown spoke of the need for black people to control their own land and their own community, and both applause and laughter erupted following his call to action: "If they build the first story, blow it up. If they sneak back at night and build three stories, burn it down. And if they get nine stories built, it's yours. Take it over, and maybe we'll let them in on weekends."[185]

---

183. Ibid., November 16, 1967.
184. Ibid., November 16, 1967.
185. Ibid., December 15, 1967.

The same issue of the *Columbia Daily Spectator* that reported H. Rap Brown's call to action also featured a staff editorial under the title, "Burn, Gym, Burn?" It advocated a tough approach toward those opposing the gymnasium in Morningside Park, and was quite unconcerned about any inherent injustice and danger in the situation. With confidence and naiveté, it declared that "the gym is not being built in Jericho, and its walls cannot be shouted down. Construction of the gym is, at this point, a *fait accompli,* and the community should realize this. Any protest they launch is bound to backfire. Columbia is certainly going to reject any future demands which the community leaders raise if they block construction of the gym. The city will certainly look with disfavor upon a protest built on the rhetoric of racism. And such a demonstration could certainly lead to a much wider melee, which the responsible leaders of Morningside and West Harlem certainly do not want."[186] The tone of the editorial was promptly termed "insulting" in a letter written by graduate student Mark D. Naison, who called its contents "dangerously provocative." "In these times," the brief, poignant letter concluded, "no white organization can enter the ghetto with condescension and threats."[187]

Among the numerous letters on the gymnasium controversy that appeared during these weeks in the columns of the *Columbia Daily Spectator*, there was one that criticized the planned athletic facility from an unexpected angle, and placed the entire project in a new perspective. The *Columbia Daily Spectator* headlined the letter "'Jock' opposes Gym." The writer, James R. Quarttrochi, was expressing the concern of Columbia College athletes about the adequacy of the projected gym's facilities. "As a 'jock'," he wrote, " I would like to take a stand against the new gymnasium on the basis of its already obsolete facilities, before construction has even begun." He compared the proposed gymnasium to other Ivy League facilities. Considering the proposed expansion of the Columbia College student body to 4,200, the seating capacity of 3,200 in the proposed gym would not even accommodate the students, and certainly not their guests. Actually, this projected increase of the college from 2,800 to the size mentioned by Quarttrochi, although still

---

186. Ibid., December 15, 1967.
187. Ibid., December 19,1967.

theoretically on the books in 1967, had already been quietly shelved. His other points, however, were valid, for instance, the absence of an indoor track. "The failings of the new gym go on and on," he wrote. "The important fact to remember is that those who have been led to believe that the new gym will solve Columbia's athletic problems are being fooled by the administration." He ended with a plea: "On behalf of all the students I ask, I beg that the administration not short-change us once again!"[188]

Although it later became apparent that there were shortcomings in the physical plans for the gymnasium and that the coaches were not entirely happy with what they would get, it was remarkable to find these sentiments revealed to the public by a Columbia College athlete, one of the select group of students who were supposedly to be best served by the whole venture. To what extent the university administration and the gym's promoters really knew what its physical properties were, despite the long haggling over space allocations, has never been clear. It would seem from Trustee McGuire's testimony to the Cox Fact Finding Commission that he, at least, assumed Columbia College athletes to be wholeheartedly behind the project that was designed, in part, to appeal to alumni pride. Yet the "jocks," like the community people, were looking the gift horse in the mouth.

---

188. Ibid., November 28, 1967.

# 8

## Up Against the Fence
### February 1968

Despite nearly a decade of news reports about the planned construction of the gymnasium in Morningside Park, the arrival of a work crew to install a fence around the site brought surprise and disbelief. But it was true, and the eight-foot cyclone fence had a finality that made hearts sink.

In the first week of February 1968, the rolls of fencing were unloaded, and workers began to establish it around the 2.1 acres, following the irregularities of the meadow's edge and heading down the hill toward Morningside Avenue. For two blocks along Morningside Drive, the concrete benches were demolished, and half of the sidewalk was cut off by the fence. Two entrances to the Park were eliminated, including the one at grade level serving the path at 114th Street used by those working at St. Luke's Hospital. The trees and rocks and the mound that had been the site of the historic blockhouse were now inaccessible behind the fence.

To avoid a confrontation, Columbia gave no advance notice of the actual groundbreaking, and no ceremony was scheduled. On February 15, the *Columbia Daily Spectator* commented: "Protests over the planned gymnasium in Morningside Park have cooled considerably with the cold weather, and may flare only slightly when the actual bull-dozing and earth-moving begins." Bob McKay gloomily agreed with this prediction, commenting "It's not a bread and butter issue," and, referring to the oil-delivery strike that was keeping much of New York, especially Harlem, without heat, he added, "People are more interested in whether they have heat in their apartments."[189]

February 1968, was, indeed, a cruel month! On February 7, three African-American students were shot dead by National Guardsmen in Orangeburg, NC, and 27 others were wounded. Although this tragic event did not have the nationwide impact of the 1970 slayings at Kent State, it affected the mood in Harlem. The African-American students at Columbia reacted with an invitation to H. Rap Brown to speak on campus for a second time. In his speech, he sought support for the victims of the "Orangeburg Massacre" and blamed institutions like Columbia for "miseducation" on the role of blacks in society. Possibly referring to the gymnasium, and similar to his speech in November, he said, "If Columbia doesn't see fit to let enough of Harlem in here, then blow it up and let them start over."[190] Brown and other African-American activists did not participate in the community protests during the next few weeks, very likely because of their preoccupation with the Orangeburg crisis.

The contract for preparation of the gymnasium site had been awarded to the Thomas Crimmins Construction Company, whose president, a Columbia alumnus, was at the time chairman of the Fairfield, CT, section of the university's $200 million fund drive. The actual construction was to be done by the George A. Fuller Company, with completion of the building expected to take two years. Columbia announced at this time that nearly half of the estimated cost of the gymnasium—now set at $11.6 million—had been raised, and that the remainder would come out of the general $200 million fund.[191]

Before the eyes of incredulous passersby, Crimmins bulldozers and a crew armed with power saws arrived on February 19 to begin waging war against nature in Morningside Park. The whine of power saws, the hacking of axes, and the moaning crashes of the big trees as they fell

---

189. *Columbia Daily Spectator*, February 15, 1968.
190. Ibid., February 16, 1968.
191. *Columbia Chronicle*, January/February 1968.

brought many to the fence to witness the destruction. Cars stopped and passengers jumped out to see what was happening. One could observe people angrily shaking the fence, and excitedly questioning the impassive foreman.

It takes a man with a power saw only minutes to cut down a tree that has grown for fifty years or more. Some of the trees were probably twice that age, having been planted when the Park was laid out. The crew moved fast, and by the end of that first day, a chaotic tangle of trunks covered most of the level area of the former meadow.[192]

Caught somewhat off guard by the unceremonious, swift start of the work, the West Harlem Morningside Park Committee decided to block the crew from entering the site the following morning. At very short notice, anybody who had shown an interest in opposing the gymnasium was contacted personally or by telephone. Suki Ports informed the news media, exaggerating the planned protest beyond her own expectations, in order to entice them to attend.

On February 20, at 8 a.m., about 20 to 30 people gathered at the entrance to the construction site at 113th Street and Morningside Drive. The gate was open, and nobody prevented the group from entering. Members of the West Harlem and Morningside Heights communities greeted each other with wan smiles. A group of students was welcomed with delight and admiration for having sacrificed early morning slumber to join in. Members of the "Expansion Committee" recently organized by Students for a Democratic Society (SDS) had been briefed by Joe Monroe. The mood, however, was subdued. The days when Suki Ports had served Japanese delicacies in Morningside Park seemed remote. As the workers began to arrive, they seemed to be astonished by the presence of the protesters, and particularly the reporters who were milling about with their photographic equipment, trying to decide if it was worth waiting in the cold for something newsworthy to happen.

Just inside the entrance, a bulldozer was parked where it had begun removal of the blockhouse mount the previous day. While its operator was warming up its engine, some of the protesters, including the author,

---

192. The Collinses photographed this destruction daily, and some of their pictures are featured in this narrative.

sat down in front of the bulldozer on the freshly turned earth. (See Figure 15.) Huddled together in the morning chill, they formed a motley group. Newsmen taped interviews with them and scribbled notes. TV cameras were busy taking in the scene in front of the machine as well as recording the screeching saws further down on the site. Sympathetic bystanders exchanged views on the apparent hopelessness of the struggle.

A handful of police were on hand, but kept themselves in the background until they were joined by several squad cars with reinforcements, and it became obvious that there would be arrests unless the group dispersed. In a dramatic gesture, Bob McKay climbed into the raised scoop of the bulldozer, thereby "resisting" arrest. His hooded figure in the scoop became the subject of a memorable photograph that was published in the next morning's *New York Times,* and also appeared in *Time* magazine.[193] (Figure 16 shows this picture of Bob McKay.)

Twelve persons were finally arrested on this occasion and charged with trespassing and disorderly conduct, including community members Bob McKay, Maria Miller, Joseph Monroe, Suki Ports, William Stanley, Marshall García, Justus Poole, and students Michael Colen, Michael Golash, Sara Eisenstein, Art Leaderman, Daniel Pope, and Pam Steinglas. The author, Christiane C. Collins, removed herself before the arrests because she was not yet an American citizen. (Charges against the community members were removed several months later, but the students were cleared shortly after the upheaval on campus.)

News coverage of the sit-in was generally sympathetic in tone. The cause seemed so hopeless that it was not only safe, but almost virtuous, to show support. The television screen brought the destruction of a scenic city park into the living rooms of many who had never heard of the long controversy raging over Gym Crow in Morningside Park. During the following days, sightseers gathered at all hours in front of the tall fence to watch the trees being felled and the paths and benches plowed under by the bulldozers. Gymnasium protesters, which included both community members and students, display their placards in Figure 17, man the barricades in Figure 18, and demonstrate in front of the Columbia President's house in Figure 19. Under the watchful eyes of

---

193. *The New York Times,* February 21, 1968. *Time Magazine,* March 8, 1968.

the police, now guarding the site around the clock after the first early morning sit-in, a sizable section of a public park was being destroyed with speed and efficiency. (See Figure 20.) The sight aroused opposition and anger in many who had previously not been involved but were aware that nature was precious and hard to find in metropolitan New York. The news media, realizing that things of more than local interest were happening, kept their sensors tuned to Morningside Park.

The West Harlem Morningside Park Committee decided to continue some form of public protest every morning at the beginning of the work-day. On many of the following cold winter mornings, a few members of the opposition would gather at Morningside Drive and 114th Street to hand out leaflets and discuss their struggle with passersby. They also argued with the crew, particularly with the African Americans among them. Never previously had the Park seen so much police protection. Police guards were placed at the entrances to the construction site, and the surrounding area was patrolled around the clock.

On the morning after the February 20th sit-in, two more persons were arrested as they blocked the entrance. One was Marshall García, a resident of Morningside Heights and long active in local tenant organizations. The other was James Latimore, chair of the Riverside Democrats, who was campaigning to become the Democratic Party's nominee for Assemblyman of the 69th District, to run against the incumbent, Daniel M. Kelly, who had voted in favor of the gymnasium legislation. This was symptomatic of how politics increasingly affected the grassroots-versus-Columbia controversy.

In this vein, one of the students who had participated in the February 20th sit-in took a leading role in arranging the early morning vigils. Michael Golash had worked on Michael Colen's political campaign the previous summer and had organized the SDS "Expansion Committee." Impatient with the casual methods of the community opposition, Golash persistently urged more rigorous action. He prepared a statement on the controversy entitled "Gym Crow," mimeographed on blue paper. This leaflet, distributed in the neighborhood, in the student dormitories, and at the gymnasium site, issued a call for support of the community protests and discussed three main reasons for opposing the gym. The first two reasons, under the headings "Separate but Unequal" and "Community Gym?" were aimed at the general public. The third, "Unplanned Obsolescence," was meant to attract the attention and support of the students. Discussing the inadequacy of the athletic facilities as planned, it gave as one of the reasons for restricted community space the allocation made for the exclusive use of the NROTC program: "The NROTC will have an armory in the gym, containing classrooms, a library, offices, and naval science equipment. Despite the controversy in recent years over the NROTC the administration has seen fit to leave these plans, conceived in 1963, unchanged." The reference was to the fact that the NROTC program at Columbia University had been under attack for some time from the students and faculty of Columbia College. Bitter protests had been mounted against NROTC and military recruitment on campus. The Columbia College faculty had taken a fairly strong stand against both the draft and NROTC, and the days of the latter seemed to be numbered.

On February 28, the students organized a protest rally for noon at the Sundial, the traditional navel of the Columbia campus. Sponsored by the Citizenship Council, SDS, and the Graduate Faculties Student Council, and aimed at the students, all community groups who opposed the gym were invited. It seemed unlikely that the students would become aroused over the gymnasium issue at a time when the war in Vietnam and the draft posed immediate threats to their lives and were draining everybody's emotional energy. However, the noon rally drew a crowd of over 250, primarily composed of students but including some faculty members and community people. After listening to the speakers, about 150 demonstrators marched to the gym site, chanting "The Park for the People" and "Gym Crow Must Go." Many elaborate placards had been prepared in advance, proclaiming the site to be "Columbia's Defoliation Zone," in reference to tactics being used in Vietnam, and castigating the project as "Unequal in the Park," a takeoff on a public relations pamphlet recently put out by Columbia bearing the slogan "Partners in the Park."

A lady from the Audubon Society, indignant for more reasons than the loss of one of the only places within miles that had attracted red cardinals, was attending her very first protest rally. With great dignity, she carried a mildly worded placard embellished with birds and flowers. She was greeted cheerfully by a bearded young man who identified himself as a member of the Sierra Club—an indication of the crisis drawing diverse factions together. At one point, a contingent of City College students joined the Columbia students, and the group moved to the walled garden behind President Kirk's residence at Morningside Drive and 116th Street. About forty of them performed a brief dance among the beds of greenery, watched aghast by the maid and butler from the upstairs window. The well-tended surroundings of the president's house provided a sharp contrast to the devastation in Morningside Park just two blocks away.

At the construction site, where the tree removal phase was over and actual excavation had begun, several police cars were waiting, and barricades had been positioned a few feet away from the chain-link fence on the sidewalk along Morningside Drive. The marchers were required to stay behind these barricades and out of the way of the traffic, which consisted almost entirely of large trucks filled with rocks and earth from the excavation. Loaded trucks exiting the gates moved north, and the empties returned south by the same route.

The first arrest came when Peter Behr, a Columbia College student, attempted to block an empty truck from reentering the gates, which were kept closed except for truck passage. There was much shoving and pushing, and the student was arrested and charged with felonious assault for having jumped on the back of a policeman. A person of slender build, Behr later insisted that he was jostled by a moving truck and fell at the feet of the policeman. Other arrests were made when some of the students succeeded in loosening poles supporting the cyclone fence.

Rev. A. Kendall Smith of Beulah Baptist Church at 125 West 130th Street in Harlem had been invited by Michael Golash to speak at the rally on campus. Impatient with the indecisive way the protest was going once the marchers had reached the gym site, Smith asked bystanders if there was an access to the construction area other than through the guarded gates. He was guided down the hill to an out-of-sight gap under the fence. Wearing his clerical garb, he crawled under the fence "as a symbolic gesture to dramatize the fact that [the site] was still a public park."[194] Accompanied by a couple of students, he sprinted up the hill and sat down in what had been the meadow. This surprise move added a new wrinkle to the demonstration, which by now had lasted more than two hours. The reverend, looking a bit dusty, "resisted" arrest as he was pushed into a paddy wagon (Figure 21.) He was charged with criminal trespassing—apparently for having entered a public park. In all, there were thirteen arrests that day, all students except Smith, which added to campus interest in the gymnasium controversy.

Although the excitement drew observers from nearby St. Luke's Hospital to its windows and balconies and spectators crowded the sidewalks, *The New York Times* devoted only a small notice to the event, describing it as a rowdy student rally.[195] Senator Paterson and Assemblyman Rangel offered to defend all those who had been arrested—a total of 27, counting both community people and students. Senator Paterson was of the opinion that, even at this late date, an increase in the opposition as well as a more intensive letter writing campaign might still persuade the city government to send a home rule message regarding the anti-gymnasium bills still pending in the State legislature.[196]

The West Harlem Morningside Park Committee was pursuing a strategy of continuous protests, designed to capture the attention of the news media, politicians, students, and potential sympathizers among the faculty. One of these was planned to take place on campus only a few days after the students' rally at the gym site. It was aimed to coincide with a gathering of local and national political figures for the eighth annual West Side Community Conference that was sponsored by Congressman William F. Ryan and the Reform Democratic Clubs of Manhattan's West Side and scheduled to take place at Columbia University's Ferris Booth Hall on Saturday, March 2, 1968. The objective of these conferences, which were open to the general public, was to present important issues to the community and provide opportunity

---

[194.] Cox Fact-Finding Commission Transcript, testimony by Rev. A. Kendall Smith, p. 2,668.

[195.] *The New York Times*, February 29, 1968.

[196.] *The New York Times*, March 3, 1968. *Columbia Daily Spectator*, March 4, 1968.

for discussion. The 1968 theme was, ironically and appropriately, "The Urban Struggle for Power." Many well-known personalities were listed for the various panels, including Roger Wilkins, Director of the Community Relations Service of the US Department of Justice, and Sargent Shriver, Director of the US Office of Economic Opportunity, was to be the speaker at the plenary session in the early afternoon. Just as Congressman Ryan was introducing Shriver, a group of protesters that included students, community people, and representatives from Harlem organizations entered the plenary session and stood along the sides of the auditorium, shouting questions at the rostrum. Congressman Ryan soon gave up, and the plenary session was closed down.[197] By the time the demonstrators reached the stage, the microphones had been turned off, and their speeches against the gymnasium received little attention from the dwindling audience. However, the boldness of the disruption and the presence of a number of representatives from the more militant black organizations in Harlem "sowed seeds of concern at Columbia University," as *The New York Times* put it.[198]

The small, but noisy and united, group that had broken up the conference was a sign that while discontent and frustration were escalating among students over the war in Vietnam, the university's involvement with the "war machine," and the problems of poverty and race, the community's anger over Columbia's attitude toward the urban neighborhoods was also mounting. Within this climate, Gym Crow emerged as the catalyst that brought everything together, providing a liaison between town and gown protests.

As noted, some university officials attempted to improve Columbia's image, but years of bungled community relations proved insurmountable. At this point, Columbia was circulating the "Partners in the Park" pamphlet on campus, in Harlem, on Morningside Heights, and to alumni. It dwelled on the program for organized teams conducted on the athletic field, giving the impression that Harlem was inhabited only

---

[197.] *The New York Times*, March 3, 1968. *Columbia Daily Spectator*, March 4, 1968.
[198.] Ibid.

by young males between 10 and 18, all members of athletic teams—no women or girls, elderly, or children.

"Partners in the Park" suggested that the gymnasium controversy and the protests were entirely a "Harlem" issue. However, on March 1, 1968, *The New York Times* printed a letter to the editor that emphasized the citywide, indeed nationwide, implications of the dispute. The letter was written by Victor Crichton, a 1953 graduate of Columbia College, who grew up in Harlem in the vicinity of Morningside Park. "I wish to state my unalterable opposition to the plan under which the City of New York is giving a large segment of Morningside Park to Columbia University for the construction of a gymnasium. I object on the basis of repeated encroachments upon park-land." Crichton lists many recent instances of encroachment on the city parks as a pattern of giving away public land, thus casting the responsibility for the Columbia gymnasium equally on the city government and the administration of his alma mater.

On March 18, the *Columbia Daily Spectator* ran a quarter-page advertisement, paid for by Crichton, that began: "Help! You can help stop construction of the gymnasium in Morningside Park! It is not too late! Write today (or telegraph) to . . ." followed by a list of city government officials. Under Crichton's auspices, a petition was circulated among Columbia students and faculty in order to stimulate discussion of the issue. Encouraged by the response to his letter in *The New York Times* and to the advertisement in the *Columbia Daily Spectator*, Crichton contacted several lawyers, among them Irving Thau, with the purpose of preparing a request for a temporary injunction—to be followed by a permanent injunction—to prevent Columbia from proceeding with construction of the gymnasium in Morningside Park. "Our attack will be, primarily, upon the lease and the insufficiency of consideration (low annual rent), though other parts of the agreement may also be attacked," Crichton explained in a letter circulated to those who had shown an interest in supporting his legal maneuver.

Although Crichton did participate in several community demonstrations, he was convinced that only legal action could accomplish anything permanently. He and Irving Thau were interested in establishing a test case that would prevent future park encroachment in New York City, and even across the nation. This strategy was warmly received by the Central Park Conservancy and the Friends of Prospect Park, who were fighting an almost continuous battle against the park encroachments advanced in the interest of essentially worthy causes.

# 9

## WINDS OF CHANGE
### March 1968

While Victor Crichton and Irving Thau were plotting legal steps, the campus newspapers printed their reactions to the recent protests. On March 6, editorials in the *Columbia Daily Spectator*, published by the students of Columbia College, and in the *Columbia Owl*, published by the students of the School of General Studies, took opposing stands on the issue of the gymnasium in Morningside Park. Under the title "Enough is Enough," the *Spectator* sided with the university's administration: "The protesters should concede. It would be nice to have larger community facilities, but that is not feasible on the park site." It continues, "and certainly, the modern community section, with its own swimming pool, and its organized recreation programs, will be preferable to 2.1 acres of debris-strewn rock."

Taking a contrary view, the *Owl's* editorial reflected the urban awareness of the students of the School of General Studies, who, incidentally, would not be eligible to use the planned gymnasium, although they may not have known this. Probably not coincidental was the fact that the dean of the School of General Studies, Clarence C. Walton, who was serving as interim director of the Urban-Minority Affairs Program, was personally strongly opposed to the gymnasium project. The faculty of the School of General Studies was the first in the university to institute a program of urban studies, and, in addition, Dean Walton had been prodding his faculty for several years to develop meaningful minority curricula. Reflecting this orientation, the editorial read in part: "We do not deny that the University needs a new gym. What we do question, however, is the immediacy of the need and the thinking that led the University to invade Morningside Park. . . . With concrete and brick, the University will convincingly demonstrate, once again, the unmitigated power this particular segment of the establishment has over the people of Harlem." To ameliorate what they considered the crisis situation in community relations, the editors of the *Owl* made "two immediate proposals":

> The first would be to institute a fact-finding committee composed of faculty, administration and community members to fully explore all possible ramifications of proposed building on Morningside Heights. The results of such fact finding would be submitted to an impartial body outside the University for final arbitration. Perhaps the courts or a city agency could fulfill such a function.
> Secondly, the University should make public the mechanisms with which it makes decisions on building plans, either through the press or by holding public meetings. Above all, the University must come to realize that it is not a private corporation that can arrogantly dismiss the needs of those that stand in the way of its precious plans. Only when Columbia begins to reconcile its educational needs with the urban environment it lives in, can it justify all its ambitious plans for the future.

The editors of the *Owl* were not alone in expressing genuine and deep concern about Columbia's urban policies, which were quite obviously leading to a crisis. Individual students and student organizations undertook efforts to "save" their university. Daniel Pellegrom, then outgoing president of the Columbia Student Council, described to the Cox

Fact Finding Commission the students' interest in better neighborhood relations. He spoke passionately of "the feeling by students that they were what may be called the conscience of the university," and said that they "believed themselves to be a part of the university that was not necessarily committed to existing university policies and could therefore speak both to the university administration and to other elements of the community and thus aid in development of solutions to the conflicts that raged."[199] Much of the mood and action on campus during the weeks following the protests was interpreted, particularly by the press, as a direct attack upon the university, while, on the contrary, many students felt that they were trying to purify their cherished alma mater.

One of several student attempts to steer the administration away from its disastrous course came from Jay Dobkin (Columbia 1968), chairman of the Citizenship Council. At a meeting with Vice President Truman, Acting Dean of the College Henry S. Coleman, and other members of the administration, he presented a student plan for shared student/community use of the entire gymnasium under the direction of the Parks Department and with a community committee in charge of space allocation and time schedules. Dobkin was apparently unaware that the possibility of joint usage of the building had been discussed at some length at the sessions in Borough President Sutton's office during the previous summer and had been labeled "impossible" by university spokesmen. Though members of the administration assured Dobkin that they would examine the plan, no action was ever taken on it.[200]

In the meantime, work on the gymnasium site had progressed from removal of trees and soil to blasting away of the so-called "ugly rocks." The detonations could be heard all over the neighborhoods, a reminder that time to salvage the Park was running out. Note here that one unfortunate consequence of the blasting was that the vibrations caused cracks and fissures in the famous dome and vaults of the Cathedral of St. John the Divine next to the ridge.

---

[199.] Cox Fact-Finding Commission Transcript, testimony by Daniel Pellegrom, 66.

[200.] *Columbia Daily Spectator*, March 12, 1968.

The West Harlem Morningside Park Committee, led by Bob McKay and Joe Monroe, continued to organize protests, and there was always a police presence. Some of the protest actions that took place in daytime hours on business days drew only the few individuals who could spare time away from their jobs and families. One of the smallest rallies, set for 1:00 p.m. on a Wednesday afternoon, drew only about a dozen people to the corner of 116th Street and Morningside Avenue, which offered a full view of the hillside that was being blasted away. The limited turnout and the inroads of the excavation created a somber mood among those marching in a circle carrying placards condemning the gymnasium; the outlook for the liberation of the gymnasium site in Morningside Park looked exceedingly dismal at this point.

When it was apparent that there would be no crowd at this rally, the assigned policemen left except for a Sergeant Sullivan. A fence separated Harlem, the city at large, and the protesters from the former playground in the Park, which was being used by the construction company to store equipment. Suddenly, a crew armed with power saws arrived and began to cut down the remaining trees on the playground—orders had been given to prepare the area for the parking of trucks. Anger brought tears to the eyes of some observing this needless destruction of the city's natural resources, and Sergeant Sullivan was overheard mumbling, his face flushed, "Don't like this any more than you do!"

Some days after the obliteration of the playground, a small cardboard sign was posted on a distant, remaining tree, announcing that a new playground would be constructed on that spot at Columbia's expense. A letter from President Kirk to the Parks Commissioner, dated January 30, 1968, affirms the university's willingness to construct a playground.[201] The attached Eggers & Higgins plan for the playground offers a rigid geometric shape unrelated to the natural surroundings and calls for paving over a substantial area of the Park. Again, there was no consultation with the families who might use the facility. The unimaginative plan, which constituted further fragmentation of the Park, was apparently accepted by the Parks Department "as is."

---

[201.] Cox Commission Transcript, exhibit.

Toward the end of March, it seemed that only a miracle or magic could prevent construction of the gymnasium. A bit of magic was actually tried on the evening of Wednesday, March 20, in the form of a torchlight protest march. At dusk, the marchers, including a contingent from Morningside Heights, began gathering at the headquarters of the West Harlem Community Organization. Joe Monroe, Bob McKay, and others handed out flashlights and homemade torches. The predominantly African-American group of about 150 torchbearers, including several children, entered Morningside Park at 114th Street in West Harlem and proceeded along the winding paths. In the darkness, the lights flickering between the trees lit up excited faces. A policeman guarding the construction site halted their progress up the hill and informed the leaders that it was illegal to carry an open flame in a public park because of fire hazard. There was suppressed laughter among those suspected of endangering the Park, because it was, after all, their intention to *prevent* the destruction of the Park. Senator Paterson and Assemblyman Rangel assured the policeman that great care would be taken in handling the torches, and that they were merely passing through on their way to the Heights. Without further objection, the march proceeded to Morningside Drive, passing President Kirk's villa and the Men's Faculty Club, where an official dinner was in progress and guests could be seen at the windows, glasses in hand, observing the procession below.

With an almost ritualistic intonation, the marchers chanted "Gym Crow must go!" as they crossed the campus to Riverside Drive and continued to the apartment building where Vice President Truman lived. Here, the protesters interrupted their march to form a tight circle in front of the building's entrance as if casting a spell on the university vice president.

When the torchbearers first crossed the campus, they barely attracted the students' attention. On their return, however, many spectators lined Campus Walk to watch what must have seemed like a ritual to exorcise evil spirits from the university. Several students joined the group for the return walk through Morningside Park to the West Harlem Community Organization to confer with the participants. On the return, the children were tired from the long walk, many torches had gone out, and one of the white students carried a sleeping baby for the African-American mother.

The torchlight event had been visually impressive and rewarding for the participants. Encouraged by the turnout, the West Harlem Morningside Park Committee organized a daytime protest a fortnight later, on Wednesday, April 3. Suki Ports produced a three-leaf mimeographed pamphlet for the occasion, offering a parody, complete with amusing illustrations, of Columbia's recent "Partners in the Park" promotion. It described the benefits to be derived by students from a projected Community-Columbia Playground to be constructed in the middle of the campus in front of Low Library. When the protest marchers reached the center of the campus, they stopped where this imaginary playground was to be located. Several black children acted out its construction with toy bulldozers and trucks. Questioned by students, other observers, and TV reporters, the youngsters gave well-informed answers on the gymnasium and related issues.

The torchlight parade and the playground charade may not have moved Columbia's administration, but the students were impressed by the ingenious street theater brought to the heart of the university by members of the African-American community and their children.

During these last weeks before the great campus crisis broke, the absence of outright support of the grassroots opposition to the gymnasium on the part of the African-American students at Columbia became increasingly puzzling.[202] The Students' Afro-American Society (SAS) had been founded in the summer of 1964 with the primary objective of providing a social and cultural focus for black students who were beginning to attend Columbia and Barnard College in somewhat more generous numbers. Preoccupied as it was with the identity of Afro-American students within a white institution, SAS remained for some time reluctant to become involved with the surrounding community. During the winter and early spring of 1967/68, however, members of the West Harlem Community Organization established contact with SAS. Although SAS

---

202. Stefan M. Bradley, *Harlem vs. Columbia University: Black Student Power in the Late 1960s* (University of Illinois Press, 2009), 272 pp. Based on recent interviews with participants and research, this study supports the author's observations.

remained, as a group, reluctant to commit, several of its members began to investigate the issues of university expansion and the gymnasium in Morningside Park. Likewise, some African-American students at Barnard College began to inform themselves by undertaking systematic research on the history and background of the controversy, as did their counterparts at Columbia College. No black students participated in the February 20th sit-in, but SAS did form an Ad Hoc Committee on the Gym about this time. According to Senator Paterson, several SAS students met with him to discuss Gym Crow, after having witnessed the protest and disruption at the West Side Community Conference. Senator Paterson remembered that the position of the African-American students at the time was that SAS could not afford any defeats, and, because the gym seemed to be a lost cause, it was not worth their time.[203] Eventually, however, the SAS leadership indicated to him that their organization would like to help the community in its struggle.

Several more activist members of SAS were pressing for greater direct political involvement at this time. These included Bill Sales and Cicero Wilson, who would later have leading roles in Columbia's spring 1968 uprising. An internal SAS newsletter circulated in early March argued against the gymnasium and challenged the black students to action: "Despite the pleas of community leaders for student support, black students have failed to respond. The community needs strong support which thus far has only been supplied by white students. It will be interesting to see if black students will give any aid or assistance to the community in its vital struggle against Columbia."[204]

It was not until April 20, when Cicero Wilson spoke at a rally in Harlem, that African-American students began to be involved in the community protests. The SAS Ad Hoc Committee on the Gym was at first so doubtful of the community's strength that it considered the most

---

[203.] Cox Fact-Finding Commission Transcript, testimony by Basil Paterson, 2,570–2,572.

[204.] Jerry L. Avorn and the Members of the Staff of the *Columbia Daily Spectator, Up Against the Ivy Wall: A History of the Columbia Crisis* (Members of the Board Associates, Robert Friedman, ed., 1968), 38.

anyone could hope for would be a 50/50 space allocation. Representatives of the community expended a great deal of effort convincing the African-American students that their stand was "NO Gym!" According to Bill Sales, the students were impressed, even incredulous, at the radicalism of the people. "They were really far ahead of us!" as Sales put it.[205]

Before the African-American students made their historic decision to join forces with the grassroots, the assassination of Martin Luther King Jr. on April 4, 1968, shattered the tenuous calm on the Columbia campus. Two days later, on Saturday, a delegation of black students delivered a letter to President Kirk at his residence, demanding that the university remain closed entirely on Tuesday, April 9, to honor the slain civil rights leader, rather than merely for the duration of the scheduled memorial service. The letter contained an ultimatum and a deadline for making a public announcement of the closing. As the deadline approached, the students tensely waited in Bill Sales' apartment near the campus.

Only a few minutes short of the deadline, a member of the administration telephoned that the request would be heeded. This action by the black students did not become known on campus until a letter to the editor of the *Columbia Spectator*, signed by SAS, and dated April 8, 1968, appeared in the newspaper the day after the memorial service. This gave the erroneous impression that the Columbia administration had followed the dictates of its own conscience when classes were ordered suspended for April 9, and a memorial service was scheduled in St. Paul's Chapel. However, even without knowledge of the black students' ultimatum, this act honoring Martin Luther King impressed some students as hypocritical and insincere in the light of recent events and Columbia's long history of blundered relations with minority groups. None of the black students attended the service in the chapel, or even remained on campus during that day, but rather fanned out into the neighborhoods. Thus, it was white SDS students who turned the service in St. Paul's Chapel into the kick-off for a tumultuous spring.

While the gathering in the chapel was in progress, Mark Rudd, the newly elected chairman of SDS, walked to the front and seized

---

[205.] Author's interview with Bill Sales, June 1971.

the lectern. He accused President Kirk and Vice President Truman of "committing a moral outrage against Dr. King's memory." He then led a group of about forty out of the Chapel in protest. Many of those remaining in their seats were nevertheless impressed by Mark Rudd's sincerity. He had expressed, perhaps crudely, feelings that were shared by many throughout the campus and the environs of the university. At this point, the Rev. John D. Cannon earned himself the disaffection of the university administration by announcing: "I know people will be asking me what I think about the disruption that took place. I want to say now that as long as I am Chaplain of this University, any student who is moved by the spirit of the truth, who wishes to speak his mind, is able to speak in this Chapel any time. So be it."[206]

The memorial service proved to be a portentous event. Not only had the white radical students crossed the Rubicon, but the religious hierarchy of East Hall had openly cast its lot with the students—or at least had insisted that students, however rudely, were articulating a message that should be heard. From this incident on, although often acting only as intermediaries or neutrals, the chaplain's office and religious advisers were to be thorns in the sides of the administration and the trustees. Several individuals connected with East Hall had been active in the bitter civil rights battles and Freedom Rides of the early 1960s in the South, and would continue to shake up their denominations long after apparent calm had returned to the Columbia campus.

That the Columbia administration was indeed duplicitous in these matters is suggested by the contents of an embittered letter to the *Columbia Daily Spectator* only three days after the Martin Luther King Jr. memorial service. Although the communication was anonymous, it was presumably written by a member of an athletic team who had attended the event and who wrote:

> At the Varsity C Club award night and banquet, held on the evening after the burial of Dr. King, Mr. Harold McGuire '27, University Trustee, informed those in attendance how happy he was to say that we

---

[206]. *Columbia Daily Spectator*, April 10, 1968.

can all look forward to the completion of the new gymnasium in Morningside Park next year, and he gave various details concerning the acquisition of this site and some of the gym's facilities. Also the Alumni Athletic Award was given to Mr. John Wheeler '36, who was praised for his adept dealing with the City and State authorities at the time the university obtained the legal rights to build on the park site. In his little talk, Mr. Wheeler praised another man, seated at the head table, as being the 'handler' of the City's park commissioners and City administrators. This arrogance, and the old Columbia cheer "Who owns New York"—as Dean Coleman assured the audience that we "do" own New York—is a reflection of the racist policies that the university is promoting on the Heights. This isn't necessarily to say that these men are complete demoniac-racist: however, their myopia adds one more spade of dirt to the grave of Dr. King, to whom many of these individuals gave their homage and "rededication" so recently.[207]

At this same banquet that celebrated certain individuals in charge of university affairs for their "handling" of city and state officials, Trustee McGuire once more brushed aside criticism of the gymnasium in Morningside Park as coming from "a small minority who don't realize that this has been passed by all the proper governmental authorities."[208] Even at this late date, in his eyes, opposition to the project was a sign of misinformation and ignorance.

It remains an open question whether Columbia expected to reconcile the arrogance expressed at the varsity award dinner with dedication to the causes and beliefs for which Martin Luther King Jr. had lived and died. It was perhaps hoped that the Center for Urban-Minority Affairs would accomplish this. In early March, the trustees had announced the

---

207. Ibid., April 12, 1968.
208. Ibid., April 11, 1968.

appointment of Franklin H. Williams Jr., formerly United States Ambassador to Ghana, one of the few African Americans of diplomatic rank, as director of the center. He was expected to assume his new position on June 1, replacing School of General Studies Dean Clarence Walton, who had served as interim director for the program since its initiation in the fall of 1967. Walton endeavored to assuage the community's disappointment at not being consulted on the director's appointment with the assurance that Ambassador Williams would "emphasize action programs rather than programs of academic study."[209] In the excitement of the next weeks, the Center for Urban-Minority Affairs and its directors would fade into the background. (In February 1969, however, Williams would take a decisive position in the final settlement of the gymnasium controversy, and the administration in Low Library would begin to regard him with apprehension.)

The radical white student members of the Columbia chapter of SDS had been active since the fall of 1966. Over the winter of 1966/67, they focused on the university's ties to the Central Intelligence Agency and the Institute for Defense Analyses as well as students' rights to due process in disciplinary matters (rather than discipline by dean's fiat without trial or hearing, which was the custom not only at Columbia but also at most, although not all, sister institutions). It was through Mike Golash and others who had been involved in Michael Colen's political campaign, and now were part of the SDS Expansion Committee, that the gymnasium was discussed at their meetings as a topic around which community support could be organized. However, an incipient division brewed within SDS, with a small faction showing greater interest in moving toward a worker-student alliance for organizing along the lines of the Progressive Labor Party. Because the gymnasium issue was associated with this faction, the majority of SDS membership had been reluctant to take up the gymnasium cause. Only after the February 20th sit-in at the construction site, when a number of its members were arrested, did SDS become interested in the gymnasium issue.

---

[209.] Ibid., March 12, 1968.

There was never a planned and coordinated strategy for grassroots opposition to the gymnasium; rather, actions were spontaneous and pragmatic. This enabled the movement to embrace diverse participants, each considering the cause from different, although equally valid, points of view. Members of the Citizenship Council and the Columbia University Student Council had gained experience in community involvement, had a long-standing interest in town/gown relations, and were consequently familiar with the gymnasium pros and cons. On the other hand, SDS came upon it relatively late and unprepared, when the controversy had already reached the proportions of a real confrontation. SDS took up the gymnasium for its political possibilities and racial implications, to the exclusion of other factors. The urgency of the moment left no time for extended argumentation, and any opportunity to involve the general student body in the wider implications of their action was disregarded by SDS rhetoricians.

The time had not yet come for combining political with environmental activism, and few Columbia students showed concern about the park encroachment aspect of the dispute. It would be incorrect to compare the case of the Morningside Park gymnasium with the later People's Park incidents in Berkeley, California. Columbia students never developed a "sense of place" for Morningside Park. Their involvement with the gymnasium struggle lacked the earthy quality of the West Coast/Berkeley events. Once the actual crisis had engulfed the Columbia campus, Morningside Park and the construction site receded to the periphery. For most students who participated in the strike and the occupation of buildings, the gymnasium issue was an abstraction, not associated with a distinct urban location. One might even assume that many of the late opponents to the gymnasium had scarcely seen the excavation site and probably had never so much as walked in the Park. In this respect, their frame of reference differed markedly from the acutely felt "sense of turf" shared by the grassroots residents, particularly by those living in West Harlem for whom the park had a distinct place value.

The students and faculty of the School of Architecture were possibly exceptions who perceived the gymnasium as representing institutional racism and a significant error in urban planning with grave social and political repercussions. Those associated with the School of Architecture had been openly critical of the way new campus construction had been carried out over the past years, and had picketed new buildings to protest their mediocre designs. For the proposed gymnasium, it was not only the matter of a single objectionable, monumental structure but also the deplorable lack of urban consideration in placing it at that particular site. The university's failure to take into account the need for planning and the implications of architectural choices was contrary to the professional principles on which the Columbia School of Architecture was proudly based.

"How Not to Build a Symbol," Ada Louise Huxtable, architectural critic for *The New York Times*, entitled her piece on the Columbia gymnasium that appeared on Sunday, March 24, 1968. "This is not the kind of symbol anyone wanted," she wrote, "It stands for one of the more disturbing problems of our troubled times—the deep and bitter split and many-layered misunderstanding between a privileged urban university and an underprivileged community—a division that the Ford Foundation has hopefully given Columbia $10 Million to heal." Huxtable delved into the background of the gymnasium controversy from its inception to the present state of affairs, and continued on a pessimistic note: "Columbia feels justified in using public parkland for a building that is perhaps one sixth for public purposes, and in its heart still thinks of itself as a privileged private club generously conferring certain optional, peripheral philanthropies. Today's university can never play that part again. It cannot avoid an involved and responsible role in its troubled neighborhoods." She concluded by calling for "a significant change in the basic understanding of this inescapable and critical community relationship."[210]

Huxtable was not alone in voicing alarm in March of 1968. The Faculty Civil Rights Group (FCRG), which was formed in April 1966 and included distinguished members of the faculty, now released to the public its report on "The Community and the Expansion of Columbia

---

[210.] Ada Louise Huxtable, "How Not to Build a Symbol," *The New York Times*, Sunday, March 24, 1968.

University."[211] This slim booklet in a Columbia-blue cover presented a carefully researched and documented study of the damaging effects of urban renewal and institutional expansion on an integrated neighborhood. Written under the direction of language Professors Peter Haidu and Robert Belnap, the report had been presented to the administration in December 1967, but had received no response. Those attending an early FCRG meeting had been inspired by John Bailey of the Architects' Renewal Committee in Harlem, whose report on his organization's activities in West Harlem touched off a lively discussion of community/ university relations.[212] FCRG's report was based on thorough research and interviews with individuals as well as organizations representing Columbia University, Morningside Heights, West Harlem, and the Hispanic communities to the south and north of Morningside Heights. Its analysis of the complex problems of urban renewal and the "expansion" policies of Columbia University is thorough and attempts to be nonpartisan. The report's public release in March 1968 caused a considerable stir on campus, as it particularly exposed Columbia's practices of tenant eviction and removal of minorities from Morningside Heights that were previously unknown by many affiliates of the university.

News media response to the FCRG report included a WINS radio editorial that called the FCRG report and community protests against construction of the gymnasium in Morningside Park clear indications that "Columbia must be doing something wrong at Morningside." Noting the "separate but unequal" approach of the athletic facility, WINS recommended that the university share the gym on a more equal basis. "And the same equal partners approach should be applied to the entire community," it continued. "When Columbia treats local residents as second class citizens, it will continue to inspire resentment and hostility. But WINS believes Columbia has a golden opportunity—and the facilities—to do much more for its community. It's an opportunity to make contributions that would benefit both the university and the neighborhood it lives in. It's an opportunity we hope Columbia takes."[213]

---

211. Faculty Civil Rights Group at Columbia University, "The Community and the Expansion of Columbia University."

212. Minutes of the meeting of the Faculty Civil Rights Group of May 11, 1966, CCC Collection, Schomburg, Box 20, #1.

213. Radio Station WINS, New York, on-air editorial, March 28/29, 1968.

Many of those affiliated with the university and even among the community opposition groups hoped that Columbia's leadership might "see the light," listen to reasonable criticism, and begin to accept suggestions. Long-time Columbia faculty as well as students and alumni were disappointed, even taken aback, at the direction their university had taken and thus exposed itself to extensive criticism. A lengthy feature story in *The Columbia Owl* by Stephen A. Stertz was indicative of the mood on campus. Entitled "Columbia vs. Morningside Heights: The Death of a Neighborhood,"[214] it presented a lively analysis of the situation based on the FCRG report as well as on interviews with Professor Haidu, Professor Charles Abrams of the Columbia Institute for Urban Environment, members of the university administration, the Rev. Dwight Smith, and other community figures.

The lack of a master plan for the university's academic as well as physical development, in particular its haphazard expansion policy, had been decried by diverse critics for several years. Ironically, just as a crisis was about to engulf the campus, the trustees announced their choice of I. M. Pei and Associates to create a comprehensive urban plan for Columbia. Wisely, Pei deferred acceptance and would eventually provide sharp commentary on Columbia's "urban planning."

In spite of professional misgivings, the faculty of the School of Architecture was late in expressing an opinion on the gymnasium in Morningside Park. Individual faculty members, especially Professor Percival Goodman, had been concerned with the problems of urban renewal and institutional expansion. Goodman had, in fact, been "disciplined" for speaking out, but his colleagues seemed to consider the gymnasium peripheral, a lost cause. As late as the spring semester of 1968, students in some design classes were assigned the expansion of the Columbia campus as an exercise, and were permitted to place projected buildings not only in Morningside Park but also in Riverside Park—so their instructors apparently considered usurping public parkland and reducing Manhattan's open space acceptable urban planning practice. Eventually, however, the School of Architecture faculty became the first,

---

214. *Columbia Owl*, March 20, 1968.

and only, faculty group to officially question the administration's policy regarding the gymnasium.

This occurred at an otherwise routine meeting of the architecture faculty on March 27, 1968, when a discussion arose concerning university planning procedures. A mildly worded resolution was passed unanimously to ask President Kirk to "reconsider" the building of the gymnasium, and a letter to that effect was sent to him on April 10. Several faculty members who were involved in wording the resolution later explained that opinions were too diverse to cite any specific reasons for reconsidering the gymnasium. According to Percival Goodman, the faculty was primarily critical of locating the structure in the Park, rather than of its design, as professional ethics did not permit public criticism of their colleagues' architecture.[215] The letter suggested that the university was in an intolerable situation, and that the language of the architecture faculty's resolution might provide a face-saving way out. However, there was no response from Low Library, even though reports on the resolution appeared in the press and a *New York Times* correspondent interviewed several members of the faculty.

At the hearings of the Cox Fact Finding Commission, Columbia Trustee Harold McGuire called the architecture faculty's resolution "a wholly irresponsible action," apparently unaware that the action was taken by a group of professionals in an atmosphere of extreme concern for their university. [216]

When news of the School of Architecture faculty resolution was passed "down the hill" to the West Harlem Community Organization as a small victory to be shared by the grassroots opposition to the gym, Margaret McNeil answered the telephone. She commented that the faculty had acted courageously, but she did not see what good it would do, "because your faculty is just as powerless as the students, except they don't know it!"[217]

---

[215.] *Columbia Daily Spectator*, April 15, 1968. *The New York Times*, April 16, 1968.

[216.] Cox Commission Report, testimony of Harold F. McGuire, 545.

[217.] Telephone conversation with the author.

On April 1, the *Columbia Daily Spectator* made its annual change of editorial boards. The new editors would prove to be highly capable as they encountered historic circumstances. Under Editor-in-Chief Robert Friedman, they took the School of Architecture resolution as a point of departure for an editorial on the gymnasium in Morningside Park that differed sharply from one published the previous month under the title "Enough is Enough." "Regardless of whether the gymnasium construction should or should not continue," they wrote on April 17, "one thing is obvious: the University's handling of the entire gymnasium affair has been abysmally bad."

# 10

## GRASSROOTS TRIUMPH
### April 20–26, 1968

Morningside Heights was now bristling with tension and a sense of foreboding. At the construction site, the blasting and excavation continued uninterrupted. Trucks rumbled out of the gates transporting rocks and the remains of the meadow to distant dumping grounds. East of the Park, Joseph Monroe and the West Harlem Morningside Park Committee were working hard to enlist the support of African-American organizations to protest Colombia University's "expansion" policies, although many of these organizations were reluctant to espouse a seemingly doomed cause that had gained a fair amount of white support. Nevertheless, the Harlem chapter of CORE decided to organize a rally to take place in Harlem on Saturday, April 20. CORE's chair, Victor Solomon, acted as master of ceremonies during more than three hours of speeches attacking Columbia's invasion of Harlem by buying real estate, "taking over" Harlem Hospital, and refusing to permit community participation in the allocation of the $10 million Ford urban grant. The rally drew a crowd of about 400, less than anticipated, but impressively bringing together a wide spectrum of black organizations that ranged, in addition to Harlem CORE, from the Mau Mau Society and the African National Pioneer Movement to the West Harlem Community Organization and other tenant groups. However divergent their political views, all the speakers, including Senator Paterson and Bob McKay, agreed that Columbia's gymnasium in Morningside Park was an invasion of Harlem turf by the white establishment, and that the "Columbia octopus" must be stopped. Cicero Wilson, recently elected head of the Students' Afro-American Society (SAS), spoke at the rally, and other SAS members attended, indicating a new direction for the organization, which had previously avoided alliance with grassroots activities.

Press attention to the rally included a scathing article by Ada Louise Huxtable for *The New York Times* summarizing Columbia's past planning and architectural blunders, including the dismal gym affair.[218] Three days after the rally, on a memorable Tuesday morning, the *Columbia Daily Spectator* printed a news analysis by Peter B. Haskell on the front page under the title "Gymnasium question unites leading activists in Harlem." Haskell called attention to a "growing feeling of militant nationalism among the Afro-Americans [which was] going to engender an opposition to the gym of a strength and unity unexpected by Columbia officials."[219] University Business Manager Joseph Nye reportedly shrugged off this latest attack on the gymnasium, repeating the university administration mantra that it was only "the small groups on either side of the question that feel and act strongly; the vast majority of the people do not care one way or the other." This view had been confirmed, in fact, by a Morningside neighborhood poll conducted the previous November by the staff of the *Columbia Daily Spectator.* Of 300 people interviewed, 47 percent had not even heard of Columbia's planned gymnasium. Of those who had heard of it, 56 percent were in favor of the project.[220] The university was relying rather heavily on this neutral, silent majority. In Nye's opinion, a rally in Harlem three days earlier that brought together a wide spectrum of black organizations was of little consequence, observing that "CORE wanted to 'keep the pot boiling' to make their views known."

The new alliance in Harlem considered the gymnasium issue a territorial conflict between black Harlem and a white Columbia that was

---

218. Ada Louise Huxtable, "Strike at Columbia Architecture School Traced to Anger over Exclusion from Planning," *New York Times*, May 20, 1968.

219. *Columbia Daily Spectator*, April 23, 1968.

220. Ibid., November 21, 1967.

acting in union with the white city and state governments. The thrust in Harlem was to obtain full control of the projected building rather than to prevent its construction altogether. The alliance set no time limit on achieving this goal and saw no reason for stopping the bulldozers—a victory could be postponed, if need be, even until the inauguration of the building. With excavation proceeding rapidly, time was running out for the cherished West Harlem Morningside Park Committee's grass-roots hope of preventing the building of the gymnasium altogether. But then, suddenly, within the span of four days, in an eruption of historic proportions, everything changed.

The events on the Columbia campus during the stormy days of April 20–26, 1968, are admirably related by some of the students who experienced the euphoria of these historic moments. Their narratives focus on agitation among students and faculty within the ivy walls, which had been growing for several years and intensified in the form of opposition to the draft and the Vietnam war.[221] However, this chronicle continues to focus on the role of the grassroots movement, which imparted a unique complexity to the crisis at Columbia and had foretold the storm of April 1968 several decades previously.

There was considerable apprehension on campus on Monday, April 22, as word circulated that SDS was planning to test President Kirk's ban on indoor demonstrations by marching the next day into Low Library. A confrontation between SDS and an anti-leftist group called "Students for a Free Campus" seemed unavoidable. President Kirk was to be presented with three demands: (1) An end to Columbia's support of IDA (Institute for Defense Analyses), a developer of counter-insurgency weapons for use abroad and in ghettoes. (2) That no one be disciplined for opposing Columbia's unjust policies. (3) A public hearing before students and faculty with full rights of due process for all concerned.[222]

Several underground campus newspapers emerged during the weeks of turmoil. Columbia's SDS students published the first one, *Up Against*

---

[221]. Notable among them are: Avorn, et al., *Up Against the Ivy Wall* and James Simon Kunen, *The Strawberry Statement: Notes of a College Revolutionary* (Random House, 1968).

[222]. Avorn, et al., *Up Against the Ivy Wall*, April 22, 1968, 33–35.

*the Ivy Wall*, on April 22. It was numbered Vol. III, no. 1 (though it had no predecessors) and bore the slogan "The year of the heroic guerilla." It included a solemn piece by Bob Feldman on "The King memorial—why we disrupted." However, it was the front page that caused the greatest reaction with a "Reply to Uncle Grayson," referring to a speech President Kirk had given recently in Charlottesville, VA, in which he charged young people with "turbulent and inchoate nihilism." The strongly worded piece, simply signed "Mark," for SDS chair Mark Rudd[223] is one of the most revealing documents of the student movement in the sixties. Promising violence and destruction, if needed, the letter reads, in part: "You are quite right in feeling that this situation is potentially 'dangerous.' For if we win, we will take control of your world, your corporation, your University and attempt to mold a world in which we and other people can live as human beings. Your power is directly threatened, since we will have to destroy that power before we take over. We begin by fighting you over your support of Vietnam and American Imperialism—IDA and the School of International Affairs. We will fight you about your control of black people in Morningside Heights, Harlem, and the campus itself. And we will fight you about the type of mis-education you are trying to channel us through."[224] (Note that this April 22 issue of the SDS publication did not mention the gymnasium controversy.)

When the march into Low Library was announced on Monday, it appeared that SDS would be the only group involved. Even on the morning of Tuesday, April 23, the demonstration expected to take place on Low Plaza at noon was presumed to be primarily an SDS rally. However, fliers distributed that morning did mention SAS participation, and the front page of that day's issue of the *Columbia Daily Spectator* suggested that, through a coalition of forces, the protest would exhibit a uniquely broad base as diverse organizations with different, although overlapping or related, grievances "came together." On the other side, the Students

---

223. Ibid., 25–27.
224. From website "SDS and SAS: Confrontational Politics," http://beatl.barnard. columbia.edu/students/his3464y/grinberg%2Bperry/sds.html

for a Free Campus, who opposed the rally, were flexing their muscles, and the university was taking security measures.

Next to the news about the impending demonstration on campus, the *Columbia Daily Spectator* placed a story dramatically entitled "The First Battle: Cit Council and CORE Plan Rally to Protest New Gym." It featured a picture of Victor Solomon of Harlem CORE and his announcement introducing an entirely new alignment of forces. Both the Columbia Citizenship Council and SDS were working with CORE, he said, to organize an anti-gymnasium rally to take place within a few days, perhaps on Thursday or the following Monday. Art Leaderman (Columbia, 1968), a member of the Citizens Council Governing Board and the SDS Steering Committee, was quoted as saying that the two organizations had jointly extended invitations to speakers from CORE "to come on Campus to discuss race issues at Columbia." The rally was intended not to prevent construction of the gymnasium but to arouse the support of students and faculty for a policy of community control of the gymnasium. SAS was not expected to participate in either of these protest actions.

The front page of the *Columbia Daily Spectator* also carried a report on yet another approach to the gymnasium issue. It was the public announcement of the attempt to prevent construction of the building in Morningside Park altogether by Victor Crichton, together with lawyer Irving Thau, seeking a court injunction against the gym. Crichton declared, "I feel that the gym is an inappropriate use of parkland by a private institution," reiterating once more his opposition to all encroachment on parkland by either public or private institutions. This position coincided with that of the West Harlem Morningside Park Committee, but differed in its reason.

Although the CORE-Citizens Council-SDS rally never materialized, and the court injunction, almost forgotten in the excitement, was not tendered until April 30, the front page of the April 23 *Columbia Spectator* proved prophetic in the sense of unrest it conveyed. Events that followed, which surprised even those who were involved in planning the April 23 protest, are often attributed to chance circumstances. In retrospect, however, it appears that the black students were operating in perfect concert and well aware of the implications of each turn of events.

The April 23 rally and its aftermath have been, and continue to be, the subject of many publications. However, the unique, but little-examined, grassroots urban movement that is the focus of this narrative illuminates aspects overlooked by other accounts, and contributes to understanding the complex realities of the controversy.

At noon on April 23, a crowd of over one thousand people comprising students, faculty, and people from the surrounding neighborhoods gathered on Low Plaza in the spring sunshine. SDS demonstrators stayed near the sundial, the traditional speaker's rostrum for Columbia students. Counter-demonstrators, mainly members of the Students for a Free Campus faction, deployed themselves on the steps of Low Library and on the terrace in front of its securely closed entrance. First to speak was Ted Gold of SDS. He was followed by Cicero Wilson, president of SAS. Wilson began with an attack on all matters white that made the predominantly white crowd feel uneasy, but what he said about the gymnasium in Morningside Park drew cheers: "This is Harlem Heights, not Morningside Heights. . . . What would you do if somebody came and took your property? Took your property as they're doing over at Morningside with this gym?" He continued by asking rhetorically, "Would you sit still? No, you'd use every means possible to get your property back—and this is what black people are engaged in right now."[225] Reminding his audience of the vulnerability of the campus, Wilson warned, "Do you realize that when you come back, there may not *be* a Columbia University? Do you think that this white citadel of hypocrisy will be bypassed if an insurrection occurs this summer?"

The authors of the retrospective publication *Up Against the Ivy Wall* observe that "in a sense, Wilson's presence at the rally was as significant as his speech."[226] SAS participation came as a surprise to campus observers, although apparently SAS members had informed SDS of their intention to participate late the night before. Senator Paterson told the Cox Fact Finding Commission that SAS students had come to his office

---

225. Avorn, et. al., *Up Against the Ivy Wall*, 39.
226. Ibid., 38.

the previous day to borrow material about the gymnasium controversy from his files, but had not told him about their plans.[227]

As noted above, neither community nor student organizations had been successful in enlisting active SAS support against the gymnasium before Cicero Wilson's appearance at the previous Saturday's protest in Harlem. By joining the action on April 22, SAS stepped out ahead of Harlem CORE and the Columbia Citizenship Council, whose major anti-gymnasium rally was planned for later that week. This unexpected SAS engagement in the gymnasium issue may have contributed to the excitement apparent among the white students when Cicero Wilson mounted the base of the sundial. For the black students, on the other hand, it was the logical climax of many weeks of reappraisal and redirection of their purpose and policy. Their commitment to the community struggle was a deliberate move, whose seriousness and importance was never in doubt.

Bill Sales, long-time radical activist and one of the SAS leaders, confirmed that although the course of events on Tuesday was greatly influenced by chance, and students' actions seemed to be guided by spur of the moment decisions, the black students knew exactly why they were participating and for what reason. The loose organization that SAS had been in the past had evolved into a "very together" group that included graduate students, like Sales, as well as students from Barnard College. Their tactics were well planned and intentional, according to Sales in a June 1971 comment to the author.

For more than a decade, Columbia's physical planning had been based on preventing just the sort of threat conjured by Cicero Wilson. Now a potential bastion—the gymnasium in Morningside Park—had become a provocation for storming the "white citadel." In the next days, the waves of African-American protest marchers invading the ivy walls drove this message home. In addition, the threat to the ivy walls came not only from without but also from within the citadel.

In a move to avoid a clash between the restless crowd of SDS students, members of SAS, and community people on one side and

---

227. Cox Fact-Finding Commission Transcript, testimony of Basil Paterson, 3,053.

Students for a Free Campus on the other, Mark Rudd was handed a letter from Vice President Truman offering a meeting at nearby McMillan Theater. The topic of the discussion was to be the "IDA SIX," regarding disciplining of the six students who demonstrated against the Institute for Defense Analyses. The students, however, were not permitted to set any ground rules before the conference; rather, they would evolve during the session. While the SDS leaders were discussing various alternatives, a large group of impatient students approached the entrances of Low Library, swerving east to an unprotected door. In retrospect, if the students had gained entrance and achieved their aim of a sit-in at the university administration building, the upheaval might never have reached campus-wide proportions. Also, SDS might have concentrated on the disciplinary concerns, and the gymnasium in Morningside Park might never have become a crucial point of contention.[228] These alternatives to the actual events remain a historical "what if," of consequence even beyond Morningside Heights.

When the students reached the east side entrance to Low Library, hastily locked by campus security guards, Mark Rudd's attempt to speak was interrupted by a shout: "To the gym, let's go to the gym site!" The voice—never identified—sounded to some like a woman's, and may have belonged to a member of the community. Juan Gonzalez believes it was a black graduate student by the name of Elsie. Bill Sales said it was a red-haired male SDS student. Mike Golash insists that it was not one voice, but many. In any case, "To the gym!" had an electrifying effect.

The closing of the entrance to Low Library played directly into the hands of the African-American students, who were intent on turning attention toward the gymnasium issue, which represented both racial and broader community concerns. As if on cue, the crowd moved toward the east campus gate at 116th Street and Amsterdam Avenue, led by Cicero Wilson and a group of black students. They were joined at 116th Street by Mark Rudd and other SDS leaders, along with a contingent of demonstrators coming from the center of the campus.

---

228. Discussion among about 50 Columbia Conservative Students at Earl Hall, October 17, 1968.

No one had expected the rally to involve the gymnasium construction site, and it was only thinly guarded. In blitzkrieg fashion, the students rushed through the open gate at the site and pulled at the cyclone fence on the slope of what had been the blockhouse hill (see Figure 22). Others went at the fence from the outside, and within minutes the chain-link enclosure was on the ground. Police reinforcements quickly appeared on the scene and tried to pry the students away from the tangled iron mesh. Trampling feet turned the soil into slippery mud, and some lost their footing as police and students scuffled. At one point there was a fierce struggle between the black students and the police, but an officer stepped in to prevent the arrests that were about to be made. Instead, a single white student was handcuffed and led away (Figure 22) after an unsuccessful attempt by his comrades to extricate him from the hands of a policeman. The prisoner, Fred Wilson, was charged with felonious assault, criminal mischief, and resisting arrest. Several of these charges were dropped when his case came to trial—his arrest was apparently an error resulting from the confusion of the moment. It is possible that before this day, Fred Wilson, who was not a member of SDS, may never have had any thoughts about the Park or the gymnasium, but now, covered with mud, he was pushed into the police van. [229]

The spontaneous call "To the Gym!" and Wilson's arrest gave an unanticipated turn to the events. The arrest bound the students more closely to the gymnasium issue, and determined their next move. While everyone was still milling at the blockhouse hill, Mark Rudd tried to make himself heard over the noise of the heavy machinery proceeding with excavation on the site. He called upon Columbia University and Sergeant Sullivan from the police to drop the charges against Fred Wilson. Rudd also reiterated the prevalent criticism against the university for building a gymnasium on public parkland and refusing full use to the community. After his address, he led the protesters back to the sundial, where they were joined by a group of about 200 SDS students led by Ted Kaptchuk and Ted Gold, who had stayed on campus.

---

[229.] Geoffrey Wilson, "Rebel on Campus: The Father of a Student Protester at Columbia University Examines His Son's Activities with Understanding and Insight," *Parents Magazine*, April 1969.

Rudd was faced with several possibilities. Kaptchuk suggested taking advantage of the crowd of 400 to 500 excited students to move the protest indoors in accord with the original SDS intention of testing President Kirk's ban on indoor demonstrations. Rudd, however, still preoccupied with Fred Wilson's arrest, yielded the sundial to Cicero Wilson, who launched a sharp attack on overt and covert racism at Columbia University, a practice shared, he said, by all, including the students. "SDS can stand on the side and support us, but the black students and the Harlem community will be the ones in the vanguard," he declared.[230] SAS members' concern over the lack of organization in the demonstration resulted in an irritable exchange between Cicero Wilson, Mark Rudd, and some other white students. In an attempt to repair the damage to the tenuous alliance between the African-American and white students, Bill Sales addressed the white students: "You did pretty well today. Hope it's not an isolated incident. It was *beautiful*. It was almost soulful. All we need is some sophistication—and some organization. The only way you win in a technological society is by your superior organization and superior commitment." By correlating the gymnasium issue and the Third World struggle, Sales pulled together certain concerns more basic to a majority of the students than the ban on indoor demonstrations and the isolated case of the gymnasium in the Park. "You strike a blow at the gym, you strike a blow for the Vietnamese people. You strike a blow at the gym, you strike a blow against the assassin of Dr. Martin Luther King, Jr. You strike a blow at Low Library, you strike a blow for the freedom fighters in Angola, Mozambique, Portuguese Guinea, Zimbabwe, South Africa."[231] Sales drew long cheers, having succeeded in both easing tension between black and white students and giving international scope to an issue involving 2.1 acres of public parkland in the heart of Manhattan. For many students not overly concerned over what they considered a purely local problem, Sales' words helped legitimize the gymnasium as a cause for protest. While peripheral to the original demonstration, the gymnasium was evolving into the catalyst uniting student factions and the community.

---

230. Avorn, et al., *Up Against the Ivy Wall,* 47ff.
231. Ibid., 43ff.

Mark Rudd, countering the criticism of incoherence, was next to speak. He reiterated the demands regarding IDA and dropping disciplinary charges against Fred Wilson, concluding, "We want them to stop that fucking gym over there." Because Low Library was by then impenetrable, Rudd suggested taking a hostage and shouted "Seize Hamilton!" Several hundred students surged into the building that housed the Columbia College administration, as well as many classrooms, and the office of their chosen hostage, Acting Dean Henry Coleman, (seen "behind bars" in Figure 23).

For many students, the episode at the construction site was their first contact with Morningside Park, and they returned to the familiar campus with a sense of relief, almost homecoming. Having taken over Hamilton Hall, the students settled into the classrooms where they normally attended lectures. During the next days, as other university buildings were taken over, students tended to group their communes within the framework of their regular activities. "Liberated" buildings provided a sense of belonging, though neither the construction site nor any other part of Morningside Park became a "liberated zone." Many writers have described Dean Coleman's captivity, as well as the complexities involved in the occupation of Hamilton Hall and other campus buildings, and their descriptions are readily available. Here, against the backdrop of student actions, we continue to focus on the fate of the gymnasium and its significance to the community's adamant opposition to its construction.

Mark Rudd formed a steering committee of eight for the occupation of Hamilton Hall: three from SAS, three from SDS, one representing the Citizenship Council, and Juan Gonzalez, representing the Latin American students. This group worked out an official statement and a list of six demands to be met before the protesters would release the Dean and leave Hamilton. According to Gonzalez, the representatives of SAS, the Citizenship Council, and he himself insisted that the gymnasium was one of the listed demands. Fliers issued from Hamilton Hall that afternoon and evening variously note the demand for an end to the gymnasium in Morningside Park in first, third, and fifth place.[232] The response to this request proved so universal and overwhelming that before long it emerged as the key demand of the six, in particular for the black students.

Various faculty members attempted to "free" Dean Coleman, whose confinement was shared by Proctor William E. Kahn and Dan Carlinsky, Director of College Relations. All three were provided with food through the windows facing College Walk. Students tended to gather in the classrooms where they had attended classes, and some sympathetic professors were invited to conduct "teach-ins." For example, George Collins was asked to discuss the urban and environmental problems related to Morningside Park, but found the atmosphere too charged for discussion. Grassroots people gathered in front of the building, providing cheer and provisions.

During the takeover of Hamilton Hall, SAS was joined by black students from Barnard College, who became ever more closely linked with, even representing, the Harlem community and its long history of struggle against Columbia's racist policies. SAS announced receipt of support from national and local black organizations, among them the Student Nonviolent Coordinating Committee, Harlem CORE, United Black Front, and the West Harlem Community Organization. As the evening wore on, the promised reinforcements began to arrive. Dean Coleman's office door was now guarded by several blacks.[233]

While many of the students in Hamilton Hall retired to sleep in the classrooms, the steering committee discussed plans for the next days. The white students had begun to feel uneasy about their control with the arrival of SAS community supporters. On the other hand, the black students were impatient with the ponderous SDS approach to decision making that relied on participatory democracy at all cost. In recent weeks, members of SDS had criticized the community's lack of

---

232. Cox Commission Report, 104ff.

233. Stefan M. Bradley, *Harlem vs. Columbia University: Black Student Power in the Late 1960s* (University of Illinois Press, 2009). Chapter 4, "On Our Own: SAS's Self-Imposed Separation," pp. 74–92, terms the Hamilton sit-in a turning point in the position of the black students in their relation to community issues.

organization, and now they were facing similar reproach from the SAS leadership.

Assured of the support of the community and black organizations, SAS became intent on taking a strong stand, suspecting the white radicals of being less committed and fearing the loss of backing from faculty and neutral students. Although both sides had anticipated a split, the white students were shaken when they were told to leave and take their own building. The departure of the white students from Hamilton Hall in the early morning of April 24 affirmed the black students' link to the Harlem community in its struggle against Columbia's racist policies. Inside Hamilton Hall, the SAS leadership maintained cool control, beginning with organization of household tasks.[234] (Figure 24 shows black students during their occupation of Hamilton Hall.)

The exit of the white students served to broaden the campus protest in a geographic as well as a political sense, with Mark Rudd and other SDS members entering Low Library through an unguarded side entrance. They made the indoor demonstration a firmer reality as they occupied the administrative headquarters of the university, settling into the offices of President Kirk and Vice President Truman. Doors were barricaded from the inside with desks and chairs, while students could easily move in and out the windows because of the wide ledge running around the building at the first floor level—McKim, Mead, & White's penetrable and inviting building designs proved eminently suited to the student occupation. The tall windows and convenient ledges provided comfortable perches for speakers, spectators, and student guards alike.

Those occupying Hamilton took the official title "The Black Students of Hamilton Hall," and for the duration of the sit-in, they spoke only under this communal title and never on an individual basis. They contacted black politicians, and soon City Hall was buzzing with telephone calls about the situation on the Columbia campus. Senator Basil Paterson was an early arrival at Hamilton Hall, and he was soon joined by Assistant Chief Inspector Eldridge Waithe, the City's highest ranking black police officer, as well as Victor Solomon of Harlem CORE.

---

[234] Ibid. and Avorn, et al., *Up Against the Ivy Wall*, 61ff.

Senator Paterson, who had previous contact with SAS on various matters including the gymnasium, was one of the first "outsiders" to be admitted inside Hamilton Hall on Wednesday morning.[235]

In spite of the cold rain that fell through most of the day, the quadrangle in front of Hamilton Hall was filled with people: students, faculty, city and university officials, activists from the community, and reporters. Students sympathetic to the sit-in formed a tight guard in front of the barricaded door, fending off students from the opposition, who frequently pelted them with eggs and other missiles. Bob McKay, who had spent the night inside Hamilton Hall, recalls the impression it made on him to see the black occupants of the building guarded by white students. Under George Hickerson's large umbrella, a group from the community huddled nearby excitedly reviewing recent events. They felt bonded, certainly with Bob McKay, like war veterans. After years of frustrating struggle, the reality of the moment was hard to believe. Spotting Bob McKay on the balcony under the banner of "Malcom X. University," they waved and cheered. His enthusiastic recognition of black and white friends in the rain below did not quite fit the disciplined restraint characterizing the mood inside Hamilton Hall.

The unity of purpose of the close-knit group in the building gave the erroneous impression of authoritarianism. Bill Sales pointed out that the extent to which individual members were attuned to each other and knew each other made traditional and formal organizational procedures unnecessary.[236] Among those who joined Columbia's black students in Hamilton were several students from Howard University, who, upon hearing news of the sit-in, had hastened from Washington, DC, to New York to offer help. They had recently occupied buildings on the Howard campus, and their experience in practical and tactical matters contributed to the smooth functioning at Hamilton Hall.

The number-one demand put forth by the Black Students of Hamilton Hall was "that construction of the gymnasium be terminated and

---

235. Cox Fact-Finding Commission Transcript, testimony by Basil Paterson, 3,053.

236. Author's interview with Bill Sales, June 1971. S.M. Bradley differs with this interpretation in the Cox Commission Report.

the slate wiped clean," and the second was "that the University use its good offices to see that charges be dropped against all persons arrested in previous demonstrations at the gym site."[237] According to Bill Sales, the white students were asked to leave "because black students wanted to hold at least one building to focus the protest on community-wide issues." Ray Brown, member of the Black Students of Hamilton Hall steering committee, looking back at the takeover, declared: "I would say that black students at this university have demonstrated that they view themselves essentially as an extension of the black community and their primary identity is with the black community and not with the university community. And in that sense there are certain obvious things that differentiate them from white students, who will generally I suppose view themselves primarily as members of an academic community. I think this is indicated by the fact that in effect all the demands made by the black students were community demands and not student power demands."[238]

Thus, Hamilton Hall became, in a sense, a forward bastion of the black community within the confines of the Columbia campus just as the gymnasium building was taken to be an outpost and bulwark of the white establishment extending academia into Harlem territory. The black students had created a beautifully matched symbolic situation. Their presence in Hamilton Hall gave "power to the people" of West Harlem, and, perhaps unintentionally, to the community people of Morningside Heights and Manhattan Valley, all equally powerless vis-à-vis the institutions. Relinquishing, perhaps only temporarily, their allegiance to the academic world, the black students allied themselves with a grassroots movement composed of black, Hispanic, and also white people of diverse economic backgrounds, bound together by profound convictions.

The Black Students of Hamilton Hall acted with astuteness and courage. They had the assured support of an impressive array of political and community leaders, and grassroots support from Harlem, the Heights, and beyond. With their choice of going it alone in Hamilton Hall, eventually asking all non-students to leave the building, they were

---

[237.] Stephen Donadio, "Columbia: Seven Interviews," *Partisan Review*, vol. XXXV, no.3, Summer 1968, 376 (interview with Ray Brown and Bill Sales).
[238.] Ibid., 377–378.

untouchable, because any action against them was bound to have considerable repercussions that would bring the promised "troops" onto the Columbia campus.

On Wednesday morning, April 24, the Columbia administration was faced with a difficult situation: the dean of Columbia College was still held hostage within a black citadel on campus, and Harlem was "battle-ready" to bring support to the students. While attention was focused on Hamilton Hall, the white students managed to establish a second front under the very noses of the Columbia administration and the police, who had been summoned to protect university property but were under orders to avoid provocation. This was not easy, because the students occupying President Kirk's office were tense, expecting the police to remove them by force. As it turned out, the police only had orders to remove a Rembrandt painting from President Kirk's office. This painting, "Portrait of a Dutch Admiral," then valued at $450,000, was probably the most important single work of art owned by Columbia University. Members of the faculty, even distinguished professors from the Department of Art History in Schermerhorn Hall adjacent to Low Library, never knew of its existence in President Kirk's office, until policemen carried it out of the building. Exit Rembrandt—students remain!

Meanwhile, President Kirk and Vice President Truman were receiving advice from Senator Paterson, Police Chief Waithe, and Barry Gottehrer from the Mayor's Urban Task Force, who had all been consulting with the Black Students of Hamilton Hall. University officials were warned of the inherent danger of the situation because of the explosive climate in Harlem where support of the students' cause continued to grow. Borough President Sutton was urging a settlement with the Black Students of Hamilton Hall, leaving the white students out of the picture for the time being. Columbia's administration, however, insisted on standing firm, especially on the matter of amnesty.

Opening a dialogue with the students was considered important by the faculty as well. Faculty members had been meeting informally in the graduate student lounge on the first floor of Philosophy Hall, a location suggested by Thomas Colahan, Vice Dean of the College, when he and members of the faculty were outdoors shivering in the rain on Wednesday morning and were informed of the black/white split. Dean

Colahan led the rain-drenched group to 501 Philosophy Hall, which became the base of operations and nerve center of what evolved into the Ad Hoc Faculty Group. One of the first steps taken on Wednesday by the group was to establish contact with the black students. This mission was carried out by Professors Immanuel Wallerstein of the Department of Sociology and Samuel Coleman of the Department of Philosophy, both members of the Faculty Civil Rights Group. Admitted into the barricaded Hamilton Hall, they spoke with the Black Students Steering Committee consisting of Columbia students Cicero Wilson, Bill Sales, Ray Brown, and Andrew Newton. The students made it clear that they would stick fast to their demands and were preparing for an indefinite sit-in. Supplies and medical items coming from the community and Harlem CORE, as well as frequent visits from black leaders, indicated that the Black Students of Hamilton Hall had wide and well-organized support. Despite the rigidity of their position, Dean Coleman was released about 3:00 p.m. on Wednesday, apparently as a result of discussions with Senator Paterson, who had informed the black students of the seriousness of kidnapping charges that could be brought against them.

Dean Coleman emerged from captivity to make a surprise appearance in Philosophy Hall at the first official meeting of the Columbia College faculty during the crisis. It was convened by President Kirk, who insisted that only regular faculty—no junior members of the teaching staff—be allowed to attend. The position of the Black Students of Hamilton Hall was outlined, followed by a lively discussion of white-student demands. Several resolutions were proposed, although President Kirk emphasized that these were purely advisory. Regarding the gymnasium, adopted resolution number five read:

> This Faculty respectfully petitions the University administration:
>
> a) to arrange the immediate suspension of on-site excavation of the gymnasium facility in Morningside Park; b) to be prepared to review the matter of the gymnasium site with a group of community spokesmen; the administration will immediately invite the Mayor to designate a group who will take counsel

with the University with respect to the location and
character of the gymnasium.

This brief overview of the faculty meeting held on Wednesday, April 24, is based on the official record prepared by Joseph L. Blau, professor in the Department of Religion and secretary of the faculty. An addendum to the official record stated that "the Trustees alone can act on resolution number five; President Kirk will ask the Chairman of the Board to consider this matter." It was evident that even in moments of great crisis, the university administration was unable to adapt itself to current conditions. The College faculty, however, had faced up to recent events and, in a sense, had redeemed its failure ever to discuss the gymnasium at any previous point, a fact noted by Dean of the Graduate Faculties George Fraenkel, who assumed the chair at the meeting when President Kirk was called away.

The recent events seemed to harden the official attitude toward the gymnasium, as indicated in the notes from a discussion with Vice President Truman that began to circulate on April 24. One of the members of SDS, who had attended the rally in Harlem the previous Saturday, met with Truman shortly after the Hamilton Hall takeover to warn him of the mood of violence surrounding the gymnasium controversy. Although the substance of the conversation was supposed to be confidential, the student, Edward Hyman ('69), distributed a personal statement the following day. He recommended giving in to community demands as the only possible way to prevent violence of even greater proportions than the sit-in and captivity of Dean Coleman. One of Truman's comments was that construction of the gymnasium in Morningside Park was a "matter of principle" both with him and with President Kirk and that they could not capitulate to such pressure. Elaborating on Columbia's legal right to built the gymnasium, the vice president reportedly said that "legality alone determines both morality and justice"—a phrase that would dog him on placards until he left the university the following year. Truman thought people should understand that, even at the risk of possible violence, "the precedent of legality over all other considerations was the rule and order of this society." Even the possibility of sabotage of the building before or after completion would not affect the administration's determination to continue with construction of the gymnasium, because it was a "matter of PRINCIPLE."[239] For the last decade, the gymnasium in Morningside Park had been advanced as a symbol of Columbia's generosity in neighborhood policy; now it had suddenly become a symbol of law and order for the university administration.

Before the conclusion of the college faculty meeting that recommended suspension of the excavation and a review of the entire gymnasium project, President Kirk and Vice President Truman were called away to meet with Sutton, Paterson, and Rangel, the three black political leaders who had been most actively involved with the gymnasium controversy, for an intensive review of the situation (it is not clear where this meeting took place, while Low Library was occupied by the students). Over the past years, local residents who made up the grassroots opposition had lost considerable faith in their elected officials; however, the closeness of these officials to the Black Students of Hamilton Hall and the firmness with which they supported the students' demands redeemed them in the eyes of their constituency. According to Bill Sales, an impressive unity developed between these political representatives, the students, and members of the community during these days, and the representatives also proved valuable as liaisons and providers of information.[240]

During the intense discussion on Wednesday afternoon, the only thing that the Columbia administration would or could promise was to call a meeting of the board of trustees as soon as possible to discuss the crisis situation. During the past twenty-four hours, President Kirk had emphasized several times that the university statutes required a three-day notice to call an official meeting of the board.

Pressured by political leaders, the faculty, and even some members of the administration, President Kirk agreed to make a special, separate offer to the Black Students of Hamilton Hall. Associate Dean Alexander

---

[239.] Text of a personal statement by Edward Hyman (Columbia, 1969) on his confidential discussion with Vice President David B. Truman, distributed on campus April 24, 1968.

[240.] Author's interview with Bill Sales, June 1971.

Platt, who favored this move, delivered a letter signed by him, rather than President Kirk or Vice President Truman. The letter read:

> To the Columbia University Students in Hamilton Hall:
>
> This is to state that the disciplinary action taken against the students presently occupying Hamilton Hall will be disciplinary probation for the academic year 1968–1969 and the remainder of the present academic year, if you leave by 10 PM tonight and, when leaving the building, supply your name by signature. Criminal charges will not be pressed if the above conditions are met.
>
> In view of the action taken by the Columbia College faculty, the President plans to ask the chairman of the Trustees to call a special meeting of the Board at the earliest practicable time to consider the faculty recommendations concerning the gymnasium.

The black students suspected that the offer might not be binding, because it did not carry President Kirk's signature. They were also aware of the hard-line approach the administration had taken during the conversations with Sutton, Paterson, and Rangel earlier that afternoon, as the latter had gone to Hamilton Hall afterward to brief the students. When the letter arrived at the occupied building, an expected rally of Harlem supporters had just been postponed because of rain. There were indications, however, that the popularity of the students' cause was growing in the black community where it was receiving a great deal of publicity. On the campus itself, the faculty was beginning to assert itself independently from the administration, and support among students continued to grow. In view of these developments, it was not surprising that the Black Students of Hamilton Hall rejected the separate settlement proposed in the letter.

Wednesday night, the campus was ringed by police and closed to all not carrying Columbia identification cards. Faculty and sympathetic students guarded Hamilton Hall from attacks by the newly formed group of right-wing students calling themselves "Majority Opposition."

At the usual Avery Hall closing hour of 10:00 p.m., the students of the School of Architecture refused to leave. Thus, it became another "liberated zone," although somewhat different in character from the buildings occupied by the other students. This occupying group, mostly graduate students, spent their time in Avery Hall discussing and planning for a better community and university environment. They were often joined by sympathetic faculty, who participated in their discussions and stayed in contact with the occupiers throughout the sit-in.[241]

A second letter from the Columbia administration, this one with President Kirk's signature, was also refused by the Black Students of Hamilton Hall. In all quarters, Wednesday night was filled with feverish activity dusk to dawn. Students took over another building, Fayerweather Hall. Concerned faculty members were anxiously aware of the need to act as a body to assume a positive mediating role, even though Columbia officials were making no effort to include faculty representatives in their discussions. The lack of an effective liaison at this critical moment between the faculty gathering in Philosophy Hall and Columbia's administration was most regrettable, and might have prevented police intervention.

On Thursday afternoon, Vice President Truman reported to about one hundred faculty members at Philosophy Hall that Columbia could not "afford" to stop the gymnasium construction, because it would cost $6 million to break the contract. This statement was disputed as ludicrous, especially by some lawyers among those attending. The next day, the *Columbia Daily Spectator* cited Henry W. Profitt, Counsel to the University, as giving a far lower estimate of the cost for halting the gym. Although both Profitt and a spokesman for the George A. Fuller Construction Company declared that it was impossible to estimate the cost of either temporarily or permanently stopping the project, they agreed that in either case it would be less than what Vice President Truman had predicted.[242] The cost of repairing the enormous damage to Olmsted's Morningside Park was not mentioned by anyone at this time. Later that year, a member of the Columbia administration, who wished to remain

---

241. Richard Rosenkranz, *Across the Barricades*, Lippincott, 1971, 2-3 and passim.
242. *Columbia Daily Spectator*, April 26, 1968.

anonymous, stated privately that the loss incurred by terminating the planned gymnasium would amount to about $2.5 million.

Truman's curt refusal to engage the faculty members in a meaningful dialogue was perhaps due to his exhaustion. Whatever the reason, it was followed that same afternoon by formation of the Ad Hoc Faculty Group (AHFG) and the group's formulation of four proposals for mediating the crisis engulfing the campus. The first requested that the trustees "implement the immediate cessation of excavation on the gymnasium site, by telephone if necessary."[243] The fact that the AHFG placed the gymnasium proposal above those involving disciplinary and other student and campus related concerns demonstrated that it was now, belatedly, recognized as the central issue. How much this was influenced by apprehension regarding support from Harlem for the Black Students of Hamilton Hall is not documented, but may be assumed—in particular, because the march canceled by rain the evening before was, by early Thursday evening, forming in front of the campus entrance at 116th Street and Broadway. College Walk's "ornamental" gates were closed, and the entrance was blocked off with police barricades. Outside the gates, a sizeable crowd was made up of black militants, community people from Harlem and Morningside Heights, and students. Their anger was fanned by speeches from the Mau Mau Society, Harlem CORE, Student Nonviolent Coordinating Committee, the United Black Front, the Peace and Freedom Party, and others. Massed inside the gates were students from the so-called "Majority Coalition," a conservative-centrist faction including many Columbia athletes. Those rallying outside the gates were intent upon marching across Campus Walk to Hamilton Hall and on to the gymnasium site in Morningside Park.

For some moments, it looked as if the shoving between the black groups attempting to break through the gates and the white students "holding the line" would erupt into serious violence. However, Dean Coleman and several faculty members were able to persuade the students inside to give way and let the march proceed through the campus, thereby defusing an explosive situation. The march across Campus Walk

---

[243.] Avorn, et al., *Up Against the Ivy Wall,* 92 and passim.

gave the black demonstrators a symbolic victory, after which most of them left Morningside Heights. The white Majority Coalition remained on campus, frustrated and angry that Dean Coleman had prevented them from defending "their" territory from the "invaders." They moved to Fayerweather Hall with the intention of dislodging the radical occupants, but members of the Ad Hoc Faculty Group rushed from nearby Philosophy Hall to persuade both irate factions to join them in their building and engage in dialogue.

Meanwhile, President Kirk and Vice President Truman were conferring over the use of police force to clear the occupied buildings.[244] Because large anti-war demonstrations were scheduled for the next three days in downtown New York City, police officials informed the Columbia administration that they would be unable to provide enough men for a campus clearing action during those three days—thus, any police actions would have to take place either Thursday night or after the weekend. Kirk and Truman chose immediate action, and informed the Ad Hoc Faculty Group of their decision to telephone Mayor Lindsay asking for the police to intervene in the campus crisis. Faculty members were stunned.

At 3:00 a.m. on Friday, April 26, Truman announced this decision on the steps of the east-side entrance to Low Library, where "To the Gym!" had been the rallying cry barely three days before, concluding, "At the request of the Mayor and without prejudice to continuation at a later time, we have suspended construction on the gymnasium pending further discussion."[245] Rather than waiting for the announced emergency meetings, as previously insisted upon, trustee approval of suspending gymnasium construction had been achieved via telephone during Thursday afternoon and evening. Although the administration emphasized that it was not terminating the project in Morningside Park, the general belief was that work on the gymnasium could not be resumed—at least not without fundamental changes in the design and purpose of the building.

---

244. It is not clear where they met while the administration's headquarters in Low Library were occupied by the students.

245. Avorn, et al., *Up Against the Ivy Wall*, 115.

In the end, there was no telephone call to Mayor Lindsay asking for the police to vacate the by now five occupied buildings (Low Library, Hamilton Hall, Fayerweather, Avery, and Mathematics—see Figure 25). Members of the Ad Hoc Faculty Group were so enraged at hearing the decision to call in the police that they initiated intense discussions with President Kirk and persuaded him to desist. His change of heart must have been due, at least in part, to a heavy scuffle between the police guarding the doors to Low Library and a group of faculty members. After a police club connected with the scalp of a young faculty member, the sight of his bleeding head contributed to President Kirk's decision to forgo police action and allow AHFG members to continue their dialogue with the Strike Coordinating Committee, which had evolved from the students, primarily SDS, in the occupied buildings.

# 11

## The Icon is Demolished
### March 3, 1969

By suspending construction of the gymnasium, the Columbia trustees considerably deflated what had become a prime demand of the student protest. Perhaps the move was intended to undercut community support for further actions by the students and to tempt the Black Students of Hamilton Hall into a separate settlement. If so, it did not succeed on either count. Though peace and quiet returned to the despoiled hillside in Morningside Park, the uproar on campus continued unabated.

On Friday, April 26, tension mounted dramatically when H. Rap Brown and Stokely Carmichael strode past an astonished group of faculty and security officers standing guard at the campus entrance at 116th Street and Amsterdam Avenue. In an effective show of support, they made a brief visit to the Black Students of Hamilton Hall. When they emerged from the occupied building, they publicly expressed their full confidence in the way the "brothers and sisters" inside were handling the situation, and then left as quickly as they had arrived. Their appearance on campus served to revive press interest in the Black Students of Hamilton Hall. Perhaps because of the air of quiet mystery hanging over the building, the media had given it little coverage during the previous few days, concentrating instead on the colorful seizure of other buildings, now including Avery, Fayerweather, and Mathematics, and the liberated life within. In Fayerweather Hall, "guerrilla theater" and an unconventional wedding took place. In improvised dress and witnessed by students with candles, the wedding of individuals named Andrea and Richard was performed by Rev. William Starr, who had been smuggled into the building.[246]

The trustees met Friday evening, and on Saturday morning, Chairman of the Board William Petersen issued a statement that pulled the rug out from under the ongoing negotiations being conducted by the Ad Hoc Faculty Group. While this group was edging toward a compromise acceptable to all sides without loss of face by anyone, Petersen's statement spread additional confusion and mistrust on the tense campus. It mentioned "a small minority of students, aided and abetted by outsiders" who were disrupting normal university life." He reaffirmed that all disciplinary power rested with the university president, and proceeded to say of the gymnasium:

> The Trustees feel that the attempts to depict the construction of that building as a matter involving a racial issue or discrimination is an attempt to create an entirely false issue by individuals who are either not conversant with, or who disregard, the facts. However, the Trustees have approved the action taken by the administration at the request of the Mayor of New York City, on Thursday, April 25, to halt construction activities temporarily. This action represented an appropriate response, and a courtesy to the chief executive of the City at a time of tension.[247]

This astonishing statement dispelled any notion that the suspension of the gymnasium construction might signal a change of heart—and actually served to stiffen the students' resolve that their conditions be met. Yet, as the weekend wore on without a settlement in sight, there were signs of weariness all around.

---

246. Avorn, et al., *Up Against the Ivy Wall*, 130.
247. Ibid., 143–144.

The Ad Hoc Faculty Group, its position now undermined by the trustees, made desperate efforts to come up with a workable basis for a settlement. Following the announcement that gymnasium construction would be suspended, the Student Strike Coordinating Committee's primary demand was for "amnesty," a demand that appeared to be unacceptable to the administration, to a good part of the faculty, and to the students opposing the demonstrators.

All this time, on-and-off negotiations were being conducted with the Black Students of Hamilton Hall, mostly by Kenneth Clark, a noted black psychologist, and Theodore Kheel, who had helped settle many labor disputes in the metropolitan area. The occupants of Hamilton Hall, however, held out in solidarity with the white students and refused a separate settlement. Instead, they sent a call to the Harlem community asking for a "real show of physical support as well as moral support." Their request brought several hundred marchers to Morningside Heights on Monday evening, just hours before the police "bust." There were rumors that one or another of the white units—Fayerweather or Avery Hall—was preparing a separate, conciliatory set of demands, but the black students, for their part, never wavered.

By Monday evening, there were signs that the predicted police bust was imminent. Detachments of the Tactical Police Force began arriving, but so did a march of several hundred supporters of the black students. Bill Sales tells of a desperate and fruitless search for a bullhorn so that the students in Hamilton Hall could address the marchers and urge them to remain near the campus to await, and perhaps divert, the expected police action.[248] Instead, Charles 37 X Kenyatta played into the hands of the police by dispersing the black rally at midnight. By then, the Hamilton Hall Steering Committee had arranged for a nonviolent exodus of the black students from the building, before any of the other occupied strongholds were touched. Before the eyes of observers that included psychologist Clark, Human Rights Commissioner Booth, representatives from Mayor Lindsay's office, and the students' lawyers, the Black Students of Hamilton Hall were quietly taken to police wagons parked on Amsterdam Avenue via the maintenance tunnels that run like catacombs under the entire campus.

---

248. Author's interview with Bill Sales, June 1971.

Once the black students were away, at about 2:30 a.m. on Tuesday, April 30, the bust began. One thousand policemen clubbed their way through the protective cordons of faculty members formed around the buildings, leaving a number of prominent academics with gashed scalps. Hundreds of students were removed forcefully and brutally. As if this were not enough violence, the police—in particular a thug-like contingent camouflaged as "jocks"—swept across the center of the campus clubbing and chasing many spectators, including faculty wives, who had heard the noise and rushed to the campus. From afar, one could hear the roar of the action and the clatter of hooves as mounted police pursued onlookers down Broadway and toward Riverside Drive.

Regardless of how much the police bust had been anticipated, the real thing was traumatic beyond the expectations of even battle-scarred civil rights marchers. The campus was left paralyzed with revulsion and despair. It was impossible to continue the academic routine. Tyler Smith, one of the architecture students who had participated in the occupation of Avery Hall, expressed a common reaction:

> Seeing how the cops acted was one thing, something I hadn't really known about before. But the thing that really affected me was the simple fact that this was how Kirk and the Trustees and Lindsay had chosen to deal with us, that this was how they'd chosen to respond to the demands of everyone, of the students, the Harlem community, the involved faculty—everyone, me included. That's what really changed my thinking, because it made me realize that it was true, everything the radicals had been saying about the way the system works in this country, about how power is used when the demands for change reach a certain level.[249]

Most sectors of the university suspended classes for the remainder of the spring semester, though students were still in evidence. Near College Walk, passersby were invited to play an original game by the Pageant

---

249. Rosenkranz, *Across the Barricades*, 41.

Players of the Theater Division of the Columbia School of the Arts. The game of "Trustees," based on the popular pastime Monopoly, was here played with real people on a large "board," with participants proceeding from "Risk" to "Free Park (Morningside)," and on to "Bust." The game's master of ceremonies, outfitted with black top hat and tails, was Joe Lovett, the white film student who had carried the black infant during the torchlight march.[250]

The Columbia protest actions brought nationwide, even international, notoriety to the gymnasium in Morningside Park. Political figures who had previously paid scant attention to the issue made their opinions known, urging the city government to look into the matter. Well-known professors of political science suddenly discovered that they had a political issue on their doorstep that they had never noticed before. Morningside Park became famous—people came to take pictures of it, and the excavation site was highlighted for tourists in sightseeing buses.

Residents of the surrounding communities staged several additional protests against Columbia's urban policies, in which students also participated. The veteran opponents of the gym in the Park, who had somewhat lost touch with each other in the turmoil of the last few days, came together, expressing incredulity at what had happened to their "lost cause." A victory of sorts had been achieved, but the community opposition regarding racism did not consider the case closed or their position vindicated. Though work on the site had been stopped, many shared Victor Crichton's opinion that the takeover of public parkland had to be challenged in court. With Irving Thau as attorney, the Morningside Park Preservation Committee, chaired by Crichton, filed suit on April 30—the day of the bust—against Columbia University and the City of New York, alleging that the land for the proposed gymnasium had been leased by the City for an "inadequate" amount of money.

On May 20, a public hearing was held before the City Council's Committee on State Legislation in an effort to persuade the committee to send a home rule message to the State Legislature for passage of the

---

250. Photograph in *Columbia Daily Spectator*, May 7, 1969.

bill sponsored by Paterson and Rangel. If passed, this bill would void the contract under which Columbia University had leased the land in Morningside Park. At the public hearing on this matter, John Wheeler, attorney and general counsel for the university, gave the storage of arms in the proposed gymnasium as the reason for the separation of the community section from the rest of the facility— letting "the cat out of the bag," as it were, according to Bob McKay. It remained doubtful, however, that the City Council would ask for home rule on the Paterson-Rangel bill, and it never did.

There was a need to pull the community together and plan for the future. Members of the West Harlem Community Organization sought to raise money—penny by penny—to replace the obliterated children's playground, and began to solicit ideas for the rehabilitation of the Park. For this purpose, and riding the crest of general interest in Morningside Park, a "Harlem Family-Community-Columbia Students" picnic was planned for Saturday, June 1, 1968. A crowd of over 200 passed through the gates at Morningside Avenue on the east side of the Park. In a festive mood, they gathered in the fenced-off construction site, "liberating" it and making it their own. Large watermelons were brought over from the headquarters of the West Harlem Community Organization. Joe Monroe strummed his guitar. Suki Ports, Bob McKay, and others improvised garden patches on the slopes of the excavation, planting flowers and vegetables. Others were busy trying to clear the level area of construction debris. Children crawled through or balanced atop the big cement pipes stored on the site. An air of happy anticipation prevailed as people discussed what could be done to repair the damage so that the community could make use of what was now considered its turf. The crater left by the blasting had destroyed the "meadow" forever, along with Olmsted's network of paths connecting Morningside Drive with the level below the embankment. The entire area had been stripped of its large trees and vegetation, and all topsoil had been removed. It seemed impossible to restore the Park to its original design. In the moonlike landscape of debris and rocks, some tried to visualize an amphitheater, surrounded by natural terraces that could accommodate a variety of events.

In the late spring of 1968, involvement with Morningside Park was lively. Just a few days after the community picnic, Columbia students chose Morningside Park as a place to celebrate after holding a counter-commencement. The official commencement transpired in the Cathedral of St. John the Divine under strict security, with Professor Richard Hofstadter substituting for President Kirk in the traditional role of speaker. Several hundred students and faculty walked out of the ceremony by prearrangement to attend an alternate festivity in front of the alma mater statue at Low Library, where they were joined by spectators that included many people from the community. It was the first time that residents from the surrounding neighborhoods were welcomed to participate in Columbia's graduation exercises—the campus was usually closed off for these events. The community people had stood by the students during the days of the sit-in, the agony of the police bust, and the strike that followed, giving practical and moral support. Now, in the bright sunshine, they cheered the students and speakers. The counter-commencement was really more than a graduation exercise. It was an affirmation of the beliefs and concerns that had motivated recent actions, and it ended with a celebratory march to Morningside Park.

The disruption of academic life at Columbia in the spring of 1968 took many by surprise, particularly some members of the faculty who were oblivious to the danger signals that had been heralding these mesmerizing events for a long time. Because the action-filled days were so densely packed with conflicting attitudes, overlapping incidents, and diverse interest groups, there was an urgent need to sort things out, to clarify what had really happened, and what, ultimately, had caused it all. Faculty efforts to try to first control and later to understand the protests resulted in several memorable university meetings. During these, as well as some "official" ones, the gymnasium issue hovered in the background. The suspension of construction gave it a back seat, especially after the traumatic bust.

On May 4, 1968, the newly created Executive Committee of the Faculties requested a fact-finding commission "to investigate and report on the disturbances on the campus during the week of April 23–30, 1968." The investigation was to cover: "1) The chronology of events up to the intervention of the police, and 2) the underlying causes of the disturbances."[251] The trustees and the administration gave their support to this project and cooperated with the commission headed by Archibald Cox, Professor of Law at Harvard University. In hearings involving 79 witnesses, 3,790 pages of transcripts were gathered, and a 222-page report, *Crisis at Columbia*, was published in October. Its shortcomings derive from the necessity of condensing an enormously complex situation with a history related in this narrative dating back to the establishment of Columbia University on Morningside Heights. Furthermore, two groups pivotal to the events refused to testify. The Black Students of Hamilton Hall formally declined because, they said, the investigating panel included neither student nor community representatives, and therefore lacked authority to "investigate the guilt of the University administration." They also repeated their primary demand regarding the gymnasium in Morningside Park.[252] The Strike Coordinating Committee also refused to cooperate with the hearings.

For members of the community, the fact-finding hearings represented a unique chance to describe Columbia's urban policies and attitude toward its neighbors to a group of influential "outsiders" and a wider public. Unfortunately, some of the testimonies contained factual errors and erroneous recall. The dates and chronology of the gymnasium in Morningside Park were jumbled. This was probably due to the fact that the witnesses had little time to prepare notes.

Though *Crisis at Columbia* did not spare criticism of the university's administration, it also did not indict those empowered with setting the philosophy and policies of Columbia as strongly as many had wished. Nevertheless, the summer of 1968 brought a different cast into Low Library. President Kirk resigned, and Andrew Cordier, a former United Nations diplomat and dean of the School of International Affairs, succeeded him as acting president. Cordier recommended dismissal of criminal charges against 400 students who had been arrested, as well as

---

[251.] As noted in *Crisis at Columbia: The Cox Commission Report of the Fact-Finding Commission Appointed to Investigate the Disturbances at Columbia University in April and May 1968*.

[252.] Avorn, et al., *Up Against the Ivy Wall*, 235–236.

reducing disciplinary charges, from suspension to censure, against many students. Notably, criminal charges against community people arrested in the sit-ins at the gymnasium construction site were not dismissed until two years later, in September 1970, after they had appeared in court numerous times.

In November, a statement over Cordier's signature on "Progress and Policy" appeared in *The Columbia Chronicle*, a fund-raising bulletin.[253] It contained thoughts on "limits to expansion," mentioning the possibility of high-rise buildings, and raised hope for a change in Columbia's planning policies. "In accord with the democratic process," it said, "the Morningside and Harlem communities should be given a free and uninhibited opportunity, divorced from the emotion of last Spring, to determine through procedures of their own choice whether in fact they do or do not want the gymnasium facilities in Morningside Park. The University will abide by the results of such a public consensus."

Among those who had opposed the gymnasium over the past years, there was a certain amount of consternation in realizing that, even at this late date, Columbia University was not certain where community sentiment lay regarding the project, and that the administration felt a public consensus was necessary. There remained the perennial question as to just how Columbia might define the "community," and who would be asked. In addition, it seemed offensive for Cordier to imply that opposing the gymnasium was an emotional, spur-of-the-moment reaction.

Victor Crichton wrote a critical piece that appeared in *The Manhattan Tribune*, recent successor to the *West Side News*, on November 30th. Cordier's letter of response, dated December 18, reiterated the sincerity of his position: "I have made it clear that the question as to whether the gym should or should not be built is a matter for the community to decide. If they should conclude, by means of their own choice, that this facility is in the interest of the recreational needs of their children, young people as well as adults, we shall then continue to consult with the community regarding the best means of implementing its construction as

253. *The Columbia Chronicle*, vol.2, no.6, November 1968.

well as the development of Morningside Park—if the community should desire such development. On the other hand, if the community does not desire the gymnasium facilities, the gymnasium will not be built on that site. This policy is so simple, so fair, and so straight-forward that there would seem no reason why there should be any confusion about it."[254]

Crichton's response to this statement was printed right next to Cordier's letter. He pointed out that Cordier referred only to the "community gym" as if there were no "Columbia gym" involved at all. The dubious justification of park encroachment was not mentioned. Crichton summarized the history of the controversy since the early fifties, showing that all along Columbia University had claimed consent and enthusiasm for the project. He feared that Columbia would "manipulate" community groups as it had in the past, as well as the State Legislature, the Mayor's office, the Parks Department, and the City Council.[255] Crichton was voicing the suspicions that any move by Columbia stirred in the neighborhoods, regardless of the sincerity of its promulgators. Unfortunately, Cordier mentioned "the development of Morningside Park" as concomitant with the possible construction of the gymnasium, which conjured up a picture of the remainder of the parkland subdivided into building lots or, less drastically, tied rehabilitation of the Park to acceptance of the gymnasium by the community. It was clear that, even after the spring events, Columbia did not yet realize that the basic principle and philosophy behind taking over public open space in the heart of a city for private construction was a matter of ethics that could hardly be resolved by a local opinion poll.

Although the community was in accord with Crichton's defense of parkland from encroachment, for those involved in the West Harlem grassroots movement, the gymnasium in Morningside Park was the icon exemplifying Columbia's racism, emblematic of its so-called "expansion" policies. For them, it was "NO gym," and they were determined to continue campaigning for this goal.

Cordier and other members of Columbia's administration were tentatively searching for a way to establish trust and reconciliation on

---

254. *The Manhattan Tribune*, January 11, 1969.
255. Ibid.

campus and within the neighborhood, although the behavior of certain trustees and officials invoked the policy that was at the root of the conflicts that had erupted so dramatically in the recent spring. In this ambiguous atmosphere, it was announced in November 1968 that the architectural firm of I. M. Pei and Partners had accepted appointment as planners for Columbia University.[256] This brought hope for a new dimension in Columbia's role as an urban institution, as Pei was considered a planner of social concern and an architect of human as well as aesthetic considerations. "Columbia is in many respects a microcosm of the city," Pei said. "Just as the central concern in the planning of a city is the welfare of its people, the plan for Columbia should consider the welfare of its constituents, which are the students, faculty and the people of the communities around it. To achieve this, extensive consultation with the various groups concerned in the planning process is absolutely necessary. Such a plan should accommodate an orderly growth of the university and the community with a minimum of dislocation leading to the creation of an environment that enhances the quality of life for all."[257]

It was clear that Pei's acceptance of this responsibility was based on the fresh context provided by the spring's events. Upon appointing Henry Cobb as "partner-in-charge" of the project, Pei declared that they were working not just on a "campus plan" but rather in the realm of "urban planning." The news that the university was at last obtaining professional guidance was cheered by those associated with the School of Architecture, who were longing to teach in an environment less contradictory to their ideals. Architecture faculty had objected for years to their lack of involvement in the university's architectural choices. (University Planning Coordinator Salmen had once declared that "the function of the Architecture School is to teach architecture, not to practice it," indicating gross ignorance of one of the university's finest professional schools.[258]) Now, at last, there was hope for rapport and

---

[256.] *Columbia University Newsletter*, November 18, 1968.

[257.] For a detailed description of I.M. Pei and Partner's reaction to the proposal of planning for Columbia University, see Bergdoll et al., *Mastering McKim's Plan*, pp. 117–129.

[258.] *Columbia Daily Spectator*, December 13, 1966.

cooperation on a professional level. During and since the Avery Hall sit-in, architecture faculty and students, with the support of the school's dean, Kenneth A. Smith, had been conducting intensive meetings that concerned restructuring the curriculum and revising its aims and organization more toward the relationship of the built urban environment to the community. Indeed, one of Pei's first proposals for proceeding with the master plan was to involve a group from the School of Architecture to provide liaison with his firm, and he personally spoke informally with faculty and students. When questioned on his opinion regarding the gymnasium in Morningside Park, he said that he felt that the site did "not belong to the University," but that if the community desired it and formulated a workable plan, there was still a possibility that it would be built. He also emphasized that he was encouraged by the "new policy" of Columbia toward the community.[259] It was, however clear that the final decision-making power in matters of expansion and planning rested with the trustees, although it was hoped that they would follow the suggestions that resulted from numerous consultations with community representatives, students, and faculty conducted by Pei and his staff.

I. M. Pei and Partners did not present "Planning for Columbia University: An Interim Report" until March 1970, after 15 months of study, and then effectively resigned June 30, 1970. Citing their discussions with a wide spectrum of constituents and community groups, their report decried the sharp separation between university and community, in particular the "concrete barriers." The Pei report did not please Columbia's administration for a variety of reasons, most likely because it contained comments such as: "Columbia is feeling the pressures of growth in every aspect of university life. On the whole, the problems have been caused by an *ad hoc* approach to space needs, which is no substitute for planning."[260] The authors of the Pei report considered the campus "incoherent and incomplete, and its space inefficiently used."[261]

---

[259.] *Columbia Daily Spectator*, December 12, 1968.

[260.] I. M. Pei and Partners, *Planning for Columbia University: An Interim Report*, March 1970.

[261.] Ibid.

In October 1968, ARCH (Architects' Renewal Committee in Harlem) had released a brochure that reported on a comprehensive study of the West Harlem neighborhood and included recommendations for urban improvements. It placed the future of Morningside Park in a wider context—"The goal of any planning for Morningside Park should be to make the Park a meaningful part of the communities surrounding it"[262]—and provided a concept for the Park that reflected this philosophy, thus professionally validating what people living in the areas surrounding the Park had been striving for over many years. The concept included a tentative plan for the gymnasium site whose focal point was an amphitheatre to be shaped by the contours left by the excavation (see Figure 26). This part of the Park concept also incorporated community suggestions, including a modest facilities building, recreational areas for all age groups (the elderly, families, teenagers, and young children), a soul food garden, picnic tables, sand pits, and a multi-purpose rink.[263]

This concept of urbanism was alien to Columbia University's antiquated, insular point of view, and the university ignored the ARCH plan altogether, because the project to build the gymnasium in Morningside was not considered terminated. There were some other unfavorable reactions to the ARCH plan as well. Many of those who had opposed the gym in the Park primarily on the basis of park encroachment complained that it introduced "too much concrete" into the parkland. The plans shown in the brochure were, indeed, rather stark and devoid of greenery, which may have been due to the schematic manner of the presentation. Proponents pointed out that the plan extended eastward, co-opting a stretch of Morningside Avenue, creating a direct, continuous transition from the streets of West Harlem into the Park area proper, thus integrating Park and community, and extending West Harlem's "turf." ARCH insisted that its plan was not a final and absolute version, rather it was meant as the basis for discussion—to be modified to conform to the overall needs of the adjoining communities.

---

[262]. *West Harlem/Morningside: A Community Proposal*, prepared by Architects' Renewal Committee in Harlem Inc. and West Harlem Community Organization Inc. (New York, September 1968).

[263]. Ibid., 39.

The architects from ARCH, with the assistance of Bob McKay, worked out a program of slide presentations to be held at various locations in West Harlem and Morningside Heights during the fall and winter of 1968/69. Unfortunately, these evening programs were poorly attended, demonstrating the difficulties of implementing participatory planning even in what were ideal circumstances.

As consideration of the ARCH plan proceeded, the gymnasium controversy continued. In February, Acting President Cordier told the *Columbia Daily Spectator* that he had conducted informal talks with several local leaders and spokesmen for the community, and that within the next couple of weeks one hundred letters requesting a formal and final opinion on the Columbia-Community Gymnasium in Morningside Park would be sent out. He would not, however, reveal the names of those who would receive the letters. Should the replies indicate opposition to the project or a "serious split," the gymnasium would not be built in the Park.[264]

The secrecy of a ballot that guaranteed anonymity to the individuals polled and left the selection of the latter up to the university aroused mistrust and ill feelings. An open discussion, rather than this type of poll, might have made the procedure legitimate in the eyes of an extremely suspicious local community.[265] To counter the rapidly mounting criticism, the decision was made to send the letters to "hundreds" rather than one hundred, and a copy would be published in *The Manhattan Tribune*—a new local newspaper that emphasized a black/white editorial policy—so that anyone could respond to the query.[266]

Neighborhood groups reacted quickly to the proposed poll. Morningsiders United, under its chair James Latimore, called an open meeting for the evening of February 27, 1969, to "educate" local residents on the issues at hand. For the first time, the university allowed a community meeting to be held on campus, in McMillan Theater, perhaps to prevent its being held in Harlem. The announced speakers included I. M. Pei, spokesmen for Columbia, political leaders opposed to the gymnasium

---

264. *Columbia Daily Spectator*, February 13, 1969.
265. Ibid., editorial comment, February 19, 1969.
266. Ibid., February 27, 1969.

project, and representatives and members of the neighborhoods. This meeting was called following a news conference in which a coalition of several Harlem groups, among them the West Harlem Community Organization, Harlem CORE, and ARCH, declared that they would ignore the poll because it would not represent community sentiment. They demanded that Columbia completely abandon all claims to land in Morningside Park, and that the Parks Department officially adopt and implement the plan proposed by ARCH, which, they insisted, was based on the wishes and needs of the community.[267]

The meeting at McMillan Theater was lively, and the program covered a range of community issues. Architect Pei did not participate, but representatives from the university attended. The most dramatic moment came when State Assemblyman Franz Leichter announced that Acting President Cordier would recommend to the trustees at their next meeting, on Monday, March 3, that Columbia should abandon all plans for constructing the gymnasium in Morningside Park. No one was prepared for this, although rumors about such a decision had begun to leak from Low Library earlier that day, when it became known that Franklin H. Williams, the Afro-American Director of Columbia's Center on Urban-Minority Affairs, had resigned from the Special Committee on Community Relations. This committee had been established quite recently, in February 1969, "to explore Columbia's relations with the community, emphasizing land use and planning, local hiring and buying, and university-sponsored services in the community." [268]

In an open letter to Acting President Cordier, Williams explained that he had agreed to serve on the Committee on Community Relations under the impression that one of his responsibilities would be to make recommendations regarding the gymnasium issue. However, neither the committee, nor he as the director of the Urban Center, nor any member of his staff had been consulted. They had, in his words, "worked conscientiously to earn the trust, respect and cooperation of the Harlem and Morningside Heights communities and of the black students here at

---

[267.] Ibid., February 26, 1969.

[268.] Columbia University Office of Public Information release, February 19, 1969.

Columbia." The letter continued: "In the process, we have had to overcome deep antagonism toward this institution, rising out of a number of issues—especially the gymnasium." Voicing his strong opposition to the poll procedure, Williams wrote, "I am anxious to impress upon you by this communication my personal disagreement with the poll; my conviction that it will create serious divisions within the Harlem community; my belief that it will result in widespread antagonism developing throughout the Harlem community and segments of our student body toward this administration, and finally, that it may seriously affect the Urban Center's ability to develop the kind of cooperative working relationship between our various schools and the surrounding community that I would like to achieve, and that you and the Board of Trustees have indicated to me that you desire."[269] This forceful letter may have been decisive in Cordier's termination of the poll procedure.

Shortly after Leichter announced Cordier's recommendation, and, ironically, just as the ARCH plan for the devastated site in Morningside Park was about to be presented to the audience, a group of about twenty black community spokesmen, including the representative from ARCH, walked out. They asserted that they did not consider Cordier's intention sufficient guarantee that the Board of Trustees would terminate the gymnasium project.[270]

At their meeting the following Monday, March 3, 1969—fifteen years after the project was first suggested—Columbia University's Board of Trustees did, however, agree unanimously to terminate the construction of the gymnasium in Morningside Park. The official announcement of this decision was accompanied by discussion of a plan advanced by Pei's team for an alternative location of the building. Once more the fear of massive relocation sent shivers down the spines of local residents, although they were assured by the architect's office that the community would be consulted. Their apprehension was allayed somewhat when the awaited Pei Master Plan was formally presented in March 1970, placing the new gymnasium underneath South Field in the middle of

269. *Columbia Daily Spectator*, February 28, 1969.
270. Ibid., March 3, 1969.

the campus. This location was later rejected because of the excessive cost the excavation would entail.

In February 1971, Columbia finally settled on an appropriate site for the building that had come to epitomize the troubles of the university. Ironically, the facility was destined to occupy almost exactly the spot identified for it when enlarged athletic quarters had first been considered more than thirty years before. The plan called for renovation of University Hall and its expansion northward and westward on the campus. The search for the gymnasium site had come full circle.

One might wonder if this simple, logical solution might have prevented the upheaval of the spring of 1968. Yet, for the grassroots movement, the gymnasium in Morningside Park was a building imbued with latent meaning as the icon of Columbia University's racist policy. A storm had been foretold for decades and that icon had now been destroyed. Time would tell if this would effectively change the university's attitude toward its neighbors and lead to an urban planning approach worthy of an eminent academic institution.

# EPILOGUE

After the stirring events of the spring of 1968, the Columbia administration was expected to change its expansion tactics and attitude toward the community and "put its house in order." The decision by university's Board of Trustees to terminate the construction of the gymnasium in Morningside Park had settled the most prominent issue for the grassroots movement. However, racially motivated expansion policies continued to be a concern.

Apart from the projected gymnasium, no issue involving Columbia University and the community matched the controversy over the so-called "Pharmacy Site" in length and intensity.[271] In the wake of the crisis of 1968, it warranted renewed attention, which heightened further in 1972. Although the School of Pharmacy had abandoned the idea of moving uptown in 1966, Columbia continued to acquire other buildings adjacent to the six-building "Pharmacy Site" and proceeded to evict their tenants. In the master plan that I.M. Pei and Associates presented to the university in 1970, they recommended making the "Pharmacy Site" an example of a new approach in cooperative planning between the university and the community.[272] A building at 130 Morningside Drive was to be rehabilitated for the relocation of tenants from other buildings that were being demolished to make way for an apartment tower to house Columbia and community residents. This plan was supported by the Morningside Renewal Council and the Morningside Tenants Committee as well as Columbia's administration. ARCH accepted the challenge of further developing the plan, and in June 1972, Columbia President William McGill (named to the post in 1970) and the Urban Renewal Council held a special meeting to develop a joint community/university project. While these promising discussions were proceeding, William Bloor, still treasurer of Columbia and in charge of all its real

---

[271.] See Chapter 4, "Morningsiders United," for its history. C.C. Collins, "Solution near on Pharmacy site?" *The Westsider*, January 11, 1973.

[272.] *Columbia Daily Spectator*, "Pei Proposes Gym for South Field, Extensive on-Campus Construction," May 7, 1969.

estate operations, ordered the eviction of all remaining tenants, whom he considered squatters, from the remaining buildings other than 130 Morningside Drive. Among them were six Jesuit priests who were removed in handcuffs. It appeared that Bloor's decision came as a surprise to those concerned, including President McGill. The Pei master plan was never implemented by Columbia University.

While the attention of those residing and working on Morningside Heights was easily diverted from the ruinous sight of the crater in Morningside Park, the devastation was ever present to those in West Harlem, and so was the fear of what might happen next. Work on the gymnasium site stopped from one day to another. Equipment was removed, but the excavation with its surrounding cyclone fence was left unaltered. Over the next year, weeds began to grow over the scarred territory, and members of the West Harlem Morningside Park Committee wondered who would be responsible for rehabilitation of the Park. Understandably, Columbia maintained a hands-off attitude—but so did the city's Parks Department.

Those who had pursued the "NO Gym" effort continued meeting to discuss possibilities based on the ARCH plan that had been made public in the fall of 1968. Without participation of the community or ARCH, the city's Parks Department in 1969 initiated a study of Morningside, St. Nicholas, and Colonial Parks to be undertaken by the Urban Research Group of the School of Architecture of the City College of New York.[273] Then, in the fall of 1971, the Parks Department proceeded to discuss the restoration of Morningside Park with Columbia University. The West Harlem Community Organization only received the news about this from a newspaper article, and immediately formed the West Harlem Coalition for Morningside Park (WHCMP) to replace the West Harlem Morningside Park Committee (WHMPC). Among the fifteen members of the new coalition were several who had long been involved in the local grass roots efforts. They included Bob McKay, West Harlem Community Organization Executive Director Margaret McNeil, Suki Ports, and the author. Other members came from a variety

---

273. Christiane C. Collins, "Morningside Park: In the Making," *The Westsider*, October 26, 1972, 1, 10.

of backgrounds and represented a range of opinions about parks and recreation. All shared the conviction that Morningside Park was an integral part of the surrounding neighborhoods and that the people should be involved in planning the future of their park.

WHCMP prepared a "Statement of Community Redevelopment Objectives and Criteria for Morningside Park" to present at a meeting with Parks Commissioner August Heckscher on February 8, 1972.[274] This important session with Commissioner Heckscher was attended by all members of WHCMP, several members of the Parks Department, President McGill of Columbia University along with members of his administration, State Senator Basil Paterson, and other political leaders. Early in the discussions, President McGill declared that the university was willing to support the wishes of the community, and that in addition to the $250,000 required in the gymnasium contract, he would personally help raise another $250,000 for the redevelopment of Morningside Park. Initially, Heckscher could not be persuaded to accept the objectives presented by WHCMP, which involved restoration of the entire park. He was, however convinced by Basil Paterson and a member of the coalition, who pointed out the historic significance and worldwide notoriety generated by the gymnasium in the Park affair.

WHCMP received technical assistance from ARCH and the CCNY study in preparing the proposal for this meeting, so the presentation included drawings and a cost breakdown. Although the Parks Department could not request additional funds from the City for that fiscal year, with the assistance of Basil Paterson and Franz Leichter, WHCMP obtained $125,000 in design funds from the Board of Estimate and the City Council . Other funds for this phase were allotted by Columbia University, the U. S. Department of Housing and Urban Development, and the Model Cities program.

During the coming months, the coalition undertook an intensive study of all aspects of Morningside Park, interviewing various experts in architecture, planning, and landscape toward developing a final rehabilitation design to present to the public at large. In the spring of 1973,

---

[274.] 3 pages typewritten. C.C. Collins Personal Collection.

Lawrence Halprin & Associates (San Francisco/New York), a private architecture and environmental planning firm of international reputation, was contracted to conduct a three-day "Take Part Workshop" sponsored by WHCMP. Halprin had gained renown for devising the "Take Part Workshop" technique as a means of involving community participants in the planning process. Jim Coleman, head of the firm's New York office, explained, "one of the primary functions of the 'workshop' is to develop a common language by which the participants can share their awareness and experience of their environment."

Preparations for the three-day workshop took several weeks. Members of WHCMP and ARCH conducted meetings with residents from the neighborhoods surrounding the park to select 25 participants who offered a wide range of viewpoints and who were willing to commit to attending the entire three days of the workshop. "Woody" (Forrest) Lee became the most active representative of ARCH, and Galen Kirkland was also heavily involved. Ernie Wright, a young architect working with ARCH, supervised construction of a 12-foot scale model of the park. The Fund for the City of New York provided a $25,000 grant to support these preparations for the Morningside Park study, ARCH contributed $15,000 in services, and the Parks Department was cooperating.

During a weekend in April 1973, study participants representing a range of ages gathered at the School on the Rock at the northern edge of Morningside Park with organizers from Halprin's office, WHCMP, ARCH, and some observers, including the author. Jim Coleman from Halprin & Associates welcomed those present and explained some of the details of the "Take Part Workshop" and its component "Awareness Scores." The first day called for bus and walking tours of Morningside Park and surrounding neighborhoods, with participants recording their observations in their score books. At various stops, they talked with store owners and addressed questions to local passersby. Awareness walks through Morningside Park singled out special aspects. Gatherings at the headquarters featured tables with craft materials for painting, model building, and other nonverbal expressions; completion of questionnaires; and animated conversations in a give-and-take atmosphere. Common shared visions for the future of the Park included preservation of the unique natural environment and development of a water feature, an amphitheater sited on the rock escarpment left by Columbia's demolition, quiet walkways, and picnic areas. Interestingly, the children participating rejected built playgrounds and preferred play spaces that would take advantage of the topography and natural features, perhaps including a waterfall. The exhilarated participants found parting from their compatriots on Sunday somewhat painful.

About a month later, the group gathered for a presentation of conclusions and possible concepts assembled by Halprin & Associates, ARCH, and WHCMP for presentation to the public, the Parks Department, and other entities, in the hope of actually realizing the rehabilitation of Morningside Park. (Figure 27 shows the Lawrence Halprin & Associates plan for the restoration of Morningside Park.)

However, there was to be further delay as unforeseen financial issues interfered with progress toward redevelopment of Morningside Park.[275] Because WHCMP was not a legally constituted group, the grant from the Fund for the City to conduct the Take Part Workshop was channeled to Halprin & Associates via ARCH. In the four months after the workshop, March to June 1973, its results in the form of a graphic proposal for physical improvements in the park and a cost estimate for their implementation and maintenance were supposed to be presented to the Parks Department. However, in May 1973, upheaval within ARCH resulted in the resignation of Woody Lee, who had worked closely and most admirably with the coalition and Halprin on the project. Several other ARCH staff members involved with the Morningside Park study also left. As a result, the project came to a standstill, as Halprin & Associates refused to proceed until ARCH completed its part of the work and paid for Halprin's services. In great distress, WHCMP tried unsuccessfully to resolve the predicament at ARCH.

---

275. The description of this episode is based on the following sources: Christiane C. Collins, "Morningside Park Rehabilitation," unpublished manuscript. Christiane C. Collins, "Morningside Park Rehab Plan Almost Ready," *The Westsider*, January 3, 1974. Richard M. Catalano, "Planning the Rehabilitation of Morningside Park," report written for the Fund for the City, November 29, 1973 (5 pages typewritten). CCC Collection, Schomburg Center.

Anxious to move the project forward, the Fund for the City provided an additional modest grant channeled to Halprin via the West Harlem Community Organization. Woody Lee, now with the Urban Development Corporation in Harlem, agreed to work with Halprin during this final phase. In January of 1973, Richard M. Clurman replaced August Heckscher as Parks Commissioner. The following fall, with ARCH out of the picture, Clurman assured Margaret McNeil, Executive Director of the West Harlem Community Organization, and Bob McKay, representing WHCMP, that the community's proposals had been endorsed and that design funds had been set aside in the capital budget effective July 1974. At this time, the funds committed and pledged for the rehabilitation of Morningside Park by the City, Columbia University, and Model Cities totaled $900,000. Clurman also promised intensive maintenance for the Park, to begin in the spring of 1975.

However, it took another decade for the Department of Parks & Recreation to compose a detailed and extensive document titled "A Conceptual Master Plan for Morningside Park."[276] This well illustrated study includes a substantial history of the Olmsted and Vaux design and the Park's subsequent transformations. It covers the events leading to the uprising of 1968 and the community's endeavors to rehabilitate Morningside Park. What the document designates as Plan 1 is based primarily on the work by Halprin & Associates, which was presented to and accepted by Commissioner Clurman in 1973. A 1982 reworking of Plan 1 by the architectural firm Bond Ryder Wilson, was designated Plan 2. (Max Bond of this firm had been associated with ARCH, and Tim Wilson had worked with Halprin & Associates on the "Take Part Workshop.") The Parks Department had contracted further modifications by the architectural firm Quennell Rothschild Associates in 1983, and it was this plan that was finally implemented in 1985.

At last, the metal fences were removed, the devastated hillside was restored, the Park landscape included a waterfall and a lagoon, comfortable paths connected the surrounding neighborhoods, and a

---

276. The City of New York Department of Parks & Recreation, "A Conceptual Master Plan for Morningside Park," prepared by Bond Ryder Wilson and Quennell Rothschild Associates, July 1985.

well-designed playground beckoned children. A new generation of people from a range of backgrounds and neighborhoods is enjoying the result of a multi-ethnic, determined grassroots movement whose conviction and vision triumphed against unbelievable odds.

## The End

# CHRONOLOGY

**1811** The Commissioners' Plan for New York City lays out a rigid grid of streets for Manhattan Island extending from 23ʳᵈ Street to 155ᵗʰ Street.

---

**1868** A proposal is submitted for a park on the upper West Side of Manhattan, where the topography of the land impedes streets.

---

**1873** A preliminary study (the "Old Plan") for Morningside Park is undertaken by Frederick Law Olmsted and Calvert Vaux. Olmsted is commissioned to design Riverside Park and Drive.

---

**1887** Olmsted and Vaux present a second, revised plan for Morningside Park.

---

**1892** Construction of the Episcopal Cathedral Church of St. John the Divine begins.

---

**1893** Columbia University announces its move from downtown Manhattan to the upper West Side, later called Morningside Heights.

---

**1894** McKim, Mead & White's Master Plan for "Columbia University in the City of New York" is accepted.

---

**1947** Morningside Heights Inc. is organized, comprising fourteen institutions with Columbia University taking the leading role.

**1953** Construction begins on a large housing complex north of 123<sup>rd</sup> Street: General Grant Houses (low income) sponsored by the New York Housing Authority and Morningside Gardens sponsored by Morningside Heights Inc. Twenty-five densely populated acres are razed for "urban renewal."

---

**1954** Columbia University closes off 116<sup>th</sup> Street between Amsterdam Avenue and Broadway.

**1954** Harrison & Abramovitz are commissioned to prepare a planning study for the "East Campus" development expansion east of Amsterdam Avenue.

---

**1955** New York City Board of Estimate and Park Commissioner Robert Moses grant permission to Columbia University for construction of an athletic field on five acres of level ground in Morningside Park.

**1956** Columbia Trustees unveil first phase of East Campus superblock.

**1958** President Kirk discusses with Commissioner Moses possible construction of a gymnasium in Morningside Park next to Columbia's athletic field.

**1959** Skidmore, Owings & Merrill present to New York City their report of a study of Morningside Heights commissioned by Morningside Heights Inc.

---

**1960** Mayor Robert Wagner sends home rule message to the State Legislature to empower City of New York to lease a tract of land in Morningside Park to Columbia University for the building of a gymnasium.

**1960** Neighborhood newspaper *The Morningsider* is founded.

---

**1961** Lease and preliminary plans for the gymnasium are submitted to various city departments for consideration. Board of Estimate authorizes lease of 2.12 acres of Morningside Park to Columbia University for the construction of a gymnasium.

**1961** Gates at entrances to Morningside Park on Morningside Drive are padlocked overnight.

---

**1962** Morningside Renewal Council (MRC) is organized.

**1962** Under pressure from the Morningside Citizens Committee, the Parks Department allocates funds for a three-stage rehabilitation of Morningside Park.

**1962–1963** Columbia University receives permission to construct tennis courts in Riverside Park below 120th Street.

**1962** Columbia's School of Pharmacy decides to move uptown, purchases six occupied apartment buildings at the tip of Morningside Drive, 121st Street, and Amsterdam Ave. "Morningsiders Six" is founded to oppose eviction.

**1963–1964** P.S. 36, the "School on the Rock," is sited on the northwest tip of Morningside Park to relieve pressure on P.S. 125. Architects A. Corwin Frost and Frederick G. Frost Jr. complete school in 1967.

---

**1964** "Morningsiders United for a Diversified, Integrated Community" is founded, consisting of non-institutionally affiliated tenants of buildings on Morningside Heights.

**1964** General Neighborhood Renewal Plan is released by the (MRC).

**1964** ARCH (Architects' Renewal Committee in Harlem) is founded.

**1964** Eight-foot-high chain-link fence is installed along the "goat path" following the upper edge of Morningside Park, as part of the "rehabilitation."

**1964** Trash is collected in Morningside Park by the community.

---

**1965** Board of Estimate approves revised General Neighborhood Renewal Plan.

**1965** Plans for the gymnasium in Morningside Park are displayed in Low Library by architects Eggers & Higgins.

**1965** Thomas P. F. Hoving succeeds Newbold Morris as Parks Commissioner.

---

**1966** Morningside Renewal Council passes a resolution opposing the gymnasium in Morningside Park.

**1966** Ad Hoc Committee on Morningside Park, chaired by Amalia Betanzos, comprises thirty member organizations, including nine from Harlem, along with the Columbia University Student Council.

**1966** Ad Hoc Committee on Morningside Park invites Park Commissioner Hoving to its first protest meeting, known as the "Funeral in Morningside Park." Hoving and Columbia students attend.

**1966** State Senator Basil Paterson and Assemblyman Percy Sutton introduce bills in Albany to repeal the 1960 law permitting New York City the right to lease 2.12 acres of public parkland to Columbia University. Lacking a home rule message, the legislature does not consider the bill. Another anti-gymnasium bill by Charles Rangel and Basil Paterson, in 1967, also will fail to be considered.

**1966** "Gym in the Park" gains importance as a political issue and among Columbia students.

**1966** Ford Foundation grants $10 million to Columbia University to support new efforts in urban and minority affairs.

**1966** Columbia President's "Council on Urban-Minority Problems" is established without community representatives.

**1966** Columbia announces ground breaking for gymnasium in November, then postpones it to early 1967.

**1966** A resolution on the gymnasium controversy presented at the fall meeting of the Columbia College faculty is received with total indifference.

**1966** Columbia Congress of Racial Equality (CORE) publishes a statement entitled "White Man's Burden?" in the *Columbia Daily Spectator* (Dec. 1, 1966).

**1966** Faculty Civil Rights Group (FCRG) is established. Ignoring the gymnasium issue, the group will publish a report on "The Community and Expansion of Columbia University" in December 1967.

---

**1967** Hoving becomes director of the Metropolitan Museum of Art.

**1967** Under the leadership of Bob McKay and Joe Monroe, the focus of opposition to the gymnasium shifts to West Harlem.

**1967** The Museum of Modern Art opens the exhibition "The New City: Architecture and Urban Renewal" with focus on Harlem.

**1967** Columbia obtains extension of "final plans" for building the gymnasium from the Board of Estimate. Meetings in Borough President Percy Sutton's office are attended by representatives of the university, political leaders, and elected officials, but no one from the community. No agreements are reached.

**1967** Morningside Renewal Council, representing sixty community organizations, votes to oppose gymnasium.

**1967** Two local newspapers merge to become *The West Side News and Morningsider*.

**1967** Columbia University accepts a deal with inventor Richard Strickland to accept royalties in return for its medical school attesting to the safety and health benefits of Strickland's cigarette filter.

**1967** The West Harlem Community Organization initiates formation of a West Harlem Morningside Park Committee co-chaired by Bob McKay and Joseph Monroe, stating total opposition to constructing the gymnasium.

**1967** Distribution of a leaflet showing a sneaker-shod crow lying on its back inscribed "Stop Columbia University GYM-CROW in Morningside Park – July 29, 1967" marks a turning point in the anti-gymnasium struggle.

**1967** The Board of Estimate permits alteration of gymnasium plans to include a community swimming pool.

**1967** The Board of Estimate permits moving the gymnasium groundbreaking deadline from November 1967 to February 28, 1968.

**1967** A letter from Morningside Urban Renewal Council Chairman Dwight Smith to Mayor Lindsay regarding the gymnasium says "public interest in this instance has been betrayed by our public officials."

**1967** Columbia University installs iron gates at both ends of "College Walk."

**1967** West Harlem Morningside Park Committee holds a rally at 116th Street and the Broadway gates; an effigy of Columbia Trustee Frank S. Hogan is burned.

**1967** The Ford Foundation grant is allocated to ten projects, including two new entities, a Center on Urban-Minority Affairs and a Development Division, without input from neighborhood leaders.

**1967** The Student Citizenship Council objects to the allocation and initiates a meeting at Columbia. Many Harlem and Morningside organizations attend. The meeting focuses on Gym Crow.

**1967** Invited by African-American students, H. Rap Brown, chairman of the Student Nonviolent Coordinating Committee, speaks at Columbia University.

**1967** Invited by the West Harlem Morningside Park Committee, H. Rap Brown attends a meeting in Harlem and calls for action to stop or take over Gym Crow.

---

**1968** Fencing is installed around 2.1 acres of Morningside Park during the first week in February, and Crimmins Construction Company begins preparation of the gymnasium building site.

**1968** African-American students invite H. Rap Brown to speak on campus for the second time.

**1968** On February 19, Crimmins bulldozers, axes, and power saws begin destruction of Morningside Park.

**1968** The West Harlem Morningside Park Committee calls for blocking crew from entering the gymnasium site on February 20. Students participate, and there is sympathetic media coverage. Bob McKay climbs into raised scoop of bulldozer, and others sit in front of it. Twelve persons are arrested. Other morning vigils follow.

**1968** On February 28, student groups, including the Citizenship Council and Students for a Democratic Society (SDS), gather at the sundial on campus for a protest that focuses on the gymnasium issue. A contingent of 150 march to the gymnasium site. A student is arrested for blocking a truck. Reverend A. Kendall Smith, in clerical garb, enters through a hidden gap in the fence and is arrested.

**1968** The West Side Community Conference, sponsored by Congressman William F. Ryan, is interrupted by protestors.

**1968** In early March, Columbia University appoints Franklin H. Williams Jr. as director of the Center for Urban and Minority Affairs, to assume the position on June 1.

**1968** In March, the Faculty Civil Rights Group, formed two years earlier, releases to the public a report entitled "The Community and the Expansion of Columbia University."

**1968** Columbia announces appointment of I. M.Pei & Associates to design a comprehensive urban plan for the university. (Pei will become a voice to be heard, but the firm's planning for Columbia will never be implemented.)

**1968** On March 20, an evening torchlight protest marches from the West Harlem Community Organization headquarters across Morningside Park to the Columbia Campus.

**1968** On March 27, the School of Architecture Faculty passes a resolution to ask President Kirk to "reconsider" building the gymnasium in Morningside Park.

**1968** On April 1, the editorial board of the *Columbia Daily Spectator* changes.

**1968** On April 3, a playground charade organized by the West Harlem Morningside Park Committee is staged on campus in front of Low Library.

**1968** On April 9, Columbia honors slain civil rights leader Martin Luther King Jr. with a memorial service in St. Paul's Chapel. No black students attend. Mark Rudd, elected leader of SDS, interrupts the service.

**1968** On April 20, Victor Solomon, chair of the Harlem chapter of CORE, organizes a rally in Harlem, drawing crowd of 400.

**1968** On Tuesday, April 23, a diverse group of over 1,000 gather for an SDS-led demonstration in front of Low Library at noon. The first speaker is Ted Gold of SDS, followed by Cicero Wilson, president of Students Afro-American Society (SAS), who electrifies the crowd. SDS is unsuccessful in an attempt to enter the side door of Low Library. Responding to a spontaneous call of "To the Gym!" the crowd moves to gymnasium site in Morningside Park. Returning to campus, Mark Rudd leads the takeover of Hamilton Hall, and Acting Dean Henry Coleman and two others become hostages. A steering "committee of eight" is formed with representatives from SAS, SDS, and the student Citizenship Council, along with Juan Gonzales representing Hispanic students.

**1968** Wednesday, April 24. SAS Supported by the Harlem community and black organizations, and intent on taking a strong stand against the gymnasium, the "Black Students of Hamilton Hall," tell the white students to leave the building. Entering through an unguarded side entrance, Mark Rudd and other SDS members then "liberate" Low Library.

**1968** On April 24, The "Ad Hoc Faculty Group" is formed for the primary purpose of contacting the Black Students of Hamilton Hall. Dean Coleman is released. The faculty petitions the university administration for immediate suspension of excavation for the gymnasium in Morningside Park.

**1968** On Thursday, April 25, the Columbia trustees vote to temporarily suspend gymnasium construction. An evening march by black militants across Campus Walk angers white students.

**1968** On Friday, April 26, at 3:00 AM, President Kirk asks Mayor Lindsay for police intervention to vacate occupied buildings, then rescinds request. The Ad Hoc Faculty Group continues its dialog with the recently formed Student Strike Coordinating Committee.

**1968** On Friday, April 26, H. Rap Brown and Stokely Carmichael briefly visit the Black Students of Hamilton Hall, who ask the Harlem community for a real show of support.

**1968** On Monday, April 28, with a police bust imminent, a non-violent exodus of the Black Students of Hamilton Hall is arranged.

**1968.** On Tuesday, April 30, at 2:30 AM, the thousand-man police bust is executed, and classes are suspended for the remainder of the spring semester.

**1968** On May 4, the Executive Committee of the Faculties requests appointment of a fact-finding commission to investigate the disturbances on the Campus. Harvard law professor Archibald Cox is tapped to lead the commission.

**1968** In late spring, students celebrate counter-commencement in Morningside Park.

**1968** On Saturday, June 1, the West Harlem Community Organization assembles a "Harlem Family-Community-Columbia Students" picnic on the construction site in Morningside Park.

**1968** In summer, Columbia President Kirk resigns, and Acting President Andrew Cordier dismisses charges against 400 students.

**1968** In the fall, the Architects' Renewal Committee in Harlem releases a comprehensive study on the future of the West Harlem neighborhood and Morningside Park.

---

**1969** Early in the year, Acting President Cordier meets with local leaders and then suggests a ballot poll on the gymnasium in Morningside Park. A coalition of West Harlem and black organizations reject the poll, and demand that Columbia abandon all claims to Morningside Park site. On February 27, at the first community meeting ever allowed to be held on campus, State Assemblyman Franz Leichter announces that Acting President Cordier will recommend to the university trustees abandonment of all plans for constructing a gymnasium in Morningside Park.

**1969** On March 3, Columbia University's Board of Trustees votes unanimously to terminate construction of the gymnasium in Morningside Park—fifteen years after the project was first suggested.

---

**1970** In September, criminal charges against community people arrested during the sit-ins at the construction site are at last dismissed.

# Glossary
## CAST OF CHARACTERS

*Because of the racial nature of the gymnasium controversy, race is indicated for politicians and community and student activists.*

BETANZOS, AMALIA– Democratic District leader, Chair of Ad Hoc Committee on Morningside Park *(Hispanic)*

BLOOR, WILLIAM – Treasurer of Columbia University

BOND RYDER WILSON – Architectural firm that, in 1982, reworked the 1973 Conceptual Master Plan for Morningside Park

BOND, J. MAX – First African American to receive architecture degrees from Harvard University

BROWN, H. RAP – Chairman of the Student Nonviolent Coordinating Committee (SNCC; the name was later changed to Student National Coordinating Committee) *(Black)*

BUCKLEY, BRUCE – Editor of *The Westsider (White)*

CANNON, JOHN D., REV. – Chaplain of Columbia University

CHAMBERLAIN, LAWRENCE – Columbia College Dean, Vice-President

CLURMAN, RICHARD M. – New York City Parks Commissioner, January to December 1973

COLEMAN, HENRY – Acting Dean of Columbia College, Hamilton Hall hostage

CORDIER, ANDREW – President of Columbia University, 1969 –1970

COX, ARCHIBALD – Chair of *Crisis at Columbia* Fact Finding Commission

CRICHTON, VICTOR – Lawyer, Morningside Park Preservation Committee

CROWELL, SUZANNE – Barnard student activist, writer for the *Columbia Daily Spectator*

EGGERS & HIGGINS – Gymnasium in the Park Architects

FELDMANN, FRIEDA – Community activist, Morningside Heights Parks and Playground Committee *(White)*

GARCIA, MARSHALL – Community activist, Morningside Heights *(Hispanic)*

GOLASH, MICHAEL – Student activist *(White)*

GONZALEZ, JUAN – Founder of Latin American Students Organization, founder of the Young Lords in East Harlem *(Hispanic)*

HALPRIN & ASSOCIATES – Environmental planners, designers of the 1973 Conceptual Master Plan for Morningside Park

HATCH, RICHARD – Architect, Founder of ARCH (Architects' to Renewal Committee in Harlem) *(White)*

HECKSCHER, AUGUST – New York City Parks Commissioner, 1967–1972

HICKERSON, GEORGE H. – Community activist, Morningside Heights *(White)*

HOVING, THOMAS P.F. – New York City Parks Commissioner, January 1966 to March 1967

HUXTABLE, ADA LOUISE – *New York Times* architecture critic

KATZ, MAUDE – Harlem resident *(Black)*

KHEEL, THEODORE W. – Lawyer, "Labor Peacemaker" *(White)*

KIRK, GRAYSON – President of Columbia University, 1954–1968

KIRKLAND, GALEN – Lawyer, ARCH *(Black)*

LEE, FOREST (WOODY) – ARCH associate *(Black)*

LEICHTER, FRANZ – State Assemblyman (D) *(White)*

LINDSAY, JOHN V. – Mayor of New York City

LYND, GLORIA – Park playground supervisor *(Black)*

McGILL, WILLIAM J. – President of Columbia University, 1970–1980

McGUIRE, HAROLD G. – Trustee of Columbia University

McKAY, ROBERT (BOB) – Community activist, West Harlem, Morningside Heights *(Black)*

McKIM, MEAD & WHITE – Architects and planners, authors of Columbia University's 1894 master plan

McNEIL, MARGARET – Executive Director of the West Harlem Community Organization (WHCO) *(Black)*

MENT, DAVID – President, Columbia University Student Council (CUSC), 1966/67

MILLER, MARIA – Community activist, West Harlem *(Black)*

MONROE, JOSEPH (JOE) – Community activist, West Harlem *(Black)*

MOSES, ROBERT – New York City Parks Commissioner, 1934–1960

MOTLEY, CONSTANCE BAKER – Civil Rights Lawyer, Federal Judge *(Black)*

OLMSTED, FREDERICK LAW – Landscape Architect

PATERSON, BASIL – State Senator (D) *(Black)*

PEI I. M. – Architect

PELLEGROM, DANIEL – President of CUSC, 1967/68

PENNAMON, EDITH – Director of West Harlem Community Organization (WHCO) *(Black)*

POOLE, JUSTUS C. (JUD) – Community activist, Morningside Heights *(White)*

POPE, DANIEL – Student activist *(White)*

PORTS, SUKI – Community activist (Morningside Heights) *(Asian)*

QUENNELL ROTHSCHILD ASSOCIATES – Landscape architects who undertook 1983 (final) modification to the Conceptual Master Plan for Morningside Park, implemented in 1985

RANGEL, CHARLES – Assemblyman *(Black)*

RUDD, MARK – Student activist, founder of Students for a Democratic Society (SDS) *(White)*

RUNYON, MARIE – Community activist (Morningside Heights) *(White)*

RYAN, WILLIAM F. – Congressman (D), 20th District *(White)*

RYDER, DON – Architect with Bond Ryder Wilson *(Black)*

SALMEN, STANLEY – Coordinator of University Planning, 1956–1967

SKIDMORE, OWINGS & MERRILL – Architects and planners, authors of a study of the Morningside Heights neighborhood commissioned by Morningside Heights Inc. and published in 1959

SMITH, A. KENDALL, REV. – Beulah Baptist Church of Harlem *(Black)*

SMITH, DWIGHT C., REV. – Chairman of the Morningside Renewal Council

SMITH, KENNETH A. – Dean, Columbia School of Architecture

SOLOMON, VICTOR – Chair of Harlem CORE (Congress of Racial Equality) *(Black)*

SOUTH, WALTER – Community activist, Morningside Heights *(White)*

STANLEY, BILL – Community activist, West Harlem *(Black)*

SUTTON, PERCY E. – Assemblyman (D), Manhattan Borough President (D) *(Black)*

THAU, IRVING – Lawyer, President of Riverside Park and Playground Committee *(White)*

TRUMAN, DAVID – Dean of Columbia College, Vice President of Columbia University

VAUX, CALVERT – Landscape Architect

WAITHE, ELDRIDGE A. – Chief Inspector, police officer *(Black)*

WALLERSTEIN, IMMANUEL – Chairman of the Faculty Civil Rights Group

WEISER, GEORGE – Community activist, Morningside Heights *(White)*

WILLIAMS, FRANKLIN H. – Lawyer, Ambassador to Ghana, Director of the Columbia Urban Center Special Committee on Community Relations *(Black)*

WILSON, CICERO – President of Student Afro-American Society (SAS) *(Black)*

WILSON, TIM – Architect with Halprin & Associates

# ORGANIZATIONS

ARCH – Architects' Renewal Committee in Harlem

CCNY – City College of New York

CFFC – Cox Fact Finding Committee

CORE – Congress of Racial Equality

CUSC – Columbia University Student Council

FCRG – Faculty Civil Rights Group

GNRP – General Neighborhood Renewal Plan

MRC – Morningside Renewal Council

NROTC – Naval Reserve Officers Training Corps

Remedco – Real estate arm of Morningside Heights Inc.

SAS – Students' Afro-American Society

SDS – Students for a Democratic Society

SNCC – Student Nonviolent Coordinating Committee

WHCMP – West Harlem Coalition for Morningside Park

WHMPC – West Harlem Morningside Park Committee

# About the Author

Christiane Crasemann Collins is a historian of twentieth-century and contemporary architecture and city planning, specializing in Central Europe and the Americas. She grew up in Chile and received degrees from Carleton College and Columbia University. She is the author, with George R. Collins, of *Camillo Sitte: The Birth of Modern City Planning*, published in 1986, and her major book, *Werner Hegemann and the Search for Universal Urbanism*, was published in 2005. Her many articles on urbanism explore the transatlantic flow of ideas.

Collins presented papers at the International Symposium of Civic Art in 2002 and at the conference on The Circulation of Ideas on Urban Aesthetics in Latin American in 2004. She has received Fulbright and Royal Institute of British Architects research awards, and she has lectured at Cornell University, Columbia University, and the Graduate School of Design at Harvard University. She lives in West Falmouth, Massachusetts.

Made in the USA
Charleston, SC
04 November 2015